THE INCORPORATION
of
AMERICA

THE INCORPORATION
of
AMERICA

Culture and Society in the Gilded Age

ALAN TRACHTENBERG

HILL AND WANG

A division of Farrar, Straus and Giroux
New York

Hill and Wang
A division of Farrar, Straus and Giroux
19 Union Square West, New York 10003

Copyright © 1982, 2007 by Alan Trachtenberg
All rights reserved
Distributed in Canada by Douglas & McIntyre Ltd.
Printed in the United States of America
First edition published in 1982 by Hill and Wang
Twenty-fifth anniversary edition, 2007

Library of Congress Cataloging-in-Publication Data
Trachtenberg, Alan.
    The incorporation of America : culture and society in the
gilded age / Alan Trachtenberg. — 25th anniversary ed.
        p.   cm.
    ISBN-13: 978-0-8090-5828-0 (pbk. : alk. paper)
    ISBN-10: 0-8090-5828-6 (pbk. : alk. paper)
    1. United States—Civilization—1865–1918.   I. Title.

E169.1.T72 2007
973.8—dc22

                                                2006046733

Designed by Nancy Dale Muldoon

www.fsgbooks.com

1   3   5   7   9   10   8   6   4   2

For my parents
and my children

CONTENTS

PREFACE
to the Twenty-fifth-Anniversary Edition

The first thing to say about *The Incorporation of America* after twenty-five years is that, apart from all else, it has put its title into circulation. That's no small accomplishment. The book was the first to recognize incorporation, a term imported from political economy, as a *cultural* phenomenon. Cultural effects began to appear almost all at once after the Civil War throughout U.S. society. Mark Twain dubbed these years with the dubious honor of the "Gilded Age." But the period was also a turning point in the country's history. The book set out to capture that elusive moment when the new first appeared under cover of the old.

The axis on which society turned was the shift from one form of capitalism to another, from predominantly self-employed proprietors to large corporations run by salaried managers. The book catches incorporation in its first bloom, so to speak, as it struggled to shake off the previous order and free its revolutionizing cultural powers. The book doesn't show America already incorporated but as becoming so. The ambience of beginning was angst, fear, menace, and violence, like all times of radical change.

The term "incorporation" gives a name to visible signs of change and less visible causes; it's both a description and an explanation. It allowed me to bring into single focus tangibles and intangibles, overt with covert, manifest with latent. It also gave a way to braid together several simultaneous stories: colonization of the West; standardization of time; linking of East and West Coast by railroad; mechanization of production; the rise of metropolis with its department stores, railroad terminals, and tall office buildings. Less tangible but no less material manifestations included new class formations and antagonisms, extreme polarization of the propertied and the propertyless, a changing middle group increasingly composed of managers, office workers, and professionals—and not least, altered meanings of keywords such as "land," "work," "city," "civic," and "incorporation" itself.

In the first instance a form of capital in its postentrepreneurial stage, incorporation refers to an emergent form of ownership in which power is distributed inwardly along hierarchical lines and outwardly in new social configurations and cultural perspectives. Significant consequences in culture followed, in how people portrayed in word, image, and stone and steel their collective lives and visions of a future. My focus was not only on change but also on conflict and contradiction. Military violence accompanied incorporation at virtually every stage: westward expansion on the graves of dispersed and extinguished native societies; class warfare in battles between workers and federal troops. There was a pervasive sense of imminent upheaval and turbulence.

My purpose was to find significant figurative patterns. Critical cultural history was how I described the project to myself: "history" in the sense of concreteness and temporality; "cultural" in the sense of a totality of relations, a "whole way of life" ("whole" not as a unified homogeneous field but as elements interrelated even where divergent and conflicted); and "critical" in the sense of skeptical, demystifying, contextual: cultural criticism in the act of becoming, in Theodor Adorno's words, "social physiognomy." My aim was to place myself inside the expressive regime, to disclose by paraphrase, by irony and paradox, the substance and tone of consciousness. How did the world of artifacts—literary texts and visual images as well as buildings and landscaped spaces (Central Park, for example)—manifest subjective and collective understandings of the national scene? The book looks at artifacts, material, verbal, and visual culture, as pedagogies that produce familiarity and habituation in their subjects. Spectacle in particular performed this function, the spectacle of public buildings and department stores displaying themselves as Renaissance palaces, of "the other half" perceived in mechanically reproduced photographs as if in a theater. Spectacle instructs by aesthetized mystification; in print as advertising or in theatricalized display it produces passive consumption of what's given in place of critical skepticism, consumers in place of engaged citizens. As Mark Twain saw the times in his novel *The Gilded Age* (1874), citizenship slipped into crisis in these post–Civil War decades, an era of mass political parties.

In the course of three decades the mainly agrarian and mercantile society of towns and small cities gave way to an industrial, metropolitan society. New systems of thought appeared; the word "system" itself became a buzzword. Institutions of "high" culture arose in marble palaces at the center of cities, emblems of the intimate terms upon which genteel culture and high wealth, also housed in marble, treated with each other. Space, time, the built environment, the meaning of goods and material things—all underwent decisive change. Professionalism offered new styles of identity. The process of radical change, the book argues, worked by contradiction. If in the spheres of production and distribution it brought increasing rationalization for the sake of control, its effects on mentality and expression included new opportunities for questioning the meaning of work, of gender, of the terms "woman" and "man." New possibilities of collective social action appeared on the horizon. Even socialism, an imagined negation of incorporation, can be taken as one of its products in the sense that the corporate form of capitalism, as Karl Marx had pointed out— and the American philosopher John Dewey agreed—prepared the ground for the next phase, the awaited "transition" to socialism.

The first twenty-five years of the life of the book, stretching from Ronald Reagan in the 1980's to George W. Bush in the early twenty-first century, seem evidence enough that *The Incorporation of America* describes the origins of our own times. By now the words of the title have a life of their own, a life steeped in contradictory prospects. Measured on a scale of material well-being, incorporation has seemed a spectacular success. But the same process that has raised the standard of living for most (not all, by a long shot) Americans also installed top-down hierarchies, inequalities of wealth and power threatening the values of democracy. Hence contradiction and paradox are as much products of incorporation as is a new professional-managerial middle class. And starting in the late 1890's, another chilling consequence has been the red demons of imperialism and war, the use of national military might to further corporate goals. While the influence of big business grew throughout the twentieth century, under Bush and his vice president, Dick Cheney, subordination of public policy to corporate interests has seemed to many at a new and distressing level.

Contemporary history clearly has added weight to the book's title. How does this book help its readers follow and grasp what is happening before our eyes? One way is by offering illuminating analogies from the past, the first age of incorporation. Recent commentators like Kevin Phillips and Paul Krugman have bemoaned the growing income gap as a kind of déjà vu of the lamentable Gilded Age. To many in government and in Congress the interests of the country and the interests of the large corporations have seemed identical. Rather than increasing the good of the country, tax cuts and other gifts to the very wealthy (many of them CEOs) have boosted the very few at the expense of the very many. The gap between the corporate oligarchy and the rest of the nation widens at a dizzying rate. Where once CEOs earned about forty times the income of their employees, the ratio is now more like four hundred times. In the 1950's the mantra was, "What's good for General Motors is good for America." The question now is whether the country has not already devolved into "America, Inc."

The irony is that the replay of Gilded Age scheming and cheating has completely distorted and mangled the view of Marx and Dewey that incorporation might presage a higher degree of social democracy. Attitudes inherited from Populism and Progressivism at the turn of the twentieth century that the corporation, as Jefferson said about cities and manufacturing, is a malignant sore on the body politic, have also returned with a vengeance. Historians Martin Sklar, James Livingston, and others have argued that such attitudes are regressive, that they distort the historical promise of the corporate form. However persuasive, this line of analysis has to contend with the return of naked greed and corporate-sponsored imperialism under Bush and Cheney.

Why the incorporation *of America*? When this book first appeared, the word "America" had become a partisan political platitude. Reagan hit his stride with theatrical flourishes that reminded voters of old beliefs in American innocence and promise—the "city on the hill," the "American Dream." "Morning in America again," he sang. I tried to neutralize the word "America" by showing how contested a word it had been. Did America stand for "union" or for "corporation"? Did the name of the nation belong to laboring people, to "producers," or to businesspeople and to the emerging class of corporate managers and upper-level professionals? The book concludes with the dramatic events of 1893–94, a year that saw both the great celebration of the new corporate world in the White City of the Chicago Columbian Exposition and its antithesis, the great railroad strike led by Eugene V. Debs, who claimed that America and union were synonymous. Twenty years earlier Walt Whitman in *Democratic Vistas* (1872) wrote that "America" and "democracy" were "convertible terms," or had better be.

Is this exceptionalism? I think there is a significant line between belief in national destiny willed by "providence" and the accrual in historical time of alternative meanings of "America," projecting alternative social and political programs. "America" and "American" remain contested terms; "Our America" has always been a debate about what Americans might be and become; "America" has never signified a single common culture. In a previous book, *Brooklyn Bridge: Fact and Symbol* (1965), I had focused on a particular industrial-urban artifact that had become a national icon; *Incorporation* widened the horizon to embrace the larger history within which the bridge underwent its initial transformation from material fact into national symbol. *Incorporation* supplemented *Brooklyn Bridge*; the two books stood to each other as a diptych of critical cultural history. My goal in both cases was to write history as "usable past," in Van Wyck Brooks's memorable phrase of 1918, usable by way of making meaningful connections between past and present. Brooks also meant by "usable" the capacity to inspire with examples of creative achievement and visions of possibility.

In a blurb in 1982, Henry Nash Smith praised this book for realizing an "ideal" of interdisciplinary synthesis often mentioned as the goal of American studies but seldom achieved. The book was indeed an experiment in interdisciplinary method, an effort to invent a cross-disciplinary framework for a conversation about what Smith rightly called "a turning point" in U.S. history, to reconstruct a colloquy among scholars from different disciplines whose separate languages, findings, insights, predispositions I hoped to put into a coherent pattern not previously identified, the pattern of incorporation. My point was to reveal relationships by which the relevance of labor history, for example, to literary criticism and to political theory would become manifest, separate particulars brought together into a meaningful whole—to change the way we interpret our world, the world that got started in the late nineteenth century.

The word "incorporation" was the key. Here in the 1880's and 1890's was a whole way of life undergoing near-volcanic change, old ideals of selfhood, obligation, and reward clashing with emerging systems and hierarchies. A way of life was at stake, a whole thing rather than an array of segmented things isolated or quarantined from each other by disciplinary rules. The subject itself produced the method. But a century later, interdisciplinary scholarship was something daring and experimental. Along with the pleasure of discovery came a certain thrill of transgression. Gertrude Stein had described artists as outlaws, living by rules of their own making. Why not bandit-historians who poached on their neighbors and wrote sentences ruled by different grammars?

American studies was then an openly transgressive enterprise (it had called itself a "movement") sitting on the edge of the academic scheme of things. Housed in "programs" rather than departments, without budgets or the power to hire and fire and give or deny tenure, typically American studies was installed at the crease between English and history, with connections to art history and perhaps political science and anthropology. Most practitioners seemed happily nestled in this state of semidependency—it provided a kind of camouflage that enabled the extraordinary flowering of scholarship that created American studies as a field of cultural study in the 1950's and 1960's in works by H. N. Smith, Leo Marx, R.W.B. Lewis, J. W. Ward, Warren Susman, William Taylor, Christopher Lasch, Neil Harris, and others. In the setting of established disciplines American studies was something added, a supplement, a gesture toward a style of discourse uncircumscribed by traditional disciplinary rules. That something else had been adumbrated by an earlier generation of "critics of culture" including Lewis Mumford, Waldo Frank, Paul Rosenfeld, and Constance Rourke, who invented ways of writing history as *experience* (in John Dewey's sense of the word: something *undergone*), the history of an era or a theme, for example, composed within the horizon of the present that included the author's own voice: Mumford's *Brown Decades*, Rourke's *American Humour*.

Incorporation harks back to this body of work. It reaches back to recover several things that had been lost. One was a sense of urgency, the belief of the earlier writers—the poets William Carlos Williams and Hart Crane were among them—that it was necessary to study the past to illuminate the present and provoke thought about the future. The critics of culture were unabashedly progressive; theirs was an ideal of scholarship in the mold of Emerson's American Scholar, "the world's eye," "the world's heart," society's "delegated intellect." Standing on the shoulders of early-twentieth-century cultural critics and more contemporary teachers like Raymond Williams (who first explored the historical meanings of "culture and society"), Henry Nash Smith, and Leo Marx, I wanted to see what might follow in the writing of history from the idea of a whole way of life undergoing tumultuous change.

What follows from incorporation? The book asks whether "America" and "union" are any longer effective terms for achieving social democracy. It's clear to me that I did not go far enough to point out how unionism and populist Americanism were compromised by their complicity in racial segregation, in discrimination by color and gender, in their recurrent embrace of chauvinistic nationalism. These qualifications of the egalitarian ideal complicate our response to Eugene Debs's words in 1894, even as we recognize the positive vision of labor opposition to corporate America: "Every honest patriotic American should understand the need to resist the 'brazen heartlessness' " of the corporations by showing active sympathy in "fellowship for the woes of others." This would be to "achieve our country," in the sense Richard Rorty has given to that notion in his own Debsian vision in *Achieving Our Country: Leftist Thought in Twentieth-Century America* (1998). But is "our country" still a viable principle of opposition?

This book hardly settles the issue but perhaps it can still usefully unsettle established convictions. Rorty's "our country" recalls a time when socialists like Debs, African-American leaders like Frederick Douglass, feminists like Susan B. Anthony and Elizabeth Cady Stanton, dissenting intellectuals and artists across the land, believed it was they, not the propertied classes, that best represented the country's symbolic name, the name of the "new world." *The Incorporation of America* continues to raise questions about the meanings of "America," even though the pursuit of that question has become unpopular in some academic circles that advocate a transnational perspective. The definition of key terms including "nation," "citizenship," "individual," "democracy," let alone "America," remains open, unsettled, and challenging. Along with all that is deplorable in the unmitigated inequality it produces, its disdain for the natural environment and impoverishment of the public realm, incorporation can still present us with visions of alternative possibility, a corporate society in the root sense of "corporate," a unified body, a collectivity, achieved according to the logic not of the capitalist market but also of an enlarged idea of equality, justice, social democracy. The challenge remains, in John Dewey's words, to choose "between a socialism that is public and one that is capitalistic." However we name the alternatives, menace or promise, the ambiguous effects of incorporation that first appeared well over a hundred years ago in "culture and society in the Gilded Age" have since radiated across the globe and present the greatest challenge to the nation and to the world in the twenty-first century.

ACKNOWLEDGMENTS

Venturing as I often do in this book beyond the usual boundaries of my work, I might not have found my way at all without the kind advice, frequent guidance, and the even more generous chiding of friends and colleagues. They are not to blame if I go astray. Warren Susman proved once more indispensable: unique as a historian, unfailing as a friend. My indebtedness to Leo Marx is long-standing and deep; for his close and sympathetic reading of the manuscript I am profoundly grateful. Jean-Christophe Agnew, John Blum, Eric Foner, and David Montgomery contributed immeasurably to whatever clarity about the historical process the book finally achieves. I am indebted as well to Sacvan Bercovitch, Charles Feidelson, and Jay Leyda for the care, deftness, pertinence, and not least the encouragement of their invaluable criticism. Owen Fiss, Winfried Flück, Eugene Goodheart, Gerhard Joseph, Ann Kibby, William Parker, and Zev Trachtenberg have earned my gratitude for extremely helpful commentaries and advice. I am also grateful to Michael Denning, Priscilla Murolo, Joel Pfister, and David Scobey for seminar papers from which I gleaned data and interpretations relevant to this study.

Working with Arthur Wang has been a particular pleasure and privilege; his good humor and wit cheered me even as his critical eye chastened my prose. Both he and Eric Foner proved formidable critics to please, which in the end pleased me. To Betty Trachtenberg I owe more than can be easily acknowledged.

Much of the writing of this book was accomplished during a

year's leave from teaching supported by the National Endowment for the Humanities and Yale University. I am grateful to the A. Whitney Griswold Faculty Research Fund of Yale University for assistance in meeting expenses incurred in preparation of the manuscript. And for gracious and skillful aid in typing the manuscript and performing sundry small tasks, I am indebted to Lorraine Estra and her staff; their help was bountiful.

Acknowledgments for the
Twenty-fifth-Anniversary Edition

I am grateful to Elisabeth Sifton for encouraging this new edition and seeing it through. Once more she has proved reliable, determined, and astonishingly crafty in every regard. It has been a privilege to work with her.

For their generosity in various ways—lending an ear, giving advice, reading drafts—I thank Casey Blake, Jim Livingston, Steve Rice, and Maren Stange, who readily lent a hand and shared knowledge with me. I cherish their collegiality and friendship. Suzanna Urminska skillfully helped with research tasks.

I remain grateful to Brook Thomas, David Leverenz, and David Shumway for their papers at the MLA panel in 2002 that marked the twentieth anniversary of this book. Brook Thomas deserves special thanks for arranging the event. So does Jim Livingston for adding a paper of his own to the forum published in *American Literary History* in 2003.

My deepest thanks to Betty for unfailing support in countless acts of tolerance and sympathy.

THE INCORPORATION
of
AMERICA

PREFACE

"The system of corporate life," Charles Francis Adams, Jr., wrote in 1869, is "a new power, for which our language contains no name." "We have no word," he noted in "A Chapter of Erie," "to express government by monied corporations." My purpose in this book can be described as an effort to find appropriate words and names for the powers which transformed American life in the three decades following the Civil War. I am less concerned than Adams with effects of "monied corporations" on either government or industry, though some of those consequences, so crucial in the emergence of modern society in America, figure in my account. I am concerned chiefly with effects of the corporate system on culture, on values and outlooks, on the "way of life." And just as my subject encompasses more than politics and economics, so my treatment of the corporate system extends beyond the technical device of incorporation in business enterprise. By "incorporation" I mean a more general process of change, the reorganization of perceptions as well as of enterprise and institutions. I mean not only the expansion of an industrial capitalist system across the continent, not only tightening systems of transport and communication, the spread of a market economy into all regions of what Robert Wiebe has called a "distended society," but also, and even predominantly, the remaking of cultural perceptions this process entailed. By "the incorporation of America" I mean, then, the emergence of a changed, more tightly struc-

3

tured society with new hierarchies of control, and also changed conceptions of that society, of America itself.

If in a literal sense incorporation refers to a specific form of industrial and business organization, in a figurative sense it encompasses a more comprehensive pattern of change. The relations between the two, between the literal and figurative meanings of incorporation, are the subject of this book. How did changing forms and methods in industry and business affect the culture of American society in the Gilded Age, the shape and texture of daily life, and the thinking of Americans?

The Gilded Age marked a significant increase in the influence of business in America, corresponding to the emergence of the modern corporate form of ownership. Based on minority ownership—that is, on the legally established authority of a small group of directors and managers to act in the name of a larger, amorphous body of otherwise unrelated stockholders—the corporation provided capitalists with a more flexible and far-reaching instrument than earlier forms of ownership such as simple partnerships and family businesses. The corporate form reaches back to classical times, but its viability for large-scale commercial and industrial enterprises did not become evident until the rapid expansion of trade and manufacturing in Europe and America in the nineteenth century. In the United States, incorporation appeared on a modest scale in the 1850's, notably in the railroad industry. By the 1870's, it had become commonplace, changing the face and character of American capitalism. The merger movement at the turn of the century was a dramatic outcome of the process inaugurated in the Gilded Age, underlining the change in the entrepreneurial history of earlier decades. That movement resulted in a major realignment of economic power. By 1904, for example, about three hundred industrial corporations had won control over more than two fifths of all manufacturing in the country, affecting the operations of about four fifths of the nation's industries. And the trend has continued, as any student of twentieth-century history well knows. By 1929, the two hundred largest corporations held 48 percent of all corporate assets (excluding banks and insurance companies) and 58 percent of net capital assets such as land, buildings, and machinery. By 1962, that ratio of ownership and control had narrowed even further, to the hundred largest corporations. In the era of multinationals,

4

certain corporations exceed many countries in wealth. Of the hundred largest economic units in the world in 1974, forty-nine were nations, and fifty-one multinational corporations.

The years covered in this book saw the beginnings of this process. In many ways a period of trauma, of change so swift and thorough that many Americans seemed unable to fathom the extent of the upheaval, the Gilded Age has seemed the age of "economic individualism," of Robber Barons and the epic scale of enterprises. The prominence of names like Rockefeller, Carnegie, Hill, Huntington, Swift, and Armour indicates that business was still thought of as a field of personal competition, of heroic endeavor, and not of corporate manipulation. The "faceless" corporation and the "organization man" had not yet arrived as public perceptions. Corporate life, as Adams observed, was still too new for Americans to recognize except in the familiar but already outmoded language of individualism. On the threshold of a process that would transform America and a good part of the world, the Gilded Age marked a watershed of clashing perspectives and practices.

Historians have long recognized that changes in business organization were associated with other historical developments such as the rise of the metropolis, a revolution in transportation and communications, and the processes of secularization, bureaucratization, and professionalization. Hardly any realm of American life remained untouched: politics, education, family life, literature, the arts. The effect of incorporation on cultural values and perceptions has not, however, been explored with the same thoroughness as, for example, the alliance of business and politics. Of course, the influence of corporate life on thought and expression is more difficult to identify, though no less significant. And any account of that influence must include subtle shifts in the meaning of prevalent ideas, ideas regarding the identity of the individual, the relation between public and private realms, and the character of the nation. Many of these changes can be traced, in turn, to a fundamental change in the meaning of "corporation."

The word refers to any association of individuals bound together into a *corpus*, a body sharing a common purpose in a common name. In the past, that purpose had usually been communal or religious; boroughs, guilds, monasteries, and bishoprics

5

were the earliest European manifestations of the corporate form. They all owed their existence, and the privileges stemming from a corporate charter, to an act of a sovereign authority. It was assumed, as it is still in nonprofit corporations, that the incorporated body earned its charter by serving the public good. The same thinking applied in the chartering of joint-stock companies in the age of exploration and colonization: the monarchs of Europe granted special charters to the great trading companies, thus encouraging the investment of private money in ventures that would promote national wealth through trade and colonies. The charters also granted monopoly privileges, and so in the American colonies the mercantilist intentions of the English trading companies aroused an antagonism toward commercial corporations which affected the granting of corporate status to private enterprises in the early decades of the nineteenth century. Until after the Civil War, indeed, the assumption was widespread that a corporate charter was a privilege to be granted only by a special act of a state legislature, and then for purposes clearly in the public interest. Incorporation was not yet thought of as a right available on application by any private enterprise. The earliest charters were thus bestowed on insurance companies, commercial banks, canal, dock, and highway companies—all concerned with the growth of cities and the expansion of internal trade. According to Stuart Bruchey, "these business corporations were no more exclusively profit-seeking associations than were the chartered joint-stock companies with which the English had pioneered in the settlement of America. They were, in fact, quasi-public agencies of the state." Even the earliest American charters (before 1815) granted to manufacturing companies were justified as acts of public service and patriotism. And during the period of internal improvements, after 1815, many states chartered tax-exempt public-service corporations to improve transportation facilities. These were often "mixed enterprises" in which the state's public funds (raised by bond issues, for example) were invested with private capital for needed turnpike, canal, and railroad projects. These corporations were still thought of as a public or semi-public institution.

The situation began to change with economic growth, especially with the westward extension of the railroad network and the rise of the factory system. With the creation of national markets in the 1850's, the corporate scheme became more important to expanding enterprises. The privilege of selling shares directly to a general public provided an efficient method of raising the capital necessary for the corporation's expansion. Its delegation of managerial authority to a board of directors allowed for venture beyond that which a small enterprise was willing to risk. Moreover, minority ownership facilitated extensions of control: horizontally, among many companies in the same industry; and vertically, by integrating industries from the extraction of raw materials to the sale of finished products within a single corporation. These refinements would become commonplace by the 1880's, after the general easing of laws governing the granting of charters. The possibilities were manifest as early as the 1840's in the pioneering large-scale textile works organized in Lowell, Massachusetts. They were, Thomas Cochran observed, "a miniature of the corporate industrial society of the twentieth century. They controlled banking, railroad, insurance, and power companies, as well as great textile mills scattered all over the state. It was the large 'modern' corporation controllable by strategically organized blocs of shares and virtually self-perpetuating boards of directors that made this concentration of power possible."

The incorporation of America did not happen without hindrance or resistance. The argument I develop is that economic incorporation wrenched American society from the moorings of familiar values, that the process proceeded by contradiction and conflict. The corporate system in business, politics, and cultural institutions engendered opposing views, however inchoate and incomplete that opposition remained. The deepest changes in these decades of swift and thorough industrialization and urbanization lay at the level of culture, difficult for contemporaries to recognize, and baffling for historians. The deepest resistances and oppositions also lay there, in the quality as well as the substance of perceptions, in the style as well as content of responses.

The antagonism which concerns me more than any other centers on the word America: a word whose meaning became the focus of controversy and struggle during an age in which the horrors of civil war remained vivid. In the eyes of those farmers, laborers, and radicals who joined in the People's Party of the 1890's, America incorporated represented a misappropriation of the name. To the Republican Party, swept to victory in 1896 under William McKinley, it represented the exact fulfillment of the name. Three years earlier, at the World's Columbian Exposition in Chicago—the event which concludes my account—an ideal shape of an incorporated America appeared in the form of a White City, while the following year, in the railroad strike of 1894, that shape and its celestial tints were challenged in blood and fire. This confrontation culminated an age of conflict that began at the end of the Civil War. From Appomattox to White City—the temporal range of this study—controversies over the meaning of America symbolized struggles over reality, over the power to define as well as control it.

I am concerned, then, with the realms of culture—our beliefs, our institutions, our social and intellectual life—in a period of great economic and social change, of political battles, of violent industrial strikes and continuing warfare against native Indians. This concern will show in my procedures. First, readers expecting a chronological narrative of incorporation will be disappointed. Instead, my account will be topical and thematic. Second, and more important, as a student of culture I am drawn especially to the figurative language by which people represent their perceptions of themselves and their worlds. Figures of speech, tropes, images, metaphors: I take these as materials of prime historical interest, for they are vehicles of self-knowledge, of the concepts upon which people act. They are also, especially in the public domain, forces in their own right, often coloring perceptions in a certain way even against all evidence. At the same time, figurative representations occupy the same social world as other forces, material and political. In each chapter I follow a procedure of narrative and analysis, setting image in relation to what we know of social fact, attempting to explicate and clarify the dialectic between mind and world, culture and society.

Each chapter takes up a feature of the social history of the era, and shows the power of images as concepts, of myths as ideology, the encompassing image and myth being that of America itself: a symbol in contention. The first chapter deals with the West as land, natural resource, and also as myth, especially "civilization" wrested from its perceived opposite, the "savage" cultures of Indians. The second concerns the machine, the actual work of machines ("mechanization") in relation to conflicted images, the dialectic of production and destruction which informed popular conceptions. Chapter 3 turns to the two major social aspects of the era, "capital" and "labor," and tries to understand each in light of its status within residual and emergent cultures, and of actual changes within the realms of business enterprise and industrial labor. The rise of the "great city," the metropolis, is taken up in Chapter 4: its rise as much into consciousness, as a place of "mystery," as into historical fact, as a place of integrated production and consumption. The idea which will flower into the White City is detected here, in the conflict between images of destructive and celestial cities in the minds of middle-class reformers. In the fifth chapter I deal explicitly with culture and its sundry relations with politics—the politics of parties and elections as well as the politics of reform and protest. While in general I use the term culture throughout the book to mean the way of life (values, perceptions, patterns of behavior, pictures of reality) of the whole society, in this chapter I bring into focus a more narrow use of the term prevalent in the upper and middle classes in these years: culture in the sense of cultivation and refinement, of formal education and trained aesthetic sensibility. This sense of the term is often known as "high" or "elite" culture, and my chief concern in this chapter is to show an evolving consensus of belief that culture indeed represents a higher sphere of activity associated with class privilege and with the older Anglo-Saxon America, a sphere distinct from the crudeness and vulgarities of common life, of trade and labor. That consensus faced a challenge, however, from a number of sources discussed in the chapter, from critics like Walt Whitman and William James, from Populist efforts to change the culture (in the wider sense of the term) of party politics, from persisting ethnic cultures in immigrant communities, and from the changes in everyday life discussed in the fourth chapter. Chapter 6 looks at the literary movement of "realism" as an aspect of the middle-class effort to grasp and define "reality," to identify America with distinct cultural meanings. The chapter focuses on William Dean Howells, and includes a discussion of Herman Melville's *Billy Budd*. My concluding chapter, the seventh, deals with the White City of 1893, its shapes and forms, its internal paradoxes, and the challenge to its cultural premises arising from Pullman in the follow-

9

ing year. The book thus proceeds from the "westward route" to its symbolic terminus in the White City: a passage through violence, turmoil, misconception, to an ironic conclusion. "Who can tell the weird and ghastly story of the last quarter of the nineteenth century," asked labor writer John Swinton in his book on Pullman in 1894: a rhetorical question which might well serve as epigraph to this effort.

1

THE WESTWARD ROUTE

I

"The Western wilds, from the Alleghenies to the Pacific," wrote the historian Frederick Jackson Turner in 1903, "constituted the richest gift ever spread out before civilized man." It was a gift, he had argued ten years earlier, from which America derived all that was distinctive in its brief history: democratic institutions, national unity, a rugged independence, and individualism. Turner had propounded his famous "frontier thesis" at a propitious moment and place: in 1893, at a meeting of the American Historical Association during the World's Columbian Exposition in Chicago. What more apt site for reflection on "the first period in American history"? Four hundred years earlier, Columbus had inaugurated the westward route; now the 1890 census disclosed that a distinct "frontier line" no longer existed. No more "Western wilds" lay ahead of the American nation.

Had the gift run out? A mere three generations earlier, it had seemed inexhaustible: Thomas Jefferson and others among the revolutionary generation guessed it would take a thousand years to reach the Pacific. They counted on free land as perpetual assurance of independence from Europe, of unending prosperity flowing from a vast inland empire. Agriculture then seemed to most Americans the truest foundation of national wealth, and uncharted acres beyond the Appalachians stirred visions of a Western "garden" tended by yeoman-farmers. The vision became policy, and through purchase, exploration, and conquest,

11

expansion proceeded steadily westward. The founders timed their calculations by a pre-industrial clock. But railroads, appearing in the 1840's and 1850's, stepped up the tempo, and the discovery of gold in California in 1849 inspired a veritable "rush" toward the western edge of the continent.

Of course, in the rush it became clear that the gift would be costly. A war with Mexico in 1848, and persistent, apparently fanatical resistance from native inhabitants, the North American Indians, indicated what price in violence and its shabby rationalizations the westward route would exact. What had seemed "vacant," "unredeemed," and "virgin" land often disclosed places of habitation by societies with different but no less self-justifying practices of land ownership and sustenance. With different notions of possession, Indians saw their land as already possessed, occupied, integrated with a human culture. The gift, in short, had to be wrested by force. The period of expansion and settlement witnessed incessant warfare. Indeed, fighting intensified in the decades following the Civil War, ending only with the collapse of Indian resistance by the early 1890's. The year 1893 marked, then, not only four hundred years of "progress" but also of destruction: the end not only of "frontier" but of independent native societies.

The westward route had drawn its unshakable sanctions from both religious and economic indicators, from "mission" as well as "progress." "The untransacted destiny of the American people is to subdue the continent," trumpeted William Gilpin in 1846; he repeated the resounding phrase in 1873 in The Mission of the North American People. Journalist, adviser to pre-Civil War Presidents, publicist for railroads and for a "Northwest Passage" to Asia, Gilpin described that destiny in providential terms: "to establish a new order in human affairs." That prospect was a key plank in the evangelical Protestant "Home Mission" movement represented by Josiah Strong, who in Our Country (1886) expatiated on Gilpin's theme: "Like the star in the East which guided the three kings with their treasures westward until at length it stood still over the cradle of the young Christ, so the star of empire, rising in the East, has ever beckoned the wealth and power of the nations westward, until today it stands still over the cradle of the young empire of the West." The star standing still would mark the end of profane time. The mission promised nothing short of sacred redemption, the remaking of "West" into a temple of God.

It was also, as Theodore Roosevelt explained in his popular *The Winning of the West* (1889), a half-mystical imperative of "race-history," a culminating moment in the drive of "the English-speaking peoples" for dominance in the world. The work of the new racial mix called "American"—an Anglo-Saxon mix in which English strains held sway—"Western conquest" had begun simultaneous with the appearance of this new breed, "at the moment when they sprang into national life." The pioneers responded to racial urges: "In obedience to the instincts working half blindly within their breasts, spurred ever onward by the fierce desires of their eager hearts, they made in the wilderness homes for their children, and by so doing wrought out the destinies of a continental nation."

In his momentous address in Chicago, Frederick Jackson Turner drew on such popular beliefs, the scattered dreams of an agrarian empire, of a providential mission for a newly forged race of white fighters and settlers. His vision coincided with Roosevelt's in many ways, though only Turner transposed the prophesied destiny into a different discourse. Reviewing Roosevelt's book in 1889, he had argued that "American history needs a connected and unified account of the progress of civilization across the continent." The nation needed, that is, a coherent, integrated story of its beginnings and its development. Connectedness, wholeness, unity: these narrative virtues, with their implied telos of closure, of a justifying meaning at the end of the tale, Turner would now embody in the language of historical interpretation. And an interpretation not merely accurate according to the canons of historical writing but serviceable according to the needs of politics and culture: the needs of the nation at a moment of crisis. "Aside from the scientific importance of such a work," he added in his review, "it would contribute to awakening a real national self-consciousness and patriotism." Neither apocalyptic in style nor explicitly visionary in purpose, Turner would speak in the tempered voice of "science," in the perspective of a belated recognition: now that the story had run its course, the historian stood poised in the White City of the Chicago Exposition to gather its meaning, to trace the "significance of the frontier in American history."

It is difficult to ignore the irony of the occasion, of Turner in Chicago, proclaiming what would become the most vital interpretation of the United States for at least the next fifty years. The moment proved a cultural as well as a scholarly event: a drama of confrontation. A scholar born and bred in the Middle West, nurtured by the rural culture of Wisconsin, where his father owned a newspaper and ran for political office, Turner urged his fellow historians to break with "eastern" intellectual proclivities, to pay more mind to "western" experience. Only recently had the profession itself emerged, with the founding of the American Historical Association in 1884. Turner himself came to his task in 1893 shaped as much by the structures of the profession as by his youth on the frontier. As a graduate student in the East, at the new center of advanced historical studies at Johns Hopkins, and as an assistant professor at the state university in Wisconsin (he would later move to Harvard), he had cut his teeth within a newly organized world of academic scholarship.

In his argument, "West" meant the pioneer sturdiness, independence, scorn of social constraint: "that coarseness and strength combined with acuteness and inquisitiveness; that practical, inventive turn of mind, quick to find expedients; that masterful grasp of material things, lacking in the artistic but powerful to effect great ends; that restless, nervous energy; that dominant individualism, working for good and for evil, and withal that buoyancy and exuberance which comes from freedom." Turner celebrated these heroic masculine traits even as he lamented the passing of the conditions which produced them. And he did so in a manner which not only described their demise but also dramatized it. For there, in the great new metropolis of Chicago, he performed a decidedly urban feat. The style itself of his discourse—neither a narrative in the grand manner nor a monograph freighted with citations, but an essay of analysis— represented the historian as a *professional,* one who performs his work according to academic standards. Moreover, the frontier thesis presupposed both a subject—"society"—and an outlook toward it neither romantic nor sentimental but "scientific," a view based on presumably sound Darwinian assumptions of evolution and organism, a subject available for research, for collective investigation. Unlike Roosevelt, Turner does not speak of "half-blind instincts" but of environment and institutions.

"In a very real sense," Richard Hofstadter has observed, "the Turner thesis and the historical profession grew up together." In its account of "progress" from simplicity to complexity, from "frontier" to "society," the thesis thus offered an account of its own origins. Indeed, Chicago itself seemed a product of the logic Turner described: "At last the slender paths of aboriginal intercourse have been broadened and interwoven into the complex mazes of modern commercial lines; the wilderness has been interpenetrated by lines of civilization growing ever more numerous. It is like the steady growth of a complex nervous system for the originally simple, inert continent." Thus the very propounding of the thesis in the new metropolis of Chicago declared the conclusion of a process, the inevitability of its end.

Thus we can see that in the contours of its argument as well as in the sinews of its sentences, the Turner thesis belongs to the new world made palpable and vivid in Chicago in 1893; it is of a piece with White City. Like the Columbian Exposition, the Turner thesis portrayed an America at a critical juncture. Both affirmed drastic change since the days when it might have been possible to imagine the nation as a society of freeholders. Both embraced the change—the rise of cities, industrial capitalism, corporate forms of business and social activities—and yet they attempted to preserve older values and traditional outlooks. Both served cultural missions: White City overtly, indeed in the very forms of culture, of high art and architecture; the Turner thesis covertly, in the guise of professional "scientific" discourse.

But the specific crisis Turner faced in the deepest levels of his argument centered on the paradox typified by Chicago. If the frontier had provided the defining experience for Americans, how would the values learned in that experience now fare in the new world of cities—a new world brought into being as if blindly by the same forces which had proffered the apparent gift of land? Would the America fashioned on the frontier survive the caldrons of the city? Turner responded to the challenge by an act of distillation. To be sure, he argued, the story of the frontier had reached its end, but the product of that experience remains. It remains in the predominant *character*, the traits of selfhood, with which the frontier experience had endowed Americans, that "dominant individualism" which now must learn to cope with novel demands. The thesis projects a national character, a type

15

of person fit for the struggles and strategies of an urban future. The prominence Turner gives to character, to a "composite nationality," in the resounding conclusion of the essay, clarifies his strategy. His response to the crisis of having reached the end of the frontier story shows in the meaning he gives to "land," treating it as he does less as an economic resource (he hardly mentions minerals and extractive industries in his 1893 essay) than as an environmental force, virtually as a character in its own right. "The wilderness masters the colonist," he writes. And the process he describes rings of a ritual event, a set of actions echoed throughout American fiction and poetry in recounted excursions into an archaic wilderness, in Cooper's tales of Natty Bumpo, in Faulkner's *The Bear*, in "The River" and "The Dance" in Hart Crane's *The Bridge*. The colonist arrives a "European," but instantly commences a descent, stepping from the railroad car into a birchbark canoe, shedding "civilized" clothing and habits. He descends, strips himself of "society," transforming himself into the very image of "land" he then sets out to transform into the image of "progress." This descent and ascent, this "continual beginning over again" and "perennial rebirth" at the "meeting point between savagery and civilization" becomes, for Turner, the authentic source not simply of a process which culminates in Chicago but of the sound fiber of American character itself. Thus, he writes, "the frontier is the line of the most rapid and effective Americanization," giving rise to "a composite nationality for the American people." The "connected and unified account" of the American past required by the times coheres, then, in the figure of the typical, the composite American.

Seeking a "connected and unified account" of the American past at a time of disunity, of economic depression and labor strife, of immigrant urban workers and impoverished rural farmers challenging a predominantly Anglo-Saxon Protestant economic and social elite, Turner thus arrived at his conception of the American character as an emblem of national coherence. The nation incorporated itself, he insisted, through that figure and its traits of inventive individualism. To be sure, the account slights crucial aspects of the Western experience stressed by later historians. It fails to acknowledge cultural multiplicity; in the Southwest alone, Anglo-Americans, Spanish Americans, Roman Catholics, Mormons, and Indians all contributed to a heterogene-

16

ous culture. It makes its claims on the basis of a decidedly partial experience—of chiefly Anglo-Saxon settlers and farmers flowing from New England into the Midwest. Moreover, the thesis ignores or obscures the real politics of the West, where, as Howard Lamar has shown, federal territorial policy held much of the region in a dependent, colonial status (prior to admission to statehood) through most of the post-Civil War period. "By 1889," writes Lamar, "every territory in the West was calling its federal officials colonial tyrants and comparing its plight to that of one of the thirteen colonies." Turner's frontier, then, is as much an invention of cultural belief as a genuine historical fact: an invention of an America "connected and unified" in the imagination if nowhere else. The invention proclaims that, even in Chicago, some fundamental residue of the nation persists, an idea of hardy manhood, of inventive genius and originality. Only partially hidden within its overtly "scientific" historical discourse, then, the Turner thesis held another discourse of uncertainty and concern over America in a time of cities, immigrants, and corporate power.

II

An invention of cultural myth, the word "West" embraced an astonishing variety of surfaces and practices, of physiognomic differences and sundry exploitations they invited. The Western lands provided resources essential as much to industrial development after the Civil War as to cultural needs of justification, incentive, and disguise. Land and minerals served economic and ideological purposes, the two merging into a single complex image of the West: a temporal site of the route from past to future, and the spatial site for revitalizing national energies. As myth and as economic entity, the West proved indispensable to the formation of a national society and a cultural mission: to fill the vacancy of the Western spaces with civilization, by means of incorporation (political as well as economic) and violence. Myth and exploitation, incorporation and violence: the processes went hand in hand.

The gift of geography to American society consisted of unimaginable natural wealth in the manifest form of a picturesque landscape. Of course, nature is manifestly neither romantic nor picturesque: the descriptive terms convey cultural meanings that live in perceptions. American painters had fastened onto conventions of landscape painting in the antebellum period with a unique intensity, and produced, in the Hudson River School, a body of work which lent to American terrain an almost mystical power. They depicted nature as the stage of dramas of growth and decay, of aspiration and defeat—and invested it with emotions appropriate to visions of national destiny. Landscape painting served as an approximation to the heroic historical canvases that academic European art crowned as the highest, most spiritual of paintings. The habit of confronting history in American nature found an even more grandiose scale, as painters and explorers turned their eyes toward views newly disclosed in expeditions in the Far West. In his experiences recounted in *Mountaineering in the High Sierras* (1872), geologist Clarence King found evidence of geological upheavals aeons old, cataclysms representing a history more antique and awesome than any possessed by European societies. In the path of America's future seemed to lie a *natural* history that gave to the Western settlement a biblical cast.

The term "natural wealth" implies another cultural perception, another way of interpreting the strata of rock and mineral deposits that gave to the mountain and desert regions of the West a look of prehistoric enchantment. Ways of interpreting the land tend to become equivalents to acting upon it, consuming it as an aesthetic object, as a resource. King's memoir registers an often tortured division of outlooks, in his case between aesthetic (and moral) perception and scientific knowledge. The division took another form in popular publications that flooded the country, especially as the nation approached the centennial year of 1876. In William Cullen Bryant's preface to *Picturesque America* (1874), a lavish two-volume set of texts and reproductions of paintings in steel engraving, we read:

By means of the overland communications lately opened between the Atlantic coast and that of the Pacific, we have now easy access to scenery of a most remarkable character. For those who would see Nature in her grandest forms of snow-clad mountain, deep valley, rocky pinnacle, precipice, and chasm, there is no longer any occasion to cross the ocean. A rapid journey by railway over the plains that stretch westward from

18

the Mississippi, brings the tourist into a region of the Rocky Mountains rivalling Switzerland in its scenery of rock piled on rock, up to the region of the clouds. But Switzerland has no such groves on its mountainsides, nor has even Libanus, with its ancient cedars, as those which raise the astonishment of the visitor to that Western region—trees of such prodigious height and enormous dimensions that, to attain their present bulk, we might imagine them to have sprouted from the seed at the time of the Trojan War.

The buried contradiction here between the appeal of wild grandeur and the comfort of mechanized access to the site where such an appeal can be satisfied is not merely comic in its blithe leap over wagon tracks and rotting carcasses that marked a mode of access only a few years past; it indicates a special kind of denial of social fact that afflicted sections of American culture in these years. Thus the railroad, the prime instrument of the large-scale industrialization which re-created American nature into "natural resources" for commodity production, appears as a chariot winging Americans on an aesthetic journey through the new empire. Tourism, already implicit in the landscape conventions, becomes yet another form of acting upon the land.

The "vast, trackless spaces," as Whitman put it, of open land, forest, and mountain—the Great Plains and the Rockies—not only fired the imagination but figured quite concretely in the industrial program. While perceptions of Western space often diminished the sense of human significance and worked their effects on the hardy folk who people the legends of Western settlement, perceptions of potential wealth inspired more calculating responses. The federal government had sponsored systematic exploration of unsettled regions as early as the Lewis and Clark expeditions in 1804–6. Mapmaking preceded settlement and had perhaps an even greater effect on conceptualization of the land than landscape paintings. About 1845, the government outfitted army explorations to find suitable routes for railroad lines to the Pacific.

The overt aim of these early probings was to chart the way to an agricultural empire—a "new garden of the world"; they explored regions for settlement and military defense. Reflecting a different emphasis and a new set of needs, explorations during the Civil War and continuing to the end of the century were concerned with natural resources; they were explicitly "scientific" expeditions, typified by the meticulously planned United States Geological Survey established in 1879. Such surveys collected detailed information about terrain, mineral and timber resources, climate, and water supply. One of the tangible products of the several postwar surveys were thousands of photographs, displayed in mammoth-sized plates and in three-dimensional stereo images, an astonishing body of work that when viewed outside the context of the reports it accompanied seems to perpetuate the landscape tradition. Many of the photographers, such as William Henry Jackson, clearly followed conventions of painting in depicting panoramic landscapes, while others, like Timothy O'Sullivan, worked more closely to the spirit of investigation of the surveys and produced more original visual reports. The photographs represent an essential aspect of the enterprise, a form of record keeping; they contributed to the federal government's policy of supplying fundamental needs of industrialization, needs for reliable data concerning raw materials, and promoted a public willingness to support government policy of conquest, settlement, and exploitation.

That policy held ambiguities and contradictions. Undertaken at first on behalf of agricultural settlement, it fostered in fact a massive industrial campaign. As Henry Nash Smith has shown, by the Civil War the West had gathered to itself connotations of a peaceful New World garden, a symbolic wish for prosperity safe from the tragedies of Europe. Fertile soil on the high plains, open spaces, seemingly "virgin" lands beckoned the independent yeoman Jefferson had celebrated as America's best hope, and seemed an assurance of permanent tranquillity. The logic of events in the 1870's and 1880's disclosed, however, not an agrarian but an industrial capitalist scenario. Penetrating the West with government encouragement, the railroad and the telegraph opened the vast spaces to production. Following the lead of the railroads, commercial and industrial businesses conceived of themselves as having the entire national space at their disposal: from raw materials for processing to goods for marketing. The process of making themselves national entailed a changed relation of corporations to agriculture, an assimilation of agricultural enterprise within productive and marketing structures. The rapid appearance of grain elevators after the

20

1850's indicated the change and its character; the need for storage facilities, and for standardized grading and weighing and inspecting, implied sales in high volume, direct purchases by dealers from farmers, and a distant exchange for commercial transaction. Agricultural products entered the commodities market and became part of an international system of buying, selling, and shipping. The farmer's work in every section of the nation thus gained a cosmopolitan character. Marketing and exchange left his hands, the work now of dealers and brokers. Where processing was necessary, as in meat and tobacco, mass producers soon incorporated the entire process, from farm to factory to consumer.

Especially with the opening of vast fertile tracts in the Western plains, farmers turned to "cash crops," attempting to anticipate prices in commodity markets centered in distant cities here and abroad. The effect of almost instantaneous telegraphic communication of prices on his plans and expectations was often cataclysmic. Controlled by private corporations, the new technologies came to be enemies of the farmer; steep rates for elevator storage, for railroad transport, for middleman services, claimed the better part of his harvests, even in years of bumper crops. Overmortgaged, overcapitalized, overmechanized, independent farmers even on the fertile plains increasingly felt the chill winds of financial disaster in the very place once promised as a New World garden.

The promise embodied in the idea of the West as a yeomen's garden had seemed so much the closer to fulfillment with the passage of the Homestead Act by the Civil War Congress in 1862, which offered 160 acres of the public domain to individuals for the nominal fee of $10. Republicans had joined with Free Soil Democrats in supporting the measure with two goals in mind: to provide an agricultural "safety valve" for surplus or discontented urban workers, and a Western population base for an enlarged domestic market for manufactured goods. Free or cheap land had tempted some labor spokesmen in the antebellum years to envision cooperative colonies in the West as an alternative to the wage system, and such a notion remained a plank of some labor organizations as late as the 1880's. But from the very beginning of the administration of the Homestead Act, it was clear that a society of small homesteaders in the West was not its functional goal. The act did not provide necessary credit for people without savings to take up their cherished 160 acres. And its clauses permitted land grabbing by speculative companies, and the eventual concentration of large tracts in private hands. As historian Fred Shannon has shown, perhaps only a tenth of the new farms settled between 1860 and 1900 were acquired under the Homestead Act; the rest were bought either directly from land or railroad companies (beneficiaries of huge land grants), or from the states.

Rather than fostering a region of family farmers, the Homestead Act would prove instrumental in furthering the incorporation of Western lands into the Eastern industrial system. Until the practice was discontinued in 1871, the Republican Congress had enthusiastically donated more than a million and a half acres of public domain in the form of "land grants" to railroad companies operating west of the Mississippi. In turn, the railroads became private colonizers in their own right, selling off large sections of their grants to individuals and companies. Responding to business lobbies, Congress passed additional acts between 1866 and 1873 virtually giving away lands and rights of access to mining and timber interests. Continuing government-sponsored surveys of exploration culminated in the establishment in 1879 of the United States Geological Survey, whose voluminous reports and maps facilitated the private development of lands rich in timber, oil, natural gas, coal, iron ore, and other minerals. Privatization of the public domain continued as large companies bought out or pushed aside individual entrepreneurs, replacing small-scale mining, timber cutting, and farming with capital-intensive methods. Hit-or-miss prospectors and miners found themselves slowly forced into day labor in Eastern-owned mines and factories employing improved machinery for more efficient extraction and processing—an experience Mark Twain recounts from his own days in the Nevada Comstock region in *Roughing It* (1871). New methods of mining, drilling, loading ores by automatic machinery, shipping oil through long-distance trunk lines, appeared in short order, stepping up the tempo of a massive conversion of nature into the means and ends of industrial production.

Thus, incorporation took swift possession of the garden, mocking those who lived by the hopes of cultural myth, and those who

22

thought of machines as chariots for tourists. Abuses in the treatment of land did arouse an outcry for control and regulation, but not until the basic apparatus of exploitation already stood in place. A movement for preservation and the protection of certain regions as national parks emerged in the 1870's; with John Wesley Powell (who explored the Grand Canyon region) and John Muir as leading advocates, Congress established Yellowstone National Park (1872) and preserved Yosemite as well (1890). Powell and others, including a growing number of landscape architects, as J. B. Jackson has pointed out, proposed plans for orderly land use of remaining public resources, especially water supplies for desert regions. But public planning was anathema to Congress and private entrepreneurs, who did not flinch from public subsidy of business. So the unimaginable wealth of nature's gift was funneled by the people's representatives into private hands.

The West poured its resources into the expanding productive system, contributing decisively to the remaking of that system into a national incorporated entity. Wheat and cattle enterprises came under control of Eastern capitalists, for whom the agricultural surplus provided a major source of new capital. Newly established meat-packing companies in Chicago and other Midwestern metropolises won direct control of the large herds which were their raw material. By the 1890's, food production and processing had joined mining as a capital-intensive, highly mechanized industry. The translation of land into capital, of what once seemed "free" into private wealth, followed the script of industrial progress, however much that script seemed at odds, in the eyes of hard-pressed farmers, with the earlier dream.

Another process of transformation occurred in the same decades: a remaking of the image of the West, a funneling of its powers into popular culture. The region emerged in popular consciousness as "Wild West," a terrain of danger, adventure, and violence. Through dime novels, themselves a modern artifact of mass production, and traveling Wild West shows such as Buffalo Bill's, the image impressed itself: the West as exotic romance. Especially through the dime novels, a cast of stock characters appeared: desperadoes, savage Indians, prospectors, Indian scouts and cavalrymen, marshals or "regulators," saloonkeepers, dance-hall madames, cowpunchers, and a mob of townsfolk, easily swayed toward lynchings and posses. These popular fantasies

23

appealed to a broad stratum of Eastern readers, for whom the West served a. an image of contrast to Eastern society. A simple Populism often colors these tales, in which villains appear as wealthy Eastern bankers and capitalists allied with the most notorious outlaws, and heroes often speak in praise of "honest workingmen," of "labor" in its contests' with "capital." Often fugitives from Eastern injustice, men prove themselves in the West, where only personal merit and ability count. The very wildness of the West allowed native ability and honesty their due. The heroic owes nothing to social station, and often outlaws prove themselves heroes in the Robin Hood mold.

Through such popular fictions, the West in its wildness retained older associations with freedom, escape from social restraint, and closeness to nature. The ideal of solitary endurance persisted, then, even in the face of rapidly encroaching Eastern business interests: persisted especially as a proto-populist image of opposition. Heroes such as Deadwood Dick easily assume roles of outlaw and lawman, of highway robber and town marshal, always maintaining his manly virtue. The prominence of disguises and false identities in the dime novel also suggests a distrust of appearances, an unwillingness to settle for fixed social roles and obligations. Not until the end of the century, when Eastern corporations had virtually accomplished their control of Western enterprises, did the image of the Western hero begin to shift, to accommodate itself to changed historical realities. And when the genre of the Western solidified into the form which would remain the staple of twentieth-century popular culture, it appeared as a fable of conservative values, a cultural equivalent to incorporation. The development is already complete in Owen Wister's *The Virginian* (1902). For Wister, Harvard graduate and intimate of Theodore Roosevelt (to whom the novel is dedicated), not only washes clean the literary crudities and thematic incoherences, indeed the very elements of popularity of the dime novel; he also turns the implicit egalitarianism of the earlier mode into an explicitly ruling-class vision. Wister's great tale of the cowboy hero who vaunts at once the values of personal honor and worldly success, who is prepared to kill to defend both his own reputation and his employer's property, completes the cultural appropriation of the West.

Wister appropriated freely from the popular tradition, clarifying character types, sharpening issues. In the dime novel the cowboy had been only one of many possible heroic roles along with scout, miner, outlaw, sheriff or marshal, detective. Fusing elements of several vocational types in his cowboy figure, including that of "foreman," or superintendent, over the band of migratory laborers who performed the cowpunching and herding on the ranches and plains, Wister re-created the cowboy as a romantic knight of the plains, a descendant of Sir Lancelot, as he put it in an article in 1895 on "the evolution of the cowpuncher." The medieval image is more than an idle allusion. The cowboy figure stands in a definite relation to the settled society of the plains— a relation of knightly deference to the aristocratic owner, the "Judge," and to his interests. The cowboy-knight knows his place and accepts it, and yet also insists fiercely on his own honor: a right permitted him and respected by the Judge. The code duello has a sacred place in Wister's West, as it did in the dime novels, and the defense of manly honor justifies the Virginian's occasional, always reluctant but always cool, quick, and efficient use of his gun, just as defense of private property justifies, indeed demands. "The last romantic figure upon our soil," Wister's cowboy hero is also a deadly killer.

III

"It is but little over half a dozen years since these lands were won from the Indians," wrote Theodore Roosevelt in *Hunting Trips of a Ranchman* (1886) about the Dakota Badlands. The compression of vast social change within such a narrow compass heightens the sense for Roosevelt that he is living *within* history:

After bloody fighting and protracted campaigns they were defeated, and the country thrown open to the whites, while the building of the Northern Pacific Railroad gave immigration an immense impetus. There were great quantities of game, especially buffalo, and the hunters who thronged in to pursue the huge herds of the latter were the rough forerunners of civilization. No longer dreading the Indians, and having the railway on which to transport the robes, they followed the buffalo in season and out, until in 1883 the herds were practically destroyed.

25

Early cattlemen found themselves doomed by the same historical process: "The broad and boundless prairies have already been bounded and will soon be made narrow." And so history seemed for Roosevelt, for Turner, for countless others contemplating the westward experience, a foreclosed event, an inevitable advance from low to high, from simple to complex, and in more senses than one, from "Indian" to "American." For Turner, "West" offered a transparent text in which "line by line . . . we read this continental page from West to East," deciphering a "record of social evolution."

It begins with the Indian and the hunter; it goes on to tell of the disintegration of savagery by the entrance of the trader, the pathfinder of civilization; we read the annals of the pastoral stage in ranch life; the exploitation of the soil by the raising of unrotated crops of corn and wheat in sparsely settled farming communities; the intensive culture of the denser farm settlement; and finally the manufacturing organization with city and factory system.

Thus "West" bespeaks a proof for "America" itself: the site where the process is laid bare, recapitulated at each successive "meeting point between savagery and civilization."

The proof was repeated over and over in countless popular prints such as "American Progress," published in 1873. Based on a painting by John Gast, the print displays a frank and simple allegory. It illustrates, in the words of an explanatory text on the reverse side, "the grand drama of Progress in the civilization, settlement and history of our own happy land." The picture shows a chase. On the left, a herd of buffalo, a bear and a coyote, and a family of Indians and their horses flee before an array of Americans in various "stages" of "progress": guide, hunter, trapper, prospector, pony-express rider, covered wagon followed by stagecoach, and a farmer in a field already under plow and oxen. Three railroad lines, representing the transcontinentals, join the flow, which originates from the city and its factories, schools, and churches. On the left, the text explains, we find "darkness, waste and confusion." And in the center of the scene, its presiding image, looms a white, diaphanous figure, "a beautiful and charming Female"—we are told—"floating Westward through the air, bearing on her forehead the 'Star of Empire.'" Her knee raised through her gown as if striding purposefully, she bears in one hand a book representing "Common Schools," and with the other "she unfolds and stretches the slender wires of the Telegraph" that are to "flash intelligence throughout the land." The Indians look back at her, the "wondrous presence" from which they flee. "The 'Star' *is too much for them.*"

In this "progress," this proof of "America," the profoundest role was reserved not for the abundance of land but for the fatal presence of the Indian. The Indian projected a fact of a different order from land and resources: a human fact of racial and cultural difference, not as easily incorporated as minerals and soil and timber. Here was a significant array of people—significant in number, in capacity to inflict damage and entail large military expense—occupying a world so entirely at odds with that of white Americans that their very opposition made a frontal encounter necessary for a definition of America itself. "Civilization" required a "savagery" against which to distinguish itself. Thus, native American Indians differed from blacks and Asians in several important regards. Blacks could be understood as a special category of American: formerly enslaved but now enfranchised and (presumably) on the way to equality. Chinese, on the other hand, were clear "aliens" whose right to occupy space in the country was completely at the mercy of American sovereignty. Blacks and Asians could be understood, also, as capable of productive labor, this being the ground of both fear of competition from labor groups and hope of ultimate assimilation. Both groups were targets of intensifying racial hostility in these years, in growing Ku Klux Klan terror and Jim Crow laws in the South, and exclusion legislation against Chinese in California. But the Indian represented a special case in that the right to space lay bound up with the very right to *exist.*

The character of that existence had presented challenges to white Europeans from the beginning. Were Indians true people, or demons, or "noble savages," happy innocents in a state of nature? Were their "tribes" similar to "nations," with whom treaties and land purchases might be negotiated? Essentially, the challenge concerned land; it came to a head very rapidly because the natives would fight fiercely and effectively against intrusions on their space, or violations of agreements reached with white governing bodies. The willingness of Indian tribes to enter into

27

compacts with white invaders indicated both a willingness and a readiness to coexist. Indeed, coexistence had altered Indian life in ways not entirely negative: the introduction of horses, for example, metal utensils and tools, woven cloth, storable and transportable food, and guns enhanced the ability to hunt, to procure food and produce clothing and shelter. But steady encroachment of white trappers, hunters, traders, and finally settlers on Indian lands increased tension and hostility and produced virtually constant warfare, with the consequence of severe changes within Indian social structure (the strengthening, for example, of chiefs and warriors, and the diminishing role of women in tribal decision making), and eventual defeat. The period after the Civil War marked the conclusion of overt hostilities (after intensified fighting in the 1870's), the forced acceptance by defeated tribes of a new reservation policy, and the onset of a long period of withdrawal and apparent passivity. The Indian, by 1893, seemed a "vanishing American."

Yet, while the figure may have receded, it hardly vanished. An Indian presence persisted as the underside, the lasting bad conscience, within the prevailing conception of "West," calling for repeated ritualistic slaying in popular "Westerns." For at all junctures the real history of expansion had translated a secret script within the idea of "progress" or "manifest destiny." Bearable only in the disguise of myth and ritual, that script revealed its potentially destructive horror in the period of intensified fighting just after the Civil War, particularly as reports of unspeakable atrocities, such as those by army troops under Colonel J. M. Chivington in a massacre at the Sand Creek reservation in Colorado in 1864, reached the East. In his first message to Congress in 1869, President Grant remarked: "A system which looks to the extinction of a race is too horrible for a nation to adopt without entailing upon itself the wrath of all Christendom and engendering in the citizen a disregard for human life and rights of others, dangerous to society." Official national policy stopped short of extermination; it settled for abolishing native ways of life and their obstructive practices of communal property holding. But even this limited form of violence could not be faced directly; it must be veiled, misunderstood as an event of another kind. The Turner thesis, which defines the land as "free" and identifies Indians with "wilderness," as a "common danger," is one such

28

veil: it fails to see Indians as other than undifferentiated "savages" in the path of "social evolution" from "frontier" to "city and factory system." To see Indians as "savage" is already to define them out of existence, to define them only in relation to their apparent opposite: "civilized" society.

The major events in Indian-white relations in these years were military and legal: more than two hundred pitched battles, not to speak of guerrilla warfare in outlying Western regions, and a reservation policy promulgated in 1887, to remain in effect until the 1930's. In each case, military action and legal solution, economic and cultural issues figured as unspoken but vital imperatives. The drama of these years was played largely on the Great Plains, but against a scenery put in place by the forced removal or expulsion of tribes east of the Mississippi in the decades before the Civil War. Executed by President Andrew Jackson in the 1830's, removal established an Indian Territory in the Southwest (now Oklahoma). The Southern tribes protested, lost an appeal to the Supreme Court, and had no choice but to accept the long march westward enforced by government troops. Chief Justice John Marshall's ruling (in 1831) was epochal: Indians were not "foreign nations" but "domestic dependent nations": "they are in a state of pupilage. Their relation to the United States resembles that of a ward to his guardian." In spite of previous treaties, Indians "occupy a territory to which we assert a title independent of their will." Or as the governor of Georgia put the matter in less judicious terms: "Treaties were expedients by which ignorant, intractable, and savage people were induced without bloodshed to yield up what civilized people had the right to possess by virtue of that command of the Creator delivered to man upon his formation—be fruitful, multiply, and replenish the earth, and subdue it."

Thus, well before the Civil War, the courts and Congress had settled the issue of conflicting "rights" by instituting as law a relation of dependency, a relation which included guarantees of protection as well as payments (in the form of annuities) for lands relinquished. "Protection," however, stood always at the mercy of "dependency," for the notion that "we assert a title independent of their will" implied that any future desire for Indian lands might well be satisfied by unilateral modification of treaties. Thus, removal imposed on Indians not only a forced abandonment of a social order and economy—many of the Eastern tribes already practiced sedentary agriculture and had a federated structure of self-government—but also an inherent legal inferiority. They were declared both inside and outside the American polity: subject to its jurisdiction, but without rights of citizenship.

The removal policy committed the government to police and military action aimed both at keeping Indians within the prescribed limits of their new territories and ostensibly protecting those limits from white incursions. But incursions increased after the Civil War as cattlemen, miners, and farmers demanded access to lands they viewed as economically desirable. The heightened friction in the West in the 1860's and 1870's resulted from stark conflicts of interest between expanding capitalist enterprises and Indian needs for sustenance. Driven westward, formerly agricultural peoples such as the Eastern Sioux were compelled to adopt a seminomadic hunting economy, based on the great roving herds of buffalo on the Great Plains. The policy of protection dwindled after the Civil War into open support of white demands to rewrite treaty boundaries, to concentrate Indian tribes within shrinking areas and enclosures called "reservations." Consistent with its economic policies of land grants and subsidies, of Homestead Act and unrestricted immigration, the federal government sponsored military campaigns to win more land and resources for exploitation. Indian policy, then, followed the logic of incorporation: expansion into space for the sake of conversion of "nature" into "raw material."

The key features of that policy in the decades after the Civil War included stepped-up military action coupled with legislative clarification of the legal status of Indian societies—their status, that is, within the purview of American polity. What needs most to be stressed is the importance of this clarification to the process of incorporation: not only as a government-sponsored clearance of an obstruction to investment and economic growth but as a crucial *cultural* definition of America itself. The method of definition was unilateral and imperial; solutions were imposed, not developed by negotiation and compromise. The problem, of course, was understood as obstruction, both by inhabitation of desirable lands and by an aggressive defense of those lands. After the Civil War, controversy arose within the national government about the most expedient solution. Earlier, in 1849, the governance of Indian affairs had been placed in the hands of the Department of the Interior; now military leaders like General William T. Sherman insisted that the Bureau of Indian Affairs be returned to the Department of War. Especially after the Sioux uprising under Chief Red Cloud in Montana and Wyoming, and the Cheyenne and Arapaho rebellion in Colorado—both following immediately after Appomattox—Sherman urged "the utter destruction and subjugation" of all Indians found outside their assigned reservations, "until they are obliterated or beg for mercy." Not only the need for costly military campaigns—millions of dollars for each expedition—but the notorious corruption of Indian agents seemed to argue for a transfer of authority to the army.

The proposal failed, and the official policy under Grant and his successors proclaimed "peace": through education, missionary work by Christians invited to replace corrupt political appointees in Indian agencies, and through a reconception of the reservation as, in John Wesley Powell's words in 1874, "a school of industry and a home for these unfortunate people." Powell and others proposed a program of "civilizing these Indians" by inducing them "to work," and requiring that they learn English in order to bring them better within the domain, and control, of "civilization": "Into their own language there is woven so much mythology and sorcery that a new one is needed in order to aid them in advancing beyond their baneful superstitions; and the ideas and thoughts of civilized life cannot be communicated to them in their own tongues," wrote Powell. And, as a decisive measure aimed at diminishing the power of tribal chiefs and thus the coherence of Indian resistance, Congress in 1871 abolished the practice of treaty making with separate tribes, thus finally denying distinct tribes the legally troublesome status of "nation." From these measures it was thought that "peace" would follow. In fact, military campaigns continued unabated, against the Sioux under Sitting Bull and Crazy Horse in the Great Plains, Geronimo and the Apaches in the Southwest, and, most tragically, against Chief Joseph and the Nez Percé tribe in Oregon. It continued until the final defeat of the half-starved Sioux

31

after a Ghost Dance ceremony in 1890, a massacre of about two hundred men, women, and children, including the old leader Sitting Bull, at Wounded Knee creek in the Black Hills.

By the 1880's, an influential reform group had begun to make itself heard, a group of well-placed reformers, philanthropists, clergymen, and their wives, who shared an 'evangelical Protestant outlook, a passion for social order, and who called themselves "Friends of the Indian." By then, the United States Army had the upper hand, and a policy which may have resulted in genocide was narrowly avoided. Genocide was in fact the logical implication and obsessive ambition of what Melville in *The Confidence Man* had called "the metaphysics of Indian-hating," a frontier habit of unremitting racial hatred. Sherman's military policy and Theodore Roosevelt's inflamed rhetoric—"treacherous, revengeful, and fiendishly cruel savages," he wrote in 1886—were stages leading to potential holocaust. Indeed, military actions, frequent armed assaults against harmless villages and women and children, massacre and atrocity—often in response to isolated guerrilla raids by desperate and vengeful young braves—had the appearance if not the official sanction of genocide. And it was an open secret that the rapid destruction of the vast buffalo herds— as many as 13 million of those imposing, shaggy creatures roamed the plains at the time of the Civil War—satisfied not only the greed of commercial hunters, leather and fur manufacturers, and railroad carriers, but government desire for a speedy resolution to the "Indian problem." Denied opportunities and land for all but marginal farming, the Plains Indians had counted on the buffalo hunt for meat, hides for clothing and shelter, bones for utensils and ornaments. "Kill every buffalo you can," advised one army officer. "Every buffalo dead is an Indian gone." "Slaughtering buffalo is a Government measure to subjugate the Indians," noted one observer. By the early 1880's, the slaughter had effectively decimated the great Southern and Northern herds. The shaggy beast receded into legend, accompanied by tidy profits for hunters and dealers in hides—and a fatal destabilization of Indian society.

The alternative to violence proposed by the "Peace Policy" had in mind, as did Grant in his remarks about the horror of genocide in 1869, the effects of such rampant slaughtering of beasts and humans on the larger society. Like their fellows among the cul-

32

tivated elite and gentry throughout America, the "peace" party feared the consequences of violence, the chaos (as they saw it) of class conflict threatening in the industrial cities. A policy of military extinction might well unleash even stormier forces of disorder, such as those which had broken out in Chicago in 1886, at the riot in Haymarket Square. Instead of exterminating Indians, they proposed membership in American society in exchange for a repudiation of Indian ways. They offered, through the Dawes Severalty Act passed by Congress in 1887, to transform Indians by education and economic support into model Americans. The Dawes Act, in short, implied a theory and pedagogical vision of America itself.

That vision manifested itself in practical terms. To every male Indian "who has voluntarily taken up . . . his residence separate and apart from any tribe . . . and has adapted the habits of civilized life," the act offered not only an allotment of land for private cultivation but the prospect of full American citizenship. It offered a choice: either abandon Indian society and culture, and thus become a "free" American, or remain an Indian, socially and legally dependent. With a perverse accuracy, the act recognized the cultural power of tribal structures, of complex kinship systems, of shamanistic religion. As an alternative, it proposed, and thus helped promulgate, what it assumed to be the typical and culturally legitimate model of the male-dominated nuclear family based on private property. Linking citizenship with both propriety and property, the Dawes Act thus implied standards for the entire society.

By setting in motion a process of detribalization, the new law disclosed perhaps the rawest nerve in white-Indian relations: the conflicting practices in regard to property, especially land. The reformers on the whole shared with Roosevelt the view that Indians lacked a civilized sense of property, of spatial boundaries. "Where the game was plenty, there they hunted," wrote Roosevelt in accents in which romance clashes with economic interest; "they followed it when it moved away . . . and to most of the land on which we found them they had no stronger claim than that of having a few years previously butchered the original occupants." Reformers spoke of the despised "communistic" system of communal property relations. The vehemence aroused by Indians, fed for generations by tales of captivities and atrocities, of

33

barbaric practices, took aim in these years of Western expansion particularly against a way of life perceived as antithetical, alien, and threatening in its implications. Again, Roosevelt provides the most vivid and blunt instances of rage. The Dawes Act, he remarked in his first message to Congress in 1901, provided "a mighty pulverizing engine to break up the tribal mass." The inner message had a wider audience in view. As he had made plain in 1889, "Indian ownership" was sometimes practiced by shiftless criminal whites as well: "To recognize the Indian ownership of the limitless prairies and forests of this continent—that is, to consider the dozen squalid savages who hunted at long intervals over a territory of a thousand square miles as owning it outright—necessarily implies a similar recognition of the claims of every white hunter, squatter, horse-thief, or wandering cattle-man." In 1886 he had warned: "The Indian should be treated in just the same way that we treat white settlers. Give each his little claim; if, as would generally happen, he declined this, why then let him share the fate of the thousands of white hunters and trappers who have lived on the game that the settlement of the country has exterminated, and let him, like those whites, who will not work, perish from the face of the earth which he cumbers." Work or perish: thus reads the inner script of the revised policy of "peace" toward the Indian.

If the Southern system of chattel slavery had obstructed industrial progress, provoking a civil war, so the Indian system of communal ownership had inspired resistance to Western expansion; it, too, required destruction, and then a policy of "reconstruction" of the defeated natives into the image of their victors: their language and costumes, their names and religion, their laws regarding work and property. By the 1890's, then, the Indian had been incorporated into America no longer simply as "savage," a fantasy object of ambivalent romantic identification or racial hatred, but as "lowest order," outcast and pariah who represented the fate of all those who do not work, do not own, do not prefer the benefits of legal status within the hierarchies of modern institutions to the prerogatives of freedom and cultural autonomy.

At the same time, and typical of the discordances of the age, knowledge of Indian cultures accumulated rapidly in these years of brutal warfare and policy formation, in the reports and monographs of the newly formed Bureau of American Ethnology (directed in its early days by John Wesley Powell). Like other academic disciplines and social sciences in these years, anthropology underwent swift professionalization, as ethnographers joined missionaries and Indian agents in native settlements, recording and analyzing their languages, customs, religions, and social structures. And scattered in their reports lay information about a way of life which might well have contributed to evolving social and cultural critiques of industrial society. Indeed, in the studies of Lewis Henry Morgan, especially in his magisterial *Ancient Society, or Researches in the Lines of Human Progress from Savagery through Barbarism to Civilization* (1877), such a contribution begins to take shape. Morgan's formulations challenged popular stereotypes of the Indian, viewing him in a perspective of history and social change deeply at odds with popular providential thought, with notions of racial superiority, and with American self-congratulatory rhetoric. Morgan carried on his research and writing despite an unlikely conventional career as a Rochester, New York, lawyer and businessman, a railroad investor and occasional member of the New York State Legislature. Refusing all university positions, he remained more or less an amateur (although he did serve as president of the prestigious American Association for the Advancement of Science), not exactly an outsider but sufficiently free of incipient professional standards to venture upon a bold theoretical enterprise in his effort to comprehend the great wealth of ethnographic data unearthed by nineteenth-century researchers. In his practical and political life, Morgan provided legal assistance to New York tribes and wrote legislation, as chairman of the State Committee on Indian Affairs, on their behalf. He never fulfilled his hope of appointment as national Commissioner of Indian Affairs.

Morgan's researches led him to a belief in the unity of mankind, and toward an evolutionary scheme in which the forms of subsistence, the level of technology, provided the basis of social change and progress. Representing earlier stages of human society and culture, the American Indian thus provided a unique opportunity for "civilized" Americans to study their own distant origins. As he put it in the preface to his remarkable study of Indian domestic architecture, *Houses and House-Life of the American Aborigines* (1881): "In studying the condition of the Indian tribes in these periods we may recover some portion of the lost history of our own race." Possessing neither the political society nor formal state of the "civilized" stage (and Morgan stresses the role of accident or fortuitous circumstances by which Semitic and Aryan peoples have arrived soonest at this condition), Indians have instead as their basic social unit what he called the gens or extended family: "a brotherhood bound together by ties of kin." Based on the arts of subsistence—hunting, gathering, some agriculture, and toolmaking—the gens functioned as communal units: "liberty, equality, and fraternity, though never formulated, were cardinal principles." About Indian dwellings he wrote: "It is evident that they were the work of the people, constructed for their own enjoyment and protection. Enforced labor never created them. On the contrary, it is the charm of all these edifices, roomy, and tasteful and remarkable as they are, that they were raised by the Indians for their own use, with willing hands, and occupied by them on terms of entire equality."

Morgan acknowledged in a letter that his work held "a tremendous thrust at privileged classes, who always have been a greater burden than society could afford to bear." "Since the advent of civilization," he wrote in the final paragraphs of *Ancient Society*, "the outgrowth of property has been so immense, its forms so diversified, its uses so expanding and its management so intelligent in the interests of its owners, that it has become, on the part of the people, an unmanageable power." Envisioning a "next higher plane of society," Morgan sees signs of its shape in forms already well established in America: "democracy in government, brotherhood in society, equality in rights and privileges, and universal education." The next plane "will be a revival, in a higher form, of the liberty, equality and fraternity of the ancient gentes."

In the face of simplistic and simplifying prevalent notions of "progress," of "civilization" and "savagery," Morgan insisted on a historical debt, "that we owe our present condition, with its multiplied means of safety and of happiness, to the struggles, the sufferings, the heroic exertions and the patient toil of our barbarous, and more remotely, of our savage ancestors." Wishing to sweep away the "misconceptions, and erroneous interpretations," the "false terminology," which have "perverted, and even caricatured" knowledge of American aboriginal history, he

36

strove to place the Indian "in his true position in the scale of human advancement." Original errors of interpretation, he worried, have been implanted, and now "romance has swept the field."

Indeed, a fabric of fantasy, nostalgia, and idealization appeared toward the end of the nineteenth century as a kind of shroud for the "vanishing American." It was a matter of faith for Huck Finn, in Mark Twain's masterpiece of 1886, that an escape from Aunt Sally's desire to "sivilize" him lay ahead, in the Indian Territory: a place imagined as one of endless adventure, play. and freedom. Such fantasies seriously misconstrued the character of Indian cultures, but they do hold an important covert insight about the majority culture rapidly consolidating its hold on American society in these years, that "to civilize" entailed destruction or abrogation of that debt Morgan speaks of. Certainly, Frederick Jackson Turner's own notion of "progress" and stages of civilization, as indeed of the "gift" of the wilderness to white America, implies a simple passing over the inert body of Indian culture on America's way to the future. In spite of Morgan's efforts, and perhaps inevitably, "Indian" remained the utmost antithesis to an America dedicated to productivity, profit, and private property.

2

MECHANIZATION TAKES COMMAND

I

Even before the Civil War, the westward trails were destined to be lined with tracks; the pony express and the covered wagon, like the mounted Plains Indian, would yield to the Iron Horse. For if the West of "myth and symbol," in Henry Nash Smith's apt terms, provided one perspective by which Americans might view their society, the machine provided another. The two images fused into a single picture of a progressive civilization fulfilling a providential mission. As John Kasson has shown, many Americans before the Civil War had believed that industrial technology and the factory system would serve as historic instruments of republican values, diffusing civic virtue and enlightenment along with material wealth. Factories, railroads, and telegraph wires seemed the very engines of a democratic future. Ritual celebrations of machinery and fervently optimistic prophecies of abundance continued throughout the Gilded Age, notably at the two great international expositions, in Philadelphia in 1876, and in Chicago in 1893.

The image of the machine, like the image of the West, proved to be a complex symbol, increasingly charged with contradictory meanings and implications. If the machine seemed the prime cause of the abundance of new products changing the character of daily life, it also seemed responsible for newly visible poverty, slums, and an unexpected wretchedness of industrial conditions. While it inspired confidence in some quarters, it also provoked dismay, often arousing hope and gloom in the same minds. For,

38

accompanying the mechanization of industry, of transportation, and of daily existence, were the most severe contrasts yet visible in American society, contrasts between "progress and poverty" (in Henry George's words), which seemed to many a mockery of the republican dream, a haunting paradox. Each act of national celebration seemed to evoke its opposite. The 1877 railroad strike, the first instance of machine smashing and class violence on a national scale, followed the 1876 Centennial Exposition, and the even fiercer Pullman strike of 1894 came fast on the heels of the World's Columbian Exposition of 1893.

It is no wonder that closer examination of popular celebrations discloses bewilderment and fear. In fiction and poetry, as Leo Marx has shown in his seminal *Machine in the Garden* (1964), serious writers before the Civil War had fastened on the image of a mechanical intrusion on a pastoral setting as a characteristic expression of a deeply troubled society. In the language of literature, a machine (railroad or steamship) bursting on a peaceful natural setting represented a symbolic version of the trauma inflicted on American society by unexpectedly rapid mechanization. The popular mode of celebration covered over all signs of trauma with expressions of confidence and fulsome praise. But confidence proved difficult to sustain in the face of the evidence.

Current events instilled doubt at the very site of celebration. A period of great economic growth, of steadily rising per capita wealth, and new urban markets feeding an expanding industrial plant, the Gilded Age was also wracked with persisting crises. An international "great depression" from 1873 to 1896 afflicted all industrial nations with chronic overproduction and dramatically falling prices, averaging one-third on all commodities. "It was," writes David Landes, "the most drastic deflation in the memory of man." A severe Wall Street crash in 1873 triggered a round of bankruptcies and failures in the United States, six thousand businesses closing in 1874 alone, and as many as nine hundred a month folding in 1878. A perilously uneven business cycle continued for more than twenty years, affecting all sections of the economy: constant market uncertainties and stiffening competition at home and abroad for business; inexplicable surpluses and declining world prices, together with tightening credit for farmers; wage cuts, extended layoffs and irregular employment, and worsening conditions, even starvation, for industrial workers.

Recurrent cycles of boom and collapse seemed as inexorable as the quickening pace of technological innovation. Thus, even in the shadow of glorious new machines displayed at the fairs, the public sense of crisis deepened.

No wonder modern machinery struck observers, especially those associated with the business community, as in Charles Francis Adams, Jr.'s words, "an incalculable force." The tempo of crisis accelerated in the 1870's. Farmers agitated through Granger clubs and the Greenback Party against the government's policy of supporting business through deflationary hard money and the gold standard. Industrial unrest reached a climax and a momentary catharsis in July 1877, when fears of a new civil war spread across the country during the great railroad strike. Provoked by a 10 percent wage cut announced without warning by the Baltimore and Ohio line, a measure to halt a declining rate of profit, the strike spread like wildfire to other lines, reaching from Baltimore to Pittsburgh, Chicago, St. Louis, Kansas City, and San Francisco. The apparently spontaneous work stoppages met with approval and support from local merchants, farmers, clergy, and politicians, tapping reserves of anger and wrath against the railroad companies. Workers in other industries joined the walkout, and for a short spell it seemed that the United States faced a mass rebellion, a recurrence of the Paris Commune of 1871 on an even vaster scale. In some communities (St. Louis, for example) committees of strikers briefly assumed control of government and railroad services.

The strike turned bloody and destructive, arousing a vehemence of response from big business and the national government even surpassing the wrath vented by strikers against railroad yards and equipment. The companies recruited local police and militia to protect their property, and pitched battles raged along the lines, although many militiamen refused to fire on the strikers, among whom they recognized relatives and friends. Finally, the newly inaugurated President, Rutherford Hayes, invoked his powers of military intervention and called out federal troops to protect "by force" (as he noted in his diary) the property of the railroad companies, among whose leaders he counted many of his closest friends and supporters. In the end, the strike left more than a hundred dead, millions of dollars of property destroyed, and a toughened company and government stand against unions. Strikers were very often fired and blacklisted, their leaders fined and jailed. The War Department issued a pamphlet on "riot duty" and constructed for the first time a system of armories in major cities to house a standing "national guard." Industrialization of the state's military force seemed a necessary adjunct to the mechanization of production.

The very extremes of effect lent to the machine an aura of supreme power, as if it were an autonomous force that held human society in its grip. In *The First Century of the Republic*, a book of essays published by *Harper's* magazine in celebration of the nation's centennial in 1876, the economist David Wells observed that "like one of our mighty rivers," mechanization was "beyond control." And indeed the display in Machinery Hall in Philadelphia that summer gave credence to the image of a flood, though without Wells's ominous note. Here, in an exposition of machines removed from their working location, a profusion of mechanisms seduced the eye: power looms, lathes, sewing machines, presses, pumps, toolmaking machines, axles, shafts, wire cables, and locomotives. The Remington Arms Company, declaring its versatility, displayed one of its newest products: Christopher Schole's new "typewriter," an astonishing device for producing neat, legible messages at the touch of a finger. The twenty-nine-year-old Thomas A. Edison, already the wunderkind of invention, disclosed his "multiplex" telegraph, capable of carrying several messages on the same slender wire. And, most memorably, Alexander Graham Bell here gave the world first notice of the greatest wonder of electrical communication: the telephone. For sheer grandeur and sublimity, however, the mechanisms of communication could not compete with the two most imposing structures in the Hall: the thirty-foot-high Corliss Double Walking-Beam Steam Engine, which powered the entire ensemble from a single source, and its counterpart, a 7,000-pound electrical pendulum clock which governed, to the second, twenty-six lesser "slave" clocks around the building. Unstinted but channeled power, and precisely regulated time: that combination seemed to hold the secret of progress.

The fairs were pedagogies, teaching the prominence of machines as instruments of a distinctively American progress. As Wells explained, mechanical progress followed laws of its own; it was not to be resisted. One of the leading economic writers of the Gilded Age, friend and adviser to Presidents, a railroad trustee, and outspoken advocate of free trade (opposed to income tax as well as tariffs), Wells often appeared in the conservative *The Nation* and the respectable *Atlantic Monthly* as an expositor of the machine age to the educated public. He argued, as he did in 1876, that legislation would prove useless against the flood of industrial goods: "Like the construction of piers and deposits of sunken wrecks, [they] simply deflect the current or constitute temporary obstructions." Even more difficult lessons lay in the daily transformations of old patterns of work, of travel, of communication. For machines in fact performed their work within extended structures, serving as parts of evolving systems, assigned precise tasks by humans. Perceived as an incalculable force in its own right, reified, fetishized, even demonized, the machine thus found a troubled place in the culture of the times.

II

The idea of an autonomous and omnipotent machine, brooking no resistance against its untold and ineluctable powers, became an article of faith. The image implied a popular social theory: the machine as a "human benefactor," a "great emancipator of man from the bondage of labor." Modern technology was mankind's "civilizing force," driving out superstition, poverty, ignorance. "Better morals, better sanitary conditions, better health, better wages," wrote Carroll D. Wright, chief of the Massachusetts Bureau of Statistics of Labor, in 1882; "these are the practical results of the factory system, as compared with what preceded it, and the results of all these have been a keener intelligence." Wright's paper, originally given as an address before the American Social Science Association, bore the title "The Factory System as an Element in Civilization."

The events of the 1870's and 1880's, however, also elicited less sanguine accounts of what the factory system had wrought. Even Wright adopted a defensive tone, warning against the seductive "poetry" and "idyllic sentiment" of many critics: "I am well aware that I speak against popular impression, and largely against popular sentiment when I assert that the factory system in every respect is vastly superior as an element in civilization to the domestic system which preceded it." Wright failed to acknowledge, however, that his account of the superior benefits of the system did not include the opportunity of workers to change their status within it; his defense assumes a permanent class of wage earners, a prospect abhorrent to believers in republican enlightenment and progress. Not surprisingly, a growing number of Americans openly questioned whether industrialization was in fact, in Henry George's words, "an unmixed good." As if in pointed rebuke of Wright's arguments and images, George observed the following year, in *Social Problems* (1883), that so-called labor-saving inventions, the "greater employment of machinery," and "greater division of labor," result in "positive evils" for the working masses, "degrading men into the position of mere feeders of machines." Machines employed in production under the present system are "absolutely injurious," "rendering the workman more dependent; depriving him of skill and of opportunities to acquire it; lessening his control over his own condition and his hope of improving it; cramping his mind, and in many cases distorting and enervating his body." True, George found the source of such evils not in machines themselves but in unjust concentrations of land ownership. In the end, he shared Wright's vision of the potential benefits of machinery, though not his conception of a permanent class of "operatives." George plainly perceived the process of degradation in factory labor as strictly mechanical, experienced as an *effect* of machinery. To a wider public than Wright had addressed, George's views seemed irrefutable.

The record of seeing, of representing the machine either in imaginative writing, in polemical discourse, or in social analysis is a record as well of implied social theories and attitudes, of responses colored by ideological predispositions. Carroll Wright addressed an audience which included enlightened manufacturers; he concluded his paper with a call for benevolent "Captains of Industry" to "carry the responsibility entrusted to them," for the "rich and powerful manufacturer ... is something more than a producer, he is an instrument of God for the upbuilding of the race." George, a native Philadelphian of middle-class birth who had wandered to California in the late 1850's, working as a seaman, printer, newspaperman, failing as a Democratic candidate for office and as the owner of an independent newspaper, wished to arouse the nation to its plight, urging the adoption of a "single tax" against land rents as the solution to the paradox whereby "laborsaving machinery everywhere fails to benefit laborers." His *Progress and Poverty*, written in the wake of the destruction, violence, and frustration of the summer of 1877, fuses evangelical fervor with simplified Ricardian economic theory; its simplicity of analysis and solution, its jeremiad rhetoric of righteousness and exhortation, helped the book find a remarkably wide audience. It reached more than 2 million readers by the end of the century. Appealing to a range of political sentiments and economic interests, George evoked a vision of older republican and entrepreneurial values restored through the "single tax" in the new corporate industrial world. Identifying "social law with moral law," he wished to show that *"laissez faire* (in its full true meaning) opens the way to a realization of the noble dreams of socialism."

George's picture of the failures of the machine and of its potential promise corresponded to the perceptions of a significant section of the society, particularly since he promised a change fundamentally within the existing order, the existing relations of capital and labor. Among representatives of older ruling groups, the picture held less promise. "It is useless for men to stand in the way of steam-engines," wrote Charles Francis Adams, Jr., in 1868. Adams, from one of the oldest Eastern families of property and former political status, would soon join forces with the engine as corporate executive of railroad and other enterprises. His less sanguine brother, Henry Adams, wrote later in *The Education of Henry Adams* (1907), regarding his own "failure," that "the whole mechanical consolidation of force ruthlessly stamped out the life of the class into which Adams was born." Devising a theory of history based on "forces," Adams crystallized the technological determinism implicit in both the popular and academic thought of his time.

Determinism appeared not only in explicit theories and observations of the role of machinery in economic prognosis; it also appeared at a deeper level of thought, in less self-conscious processes of mind. Images of machinery filtered into the language, increasingly providing convenient and telling metaphors for society and individuals. Carroll Wright's conception of the factory implied a more embracing image: society as a factory. He described the factory as a "legitimate outgrowth of the universal tendency to association which is inherent in our nature." Buried here is a Spencerian notion of evolution from simple to complex forms, from independence to interdependence, from simple tools to intricate machines. The social division of labor, then, as exemplified by machine production in factories, is made to seem *natural*, an inevitable and "legitimate" evolution. The notion of the self consisting of a material "mechanism" had been present in American and European thought since the late eighteenth century; now the image struck a note which resonated with perceptions of expanding factories, railroads, and dynamos. "The more we examine the mechanism of thought," wrote Oliver Wendell Holmes in a Phi Beta Kappa address in 1870, "the more we shall see that the automatic, unconscious action of the mind enters largely into all its processes." Acceptable because undeniable in the world of thought, continued the famous literary doctor and experimental scientist, this idea of mechanism must be rejected in the "moral world," which "includes nothing but the exercise of choice." Holmes responded to the "confusion" worked by "materialism" on moral issues, by insisting so forcefully on the priority of choice in questions of good and bad precisely because of the threat of "mechanism" to the very concept of a moral universe.

The prospect of a mechanization of moral choice raised fears particularly among Americans clinging to a Protestant belief in free will, in the efficacy of human effort, and especially in the value of a properly trained and disciplined "character." Preservation of a belief in a "moral universe" in which rewards and punishments flowed from character and moral choice assumed an urgency in these years of massive mechanization. For, as Holmes recognized, images of mechanism now appeared throughout daily life and everyday discourse.

"Whatever constantly enters into the daily life soon becomes an unnoticed part of it," observed Charles Francis Adams, Jr., about the railroad system, "so much a part of our everyday acts and thoughts that they have become familiar." Indeed, the familiarization of American society with machinery represents one of the major cultural processes of these years, even in such simple matters as riding in streetcars and elevators, getting used to packaged processed foods and the style of machine-made clothing, let alone growing accustomed to new harsh sounds and noxious odors near factories and railroad terminals. The proliferation of new machines and machine-made tools for industrial and agricultural production marked an even more drastic upheaval in the forms, rhythms, and patterns of physical labor.

Perhaps more expressive of changing cultural perceptions because of its greater diffusion than serious or "high" literature, popular fiction and folklore in these years represented machinery especially in its sheer power and exemption from human vulnerability. In regional folktales and ballads, such figures as the lumberjack Paul Bunyan, the railroad worker John Henry, the locomotive engineer Casey Jones pit their strength and skill and daring against the machine.

Dime-novel Western adventures depict orgies of shootings and killings with every variety of automatic repeating weapons, each named precisely. A magical machine, endowing its owner with ultimate powers of "civilization" against "savagery," the gun not only won the West in such fictions (as it did in fact) but helped make the notion of repeatability, of automation, familiar. Indeed, as recent scholars have remarked, the interchangeability of plots and characters in dime novels parallels the standardization of machine production that became a central feature of factory life in the 1880's. Dime novels also provided a field for technological fantasy; beginning with *The Huge Hunter,* or *The Steam Man of the Prairies* in 1865, these novels included inventors (often boys) as standard fare, along with robots (like the ten-foot steam man), armored flying vessels, electrified wire, and remote-control weapons. The fiction provided vicarious mechanical thrills along with fantasies of control and power. Machines are imagined as exotic instruments of destruction, only obliquely linked to the means of production revolutionizing the industrial system.

The fictive imagination of terror, of technological cataclysm, served as a form of familiarization. The implications of a technologized world and its potential for explosion was not lost on more troubled observers, who felt themselves on a precarious bridge between an earlier America and the present. Like Holmes, the novelist William Dean Howells worried about the intrusion of mechanism on morality. Viewing New York City from an elevated car, Basil March in Howells's *A Hazard of New Fortunes* (1890) has a sudden perception of a "lawless, godless" world, "the

46

absence of intelligent, comprehensive purpose in the huge disorder." March preserves his belief in a moral order, however, by concluding that such is the "chaos to which the individual selfishness must always lead," denying his earlier perception that "accident and then exigency seemed the forces at work" in the city. Howells's terror is hardly enjoyable; it arises from the sudden fear that moral choice, the acts of good people of sound character, might not prevail against the "accidents" of mechanized life. This passage and others from *A Hazard of New Fortunes* suggest how far toward cultural despair Howells had traveled since his response in Machinery Hall at the 1876 Centennial Exposition to one of the most colossal machines of the times. He wrote then of the "vast and almost silent grandeur," the "unerring intelligence," of the Corliss engine, struck by its apparent gentleness. And when the thought occurs that this "prodigious Afreet" could crush its attendant engineer "past all resemblance of humanity," it is swiftly repressed by an emotion of national pride in the "glorious triumphs of skill and invention" displayed in Philadelphia: pride, and a confident vision of cultural progress. "Yes," he writes, "it is still in these things of iron and steel that the national genius most freely speaks by; and by the inspired marbles, the breathing canvasses, the great literature; for the moment America is voluble in the strong metals and their infinite uses."

Howells's nervousness about that volubility, even as he embraces it as benign, was shared by many among his readers in the *Atlantic Monthly* and *Harper's*, the most respectable of the middle-class journals of opinion and letters in those years. Indeed, nervousness provoked by modern mechanical life provided the theme of the widely read medical treatise by George M. Beard in 1884. A pioneering work in the study of neurasthenia, *American Nervousness* builds its case through an elaborate mechanical metaphor: the nervous system is like a machine presently under strain in response to the pressures of the machinery of civilized life. Like Thomas Edison's central electric-light generator, wrote Beard (a friend of the inventor), "the nervous system of man is the centre of the nerve-force supplying all the organs of the body." "Modern nervousness," he explains, "is the cry of the system struggling with its environment," with all the pressures exerted on striving Americans by the telegraph and railroad and printing press. Simply to be on time, Beard argues, exacts a toll from the human system.

A treatise on causes of the breakdowns, distemper, anxieties becoming more common among the urban middle classes, Beard's book reveals yet another cause, social and cultural rather than technological, or of a genuine nervousness the author himself shares. He explains that by American he really means only "a fraction of American society," the "four million" salaried "brain-workers," those educated few who strive for "eminence or wealth" and wrestle with dilemmas of religion in an age of science. Excluding "muscle-workers," the "lower orders" who may succumb to "insanity of the incurable kind" but not "American nervousness," Beard makes nervousness a badge of distinction. He also discloses another source of severe anxiety prevalent among middle- and upper-class Americans, that of impending chaos, the rule of accident, exigency, and rampant city mobs. "All our civilization hangs by a thread; the activity and force of the very few make us what we are as a nation; and if, through degeneracy, the descendents of these few revert to the condition of their not very remote ancestors, all our haughty civilization will be wiped away."

The fear of cataclysm implicit here is not so much technological as social: a fear manifest throughout the popular media after 1877 of uprisings and insurrection, of a smoldering volcano under the streets. For David Wells, writing in 1885, such popular disturbances as the agitation for an eight-hour day and talk of socialism "seem full of menace of a mustering of the barbarians from within rather than as of old from without, for an attack on the whole present organization of society, and even the permanency of civilization itself." Henry George, too, concluded *Progress and Poverty* with a picture of potential collapse, of "carnivals of destruction." "Whence shall come the new barbarians," he asked. "Go through the squalid quarters of great cities, and you may see, even now, their gathering hordes! How shall learning perish? Men will cease to read, and books will kindle fires and be turned into cartridges!" The association of social unrest with the imagery of technological violence, of new city crowds with ignorance and contempt for culture (or regression to "savagery"), fired the imagination with a nightmarish narrative of impending apocalypse.

In all its guises, the machine had made the future seem problematic, and among the responses in the realm of culture were a growing number of future-oriented stories, utopian and science-fiction. Some, like Ignatius Donnelly's *Caesar's Column* (1889), portrayed class war fought with weapons of new magnitudes of destruction. More typical, as Neil Harris has shown, were tales of futures in which machines took charge for human benefit. On the whole, as Harris writes about the outpouring of futurist writings in the 1880's and onward, technology serves as "an enabling condition for the description of other worlds," the rational efficiency of machines teaching a lesson in eradicating human misery. Such works project modern anxieties about violence and disorder only to dispel them, often by fusing machines with mystical religions. Such a fusion "had a common objective: the allaying of human anxieties, and most of all, anxieties about aggression, accident, old age, and death." On the whole, this body of popular romance and utopian speculation fastened on science and the machine as a hope for rationality, for the control so wanted in present affairs.

This hope is strongest in the most influential utopian novel of the era, Edward Bellamy's *Looking Backward* (1888). Joining romance to a detailed account of a future society, the book appealed precisely to anxieties about mechanization and sordid cities by constructing a rational Christian alternative in Boston of A.D. 2000, superimposed on the contemporary city. The book follows the conversion of its upper-class, disaffected hero, Julian West, to the new (but familiarly traditional) "religion of solidarity." One of Beard's "nervous Americans," West awakens from mesmerically induced sleep (he suffered from the modern ailment of insomnia) in a sealed chamber deep in the recesses of his house, to discover himself in the future, a new house on the site of his own (which had been destroyed in a fire through which he slept, like Rip Van Winkle, into a new generation), and a new society in place. West learns from his host, Dr. Leete, that the new order had appeared simply and peacefully when Americans decided they had had enough of nervous-making economic crises, unhappiness, and threatening inequality. By a happy union of "solidarity" (the religious element) and rationality (the mechanical element), they devised a system of public ownership aptly called "nationalism." Taking its moral values from "solidarity," the system obeyed the rational forms and dictates of the machine—a logical evolution, Bellamy argues, from the factory system and corporate structures of the year 1887. Now the government is a Great Trust, and while local and family life has been decentralized, production and distribution have been placed under complete state control.

"Nowadays," the born-again Julian West observes, "everybody is part of a system with a distinct place and function." Production is managed through an "Industrial Army," a compulsory work force organized in strict military fashion, with hierarchies of command (based on merit and effort). The period of service is regimented but brief, leading the English socialist William Morris to comment in a review that Bellamy still accepted the industrial capitalist notion of work as "a mere adjunct of life," rather than "the necessary and indispensable instrument of human happiness." Happiness in *Looking Backward* is identified entirely with leisure and consumption—the consumption of religious emotions of "solidarity" as much as of the cornucopia of goods produced by the productive system. That system, though its organization is described in detail, remains invisible; West never visits the actual factories, though he tours the giant warehouses or department stores, where people no longer waste their time "shopping"; they trade credits earned in compulsory labor for goods already ordered. "It is like a gigantic mill, into the hopper of which goods are being poured by the train-load and ship-load, to issue at the other end in packages of pounds and ounces, yards and inches, pints and gallons, corresponding to the infinitely complex personal needs of half a million people." Infinitely complex, those needs remain measurable by standardized weights.

Bellamy's criticism aims at waste, haste, inefficiency, and injustice: at social organization, not at the machine. Like George's, his vision redeems the machine from a wasteful system. Moreover, in the most emotionally decisive maneuver of the book, Bellamy further deploys the machine to redeem the nation: "to realize the idea of the nation with a grandeur and completeness never before conceived . . . as a family, a vital union, a common life." Thus, West cures his nervousness in a restored family, peacefully consuming its machine-provided pleasures in safety and security—that is, in a fable of socialism (though Bellamy avoided that inflammatory word) amenable to middle-class America.

50

Bellamy's is a fable of hope, of social happiness. Mark Twain's venture into speculative romance, *A Connecticut Yankee in King Arthur's Court* (1889), is the obverse, its conclusion an unmitigated disaster of human carnage and emotional confusion. A complex and richly contradictory book, the novel also takes a backward look, into the Middle Ages. It pits nineteenth-century "ingenuity" and republicanism, in the person of Hank Morgan, against sixth-century superstition and monarchy. Foreman at a Hartford gun factory who is transposed to Camelot by a blow on the head from one of the "rough men" he supervises, Morgan combines in his person the republican ideology, fierce individualism, and practical inventiveness which had once, before the Civil War, seemed a stable set of bourgeois character traits. Inventor, businessman, and ideologue, Morgan sets out with sublime confidence to reform Arthurian England, to modernize its thinking and politics as well as its productive energies. Though at first a vehicle for satire aimed at the chivalric absurdities of Arthurian romance, and an assertion of the superiority of a down-to-earth practical wisdom against the inflated language and forms of deference associated with feudalism, Morgan soon takes up reform in earnest. Mechanism provides the chief image of his work, of his spectacular "effects" as well as his schools known as "Man-Factories," his newspapers, telephones, smoking factories, and stock exchange. Through all the comedy and exhortation to "freedom," as Darko Suvin observes, the book's imagery bursts with volcanic explosions, prefiguring the cataclysmic conclusion. Anticipating a counterrevolution by the Church, Morgan builds a fortification of electrified barbed wire topped with Gatling guns—devices borrowed intact from dime-novel fantasies of destruction. In the end, the Yankee and his small elite of faithful followers (who address him as The Boss) find themselves trapped behind "a solid wall of the dead—a bulwark, a breast-work, of corpses."

The Yankee's liberating project, as the industrial enterprise itself threatened to do in the eyes of Henry George and others, collapses in paradox: "We were in a trap you see—a trap of our making." In these final words of Clarence, one of the faithful, Mark Twain provides a grotesque metaphor for his own age. In the end, the book's argument itself collapses in a muddle, as neither Morgan nor Mark Twain is able to sort out the causes of failure. But the predicament the book dramatizes, of machine-making a human future, resonated grimly with realities of the day. Had "to produce" come to mean "to destroy"?

III

Such figurative associations of machines with violence suggest profound tensions among Americans who, like Mark Twain, otherwise saluted modern technology as a boon to republican ideals. Metaphors of wreckage and self-destruction seem to express unresolved cultural dilemmas, conflicting value systems such as those described by Leo Marx as "machine" and "garden," the values of mechanical progress and those of pastoral harmony in a peaceful landscape. But the coexistence of figures of destruction, of "dark Satanic mills," with those of unbounded Promethean production, also points in the direction of the Promethean effort itself, toward the character of the mechanization process. Subtle interweavings of destruction and creation formed the inner logic of the industrial capitalist system, a logic less conspicuous but nonetheless compelling in its consequences than the more dramatic versions of contradiction evoked by Henry George and Edward Bellamy. As analysts here and in Europe had begun to discover, that system possessed a baffling unconscious energy which resulted in recurrent cycles of expansion and contraction, inflation and deflation, confidence and depression. Such aberrations seemed to follow from precisely those increases in productive power which marked the industrial world in these years.

If Americans seemed especially intense in their response to mechanization, especially obsessed with alternating images of mechanical plenitude and devastation, an explanation lies in the special circumstances of native industrialization, its speed, its scale, its thoroughness within a brief period. Suffering fewer social barriers, possessing the largest domestic region convertible to a national market without internal restriction, by the end of the century American industry rapidly surpassed its chief European rivals, England and Germany. Figures of absolute increase signified the triumph: the production of raw steel rising from 13 tons in 1860 to near 5,000 in 1890, and of steel rails multiplying ten times in the same years; total agricultural output tripling between 1870 and 1900. Agriculture showed the most dramatic and immediate evidence. A single mechanized farmer in 1896 was able to reap more wheat than eighteen men working with horses and hand equipment sixty years earlier. As output increased, more land came under cultivation (increasing almost fivefold between 1850 and 1900, from about 15 to 37 percent of the total area of the country), and the proportion of the agricultural work force (including owners, tenants, and managers) declined precipitously from its height of 44 percent in 1880. In the critical decade of the 1880's, the balance began its historic shift in favor of nonfarm labor; heavy Northern investment, in machines to produce cash crops such as cotton, tobacco, grain, and cattle (their steep profits flowing as capital into industrial expansion), stimulated this process of displacement into crowded cities already bursting with rural immigrants from overseas.

But such figures of expansion tell only the outside story. The inner story concerned not only absolute increase but a revolutionary rise in *productivity.* "We have increased the power of production with a given amount of personal effort throughout the country," observed David Wells in 1885, "probably at least twenty-five, and possibly forty percent." In such figures the American propensity for mechanical improvement seemed to bear its most impressive fruit.

Of course, that propensity characterized the entire industrial world, but it had been a special mark of American manufacturing since its beginnings. With a scarcity of skilled labor, of craftsmen and artisans with accumulated experience in nascent industrial processes such as spinning, weaving, and milling, American circumstances placed a premium on mechanical invention and improvement. Scarcity of skills together with cheapness of land had maintained a relatively high cost of labor in the young United States. Moreover, as H. J. Habakkuk has explained, the relative absence of customary work processes and of formal engineering and scientific academies provided incentives for invention, for the devising of machines and techniques to compensate for labor scarcity. Without an inherited aristocratic social order, the new country held out more hope to entrepreneurs for social acceptance as well as material rewards. Many early industrial entrepreneurs had begun their working lives as craftsmen, mechanics with a knack for invention, and had risen to wealth and status as

53

a result of their mechanical skill and entrepreneurial expertise. With mechanical efficiency a greater economic need in the United States than in Europe, and with business a freer field of endeavor, American inventor-manufacturers such as Eli Whitney and Elias Howe developed and refined the practice of interchangeable parts (originally in the making of small arms) considerably before their European counterparts. By the 1850's, the practical Yankee inventor-entrepreneur, the tinkerer with an eye on profit, had come to seem an American type, proof of the republican principle that self-taught men of skill and ingenuity might rise to wealth and social position.

The prominence of mechanical skill made it seem to many that the dramatic increases in productivity during the years of explosive growth after the Civil War arose from the logic of invention, of mechanical improvement itself. But new economic conditions in fact marked a radical discontinuity with the past difficult for many Americans to grasp. The new breed of business leaders were often skilled in finance, in market manipulation, in corporate organization: entrepreneurial skills on a scale unimaginable to most manufacturers before the war. Moreover, they conducted their daily business through a growing system of managers, accountants, supervisors, lawyers: a burgeoning structure of business offices increasingly removed from the machines and labor in the factory itself. The process of invention and technological change lay increasingly in the hands of university-trained engineers and applied scientists, representing an entire new institutional formation which had mushroomed during and after the war. And industrial laborers now tended to be men and women without traditional skills, operators and machine tenders, with little hope of significant social improvement through their own talents and efforts. In short, the increasingly rigid social stratification that accompanied the dramatic rise in industrial productivity confused, angered, and frustrated masses of Americans, a growing percentage of them recent immigrants recruited into the very industrial system which seemed destined to dash their hopes of social improvement.

Technological determinism implied that machines demanded their own improvement, that they controlled the forms of production and drove their owners and workers. Americans were taught to view their machines as independent agencies of power, causes of "progress." Machines seemed fixed in shape, definite self-propelled objects in space. In fact, however, machinery underwent constant change in appearance, in function, in design. Machines were working parts of a dynamic system. And the motives for change, the source of industrial dynamism, lay not in the inanimate machine but in the economic necessities perceived by its owners. Higher rates of productivity through economies of scale and velocity, through greater exploitation of machinery and reorganization of both factory labor and corporate structures, were deliberate goals chosen by business leaders out of economic need. "Goaded by necessity and spurred by the prospect of higher returns," as David Landes writes, industrialists undertook a concerted quest for higher productivity. That quest proved the inner engine of mechanization.

Even minute increases in the rate of productivity might result in greater market advantages. The American fascination with the machine either in its Promethean or in its demonic aspect tended to divert attention from the countless small innovations at the work place, changes both in machinery and the design of work, accreting into major new patterns of production. The belief that viewed "progress" as a relation between new machines and old, a matter of replacing the outmoded by the novel, obscured the transformations of labor, of the human relation to production, each mechanical improvement represented. Technological change in these years consisted of a vast interrelated pattern of novelty, developments in metallurgy, mining, chemistry, hydraulics, electricity feeding back into each other. The result was new materials—such as hard steel, new lubricants for high-powered machines, new abrasives for grinding, new machine parts such as ball bearings—and improved machines, turret lathes, and milling machines for the precision-making of machines and tools themselves. With steam power prevailing in the 1870's, machines grew bigger and faster, and factories resembled jungles of shafts, belts, axles, and gears to transmit power from immense prime movers. By the late 1880's, industrial applications of electricity had already appeared, especially after the development, by Edison and others, of a central generating source. Electricity offered new possibilities of conversion of power into heat, light, and motion, and permitted new efficiencies and economies in the design of factories, including decentralization, dispersion of work areas, and assembly lines. In both the transformative (textiles, chemicals, food processing, glass making) and assembling (construction, clothing, shoe, machine making) industries, electricity worked major alterations in the forms of labor.

The most immediate consequences of changes in materials, power, shape and size and location of the machine,.and the degree of skill necessary for its operation, were felt in the industrial plants. Unsettled economic conditions made manufacturers obsessed with efficiency, with the breaking of bottlenecks, the logistics of work flow, the standardization of parts, measurements, and human effort. Throughout these years, cost-accounting concerns became more prominent, until by the 1890's the corporate office virtually dominated the work place, imposing demands for speed, regularity, and quotas of output. As a result, human effort fell more and more into mechanical categories, as if the laborer might also be conceived as an interchangeable part. Furious efforts to cut labor costs led to the announcement of severe work rules, the replacement of traditional craftsmen by unskilled or semiskilled labor: the effort, that is, to lower the cost of wages by increasing investment in the fixed capital of new machinery. Such developments, including the redesign of factory spaces for the sake of greater mechanical efficiency, set the stage for several of the fiercest labor struggles of the 1880's and 1890's. The process of continual refinement and rationalization of machinery, leading to twentieth-century automation, represented to industrial workers a steady erosion of their autonomy, their control, and their crafts.

In the record, then, of mechanical change lay an intermingling of production and destruction, the scrapping of old machines, old processes, and old human skills. An inevitable wreckage accompanied the "progress in manufacturing" David Wells had described as a "mighty river." That image hinted at unconscious meanings, the figure of speech disclosing more than Wells himself recognized. "Like one of our mighty rivers," he wrote in 1876 about manufacturing, "its movement is beyond control." All efforts at control would, "like the construction of piers and the deposits of sunken wrecks, simply deflect the current or constitute temporary obstruction." Wells employs such figures of speech to enforce his message against protective tariffs. Yet the figures intrude another message. The simile linking manufacturing and "our mighty rivers" tells us, for example, that machinery shares a kinship with nature, especially an American ("our") nature. The simile also alludes to the association of machines with water power: steam had displaced water by 1876, but just seven years earlier almost half the American manufacturing establishments drew power from waterwheels and turbines. In Wells's mind the process entailed calculated destruction for the sake of preserving profits. "Abandonment of large quantities of costly machinery," he explained further in an essay of 1885, is often "a matter of absolute economical necessity." Destruction of the old prevents "the destruction of a much greater amount of capital by industrial rivalry." Thus, the symbiotic relation between destruction and production illustrated a universal principle: "The destruction of what has once been wealth often marks a greater step in the progress of civilization than any great increase in material accumulation."

In these years the mighty river of industrial expansion threatened to take dominion everywhere, converting all labor to mechanical labor, to the production of commodities for distant markets. The spread of the machine meant the spread of the market: more of the continent and the society brought under the domain of political economy and its unconscious logic Wells explicated so vividly. Along with regional and local autonomy, age-old notions of space and time felt the impact of mechanization as a violent wrenching of the familiar. As more efficient machine production required greater attention to uniform parts and units of measurement, standardization of basic perceptions infiltrated the society. And the chief agent of such cultural changes was, of course, the most conspicuous machine of the age: the steam-driven locomotive, with its train of cars.

It is not difficult to account for the prominence of the railroad as the age's symbol of mechanization and of economic and political change. Railroad companies were the earliest giant corporations, the field of enterprise in which first appeared a new breed of men—the Cookes, Stanfords, Huntingtons, and Hills—of unprecedented personal wealth and untrammeled power. Not only did the railroad system make modern technology visible, intruding it as a physical presence in daily life, but it also offered means of exercising unexampled ruthlessness of economic power. In railroad monopolies, combinations, conspiracies to set rates and control traffic, lobbies to bribe public officials and buy legislatures, the nation had its first taste of robber barons on a grand scale.

At the same time the railroad system provided the age with fundamental lessons in physical and economic coordination. Its physical plant in these years represented the very best mechanical invention and improvement: greater load-bearing capabilities, higher speeds, and longer trains, following from air brakes, automatic couplers, block-signaling apparatus, standard-gauge tracks. Although often overcapitalized in the 1860's (through "watered stock," a favorite device of Wall Street speculators), the railroad system expanded into several national networks, providing major stimulation to basic industries like steel, construction, and machine making. In its corporate organization the system stressed coordination and interdependence, the railroad companies being the first to rationalize their business offices into central- and regional-sales, freight, passenger, and legal divisions. Resolutely private entities, even though they thrived on outlays of public funds and privileges through government agencies, the companies organized themselves along strict military lines; indeed, former Civil War generals often served as presidents and directors of operations. They emerged by the 1870's as competing private structures employing hundreds of thousands of citizens as managers, civil and mechanical engineers, lawyers, firemen and conductors, yard and gang laborers. Models of a new corporate world, they seemed the epitome of the modern machine.

Their prominence in America also followed from unique geographical conditions: the vast spaces to be traversed as cheap land, before the Civil War, encouraged far-flung settlements. As George Taylor has shown, a revolution in transportation proved necessary before "the almost explosive rush of industrial expansion which characterized the later decades of the century." Unlike the European situation, where mechanized transport appropriated existing roads and horse tracks as it overturned an older society and culture, here the railroad seemed to "open" places for settlement, for raw materials and transport to markets. As Wolfgang Schivelbusch observes about the American difference: "The mechanization of transport is not seen, as in Europe, as the destruction of a traditional culture, but as a means to gaining a new civilization from a hitherto worthless (because inaccessible) wilderness." The American railroad seemed to create new spaces, new regions of comprehension and economic value, and finally to incorporate a prehistoric geological terrain into historical time.

The exact economic value of this massive process has been a matter of some controversy among economic historians, Robert Fogel arguing that the "net benefit" of the displacement of the canal system by the railroad being "much less than is usually presumed." But there is no doubt that the railroad "increased the *economic accessibility*" of raw material. The railroads proved decisive in this era in facilitating that "interchange of matter" from one location to another (as Karl Marx put it), essential to industrial production. This change of location of raw materials and then of goods represented a radical breaking of spatial barriers, barriers of local and regional terrain and cultural difference. Thus, the external economy provided by the railroad in its increased velocity of transport included the incorporation of space and time as factors among the elements of production: the necessary act of overcoming barriers, of virtually annihilating space or distance by reconceiving it as time (places becoming identified as scheduled moments of departure and arrival), emerging as the major capital industry in the age of steam.

The necessity of pushing aside old concepts asserted itself especially in the establishment of standard time zones in 1883. Until that year, "local mean time" ruled across the continent, as it did throughout the world. Each locale assumed responsibility for setting its own time by tested methods of solar readings. Bells and clocks struck noon, for example, when the sun stood directly overhead: never exactly the same moment from place to place or week to week. Local life arranged itself in relation to the most influential community timepieces: church bells and steeple clocks, and after the 1840's, the cupolas and stark brick bell towers of mills and factories. The latter testified to a new importance assigned to time by the factory system, to promptness, regularity of work habits, and most of all, to the conversion of work into time-wages occurring within factory walls. But stubborn local standards persisted, and overlappings of regional times set by the larger cities and local times in the hinterlands formed a crazy-quilt pattern across the nation.

The necessity of regulating times appeared with the railroad; especially after the first transcontinental hookup in 1869, the situation seemed increasingly eccentric, to the point of danger and economic loss. Obviously, a railroad passing from New York to Chicago could not adjust itself to the dozens of local times different from each other by fractions of minutes (11 minutes 45 seconds, between Boston and New York, for example). Railroad corporations set their own times. By early 1883, there were about fifty such distinct private universes of time, each streaming on wheels through the countryside, oblivious of the others. Railroad-stations, which quickly became the most influential source of time in the larger cities, often displayed several clocks, each indicating the time on specific lines, and one declaring the presumed local :'me.

The issue came to a head in these years: not coincidentally, years of increasingly destructive competition in which the smallest factors of technical innovation in production or distribution might make the difference between success and failure. It seemed in everyone's interest to eliminate the disadvantage of eccentric time. The American Society of Civil Engineers joined with the American Association for the Advancement of Science and similar groups to give the approval of science to standard time zones. In 1882 the engineers reported: "Mistakes in the hour of the day are frequent. In every city or town, in every State, discrepancies are met which produce great aggregate inconvenience. Thousands of engagements are broken. Innumerable disappointments and losses result." In 1883 the railroads acted and, by joint decision, placed the country—without act of Congress, President, or the courts—under a scheme of four "standard time zones." This, of course, was "railroad time." Most communities adjusted their clocks at the railroad's behest (Chicago held out for a brief spell), and where local time did not immediately fall before the rush of the industrial machine, it remained only as a kind of twitch of residual "nervousness."

IV

In 1871, Walt Whitman, still in a mood of buoyant but guarded optimism about the future of America and his own role as bard of its democratic hopes, published one of his more ebullient

60

poems. But while ostensibly a celebration of recent technological feats, the Atlantic cable, the Suez Canal, the Union Pacific Railroad, "Passage to India" holds in reserve buried doubts and misgivings. A poem of "progress," it reverts obsessively to the "past"; a praise of accomplishment, it fastens on defeat: the "sad shade" of Columbus, the "unloving earth, without a throb to answer ours, / Cold earth, the place of graves." It sings "the great achievements of the present . . . the strong light works of engineers," yet finds them all useless apart from other works of the poet, "the true son of God," who will assure that "Nature and Man shall be disjoin'd and diffused no more." The poet seems to complete the work of the engineer—or does he remedy it, restoring what the machine has split asunder? The poem leaves this question unresolved, but ends with a prayer and a vision of a farther journey, a spiritual voyage launched "out of myself," toward a transcendent "Rondure" and solutions to "ye aged fierce enigmas" of life and death.

Doubts are registered in the lower frequencies of the poem. And even more ambiguous than the relation between poet and engineer is the idea of modern technology itself. On one hand, the poem speaks in the accents of celebration; then it seems to undercut the value of the magnificient engineering achievements by subordinating them to the work of the *poet*, whose constructions are of thin air. Whitman accurately perceives the political input of the communications and transportation revolutions, recognizing that they constituted a single world system, a global perspective, a "Rondure." Yet these awesome connections in space and the transcendence of time evoke fears of a widening gap between man and nature, a deeper alienation from earth. The poem makes no mention of either social or psychological effects of the new modes of travel and communication—no mention of markets and labor, of jolts to the nerves and altered perceptions of time and space—but produces a feeling of disjunction and dislocation, nevertheless.

In speaking of a redemptive' poet, a "son of God," a farther journey, Whitman seems to propose a solution to a problem only dimly perceived: the unspoken implications of modern industrial technology. For while his "engineer" seems a single-minded artificer of a grand system of connecting links, cables, canals, and spans, such acts of construction belonged as well to the rapidly

61

consolidating system of mechanical production. Whitman misses that association: the role of science and technology in the socio-economic dialectic of industrial production. In light of that role, the "Rondurc" described by engineering feats also obliterates the local, the regional, the immediate relation to an intimate "nature." It also represents a profoundly altered character of human labor itself.

The visionary mode of Whitman's celebration does not permit the sort of irony with which Herman Melville perceived modern machinery. Melville's poem on the mechanized iron-sided battle-ships employed in the Civil War, "A Utilitarian's View of the Monitor's Fight" (1866), views technology in the light of what it has displaced. The title links the phenomenon the poem describes to a leading nineteenth-century ideology popular among American businessmen, Jeremy Bentham's "calculus" of counting benefits against costs, of judging value by practical effects. "Plain mechanic power / Plied cogently," writes Melville in the ironic guise of a "Utilitarian," transforms "warriors" into "operatives" and war itself into a kind of factory labor. Indeed, "cogently" implies not only deadly accuracy but an end to the distinction between battle and work, between destruction and creation: "No passion; all went on by crank, / Pivot, and screw, and calculations of caloric." The heat of engines replaces the heat of human passion, and "calculations" now govern where once emotion ruled. By implication, the diminishment of warfare to industrial work results in the conversion of workers into mechanical parts, into mirror images of their machines: a hellish prospect Melville had imagined more than a decade earlier in his story, "Paradise of Bachelors and the Tartarus of Maids," in which female "operatives" of a paper-making factory appear as grim, impoverished counterparts to a group of smug, prosperous, and well-fed male lawyers.

Such premonitions of the rule of calculation anticipated the decisive developments in the 1870's and 1880's. In the quest for greater productivity, for more efficient machines, more output per unit of cost, calculation of several kinds played an increasingly significant role. With the enlarged role of the accounting office in decisions relevant to materials and labor, transportation, advertising, and sales, mathematical considerations entered the business world in a major way. At an opposite pole to commerce, another kind of abstract calculation appeared in an enlarged and more systematic role for science, for basic research as well as applied science and engineering. Professional, white-collar personnel expanded the size and influence of office and laboratory, both increasingly distant from the shop floor but increasingly pertinent to the daily arrangements and pace of factory life. Calculations of economy and of science developed into professional processes with their own skills and rules, but in the end their effects were felt in the changing relations between human labor and machines, in the steady encroachment of mechanization on the forms of work, of everyday life, and social transactions throughout America.

The enhanced importance of refined and reliable calculations implied a position of new significance for knowledge, a critical role for trained abstract thought within the productive system. This development appeared in an intricate process of institutional change: the appearance of new schools, of new relations between formal education and corporate industries, and greater accessibility of science to industry. Events in the 1870's and 1880's prepared the way for the turn-of-the-century research laboratory as an integral component of the electrical and chemical industries. The role of scientific method and knowledge within industries expanded, however, not primarily from schools and laboratories themselves, but from new perceptions on the part of industrial managers of the advantages of scientific calculation in their quest for greater productivity, a quest itself spurred by more systematic and rationalized methods of economic calculation.

The incorporation of basic science and formal technological training with industrial production quickened dramatically during these decades of economic uncertainty. During the earlier stages of industrialization, science and technology had seemed wholly separate and often antagonistic fields, theoretical scientists (often gentlemen amateurs) holding themselves aloof from either direct mechanical application or entrepreneurship. Even as late as the early nineteenth century, craftsmen-inventors such as Elias Howe and Oliver Evans ruled over technological innovation, using an on-the-job cut-and-try technique of experimentation. Such figures predominated especially in America, where formal science bore the onus of impracticality and remoteness from human need. In fact, however, practical innovators were less ignorant and disdainful of basic principles than the popular

63

notion recognized, and trained university scientists, particularly geologists, served as consultants for mining and railroad companies even before the Civil War. Even as the image of the self-taught cut-and-try inventor remained uppermost in popular thought as more distinctly American than the "gentleman scientist" or pure experimentalist, the currents began to converge. Graduate programs in science developed at major universities, and specialized schools of engineering supported by private funds, such as Massachusetts Institute of Technology (1866), proliferated; by 1900, the list of technical institutes included Case, Carnegie, Stevens, and Worcester Polytechnical Institute. With their close ties to private industries, their willingness to design their curricula to meet industrial needs, such schools fostered specialization of functions, a process reflected in the new professional societies splitting off from the original American Society of Civil Engineers (founded in 1852): mining, mechanical, electrical, and naval engineers all forming distinct societies with their own journals and meetings in these years.

Engineering thus transformed itself from its earlier empiricism and artisanship in order to mediate the vast structural changes in mechanical production compelled by economic need. "The artisan was replaced in the vanguard of technological progress by a new breed," writes Edwin Layton. "In place of oral traditions passed from master to apprentice, the new technologist substituted a college education, a professional organization, and a technical literature patterned on that of science." The schools, the professional societies, the new roles of responsibility within corporate hierarchies, fostered a new quality of mind and outlook: disciplined, systematic, administrative. Trained to combine the findings of formal science with economic, legal, and logistical considerations, rhe new engineers brought into industry an apparently detached, objective, and highly specialized approach to solving problems. But whether designing the flow of work in factories or rating the output of machines, the engineer served finally a chronic need of the industrial system: to impose system and order, through improved machinery, for the sake of assuring a reliable return on investments. As David Noble has argued, the new institutional ties between engineering and industry served that need of capitalists, more dire in time of crisis, "routinely to anticipate the future in order to survive."

The consequences were felt throughout the society and culture: most notably in the increasing specialization of knowledge, its fragmentation into arcane regions of technique and learning, and in the growing concentration of the power accompanying specialized knowledge and skills within private corporations. In the 1870's and 1880's, however, this process remained fairly hidden from view. With public attention focused on severe economic fluctuations, rising tensions between capital and labor, and the colorful if morally dubious lives of captains of industry, the steady incorporation of institutionalized rationality into the system went generally unnoticed. Moreover, persisting popular images of business success through self-help, luck and pluck, and venturesome risk taking, left little room for the concept of controlled and systematic anticipation of the future.

It remained a common belief that the system owed its dynamism and innovations to the personal "genius" of prominent individuals like Thomas A. Edison. One of the most popular Americans of his own time and since, Edison in his public guise represented a form of knowledge starkly at odds with new realities; indeed, at odds even with the truth about his own activities. Like the image of the isolated machine with its alternating demonic and Promethean currents, popular perceptions of Edison distorted the underlying logic of events, making "progress" seem both more accidental and more innocent.

Already renowned by the 1876 exposition for his multiflex telegraph, his improved ticker tape, his many patented devices, and his success as a manufacturer of his own stock-quotation printer, Edison rose to genuine fame with the invention of the phonograph in 1877 (he was then thirty years old). With his talking machine and, in 1879, the electric light bulb, Edison attracted perhaps the widest attention of the age in the press, journals, and popular books. In these years, the Edison legend took shape: the stories of his childhood experiments in rural Ohio with chemistry and electricity, his exploits as a trainboy on the Grand Truck Railroad of Canada and Central Michigan, the newspaper he published on board the train, his self-taught mastery of mechanics and electricity, his years of study, wandering, working at odd jobs, until his arrival in New York in 1868 and his invention of a stock-quotation printer which won the attention of Western Union and launched his career. The periodical literature stressed two key elements of Edison's success: his natural genius, flourishing without formal school training, and his instinctual entrepreneurship which led him unerringly to *useful*, that is to say, marketable inventions. Thus, the public Edison seemed to embody in perfect combination precisely what many at the time felt America to be losing, its rural Protestant virtues of the self-made man, and what it was gaining in the way of material improvements. Edison seemed to hold together the old and new, the world of the tinkerer and the world of modern industry; the age of steam (his youth on the railroad) and the coming age of electricity. He made the new America of cities and complicated machinery seem to evolve in an orderly fashion from the old America of country towns and youthful high jinks on country railroads.

As a form of popular knowledge and a version of the new industrial realities, the most critical feature of the Edison image concerned the origins of invention. In 1876, Edison had sold his manufacturing business in Newark and withdrew with a small group of helpers to Menlo Park, a quiet New Jersey town about an hour by railroad from New York, where he established the first significant industrial-research laboratory in America. After five years he moved to larger, better-equipped buildings in Orange, New Jersey, but the period at Menlo Park from 1876 to 1881 proved the most fertile of his career, yielding the most dramatic products of his labors: the phonograph, the improved telephone, the incandescent lamp, and the basic elements of a central power-generating system. It was during these years, too, that Edison assumed his best-known role, as "Wizard of Menlo Park." And in their accounts of the wizard, popular stories in the press and journals portrayed a character part Prometheus, bringing light, and part Faust, tainted with satanic association. The setting itself —the mysterious fire-lit laboratories in wooden buildings within a peaceful rural landscape—enhanced the demonic aura. But demonism was no more than a whiff, dissolved by descriptions of the guileless, open-faced, wry and salty Midwestern boy-man Edison turned out to be. Instead, the wizard image served another primary function: to account for the origins of Edison's inventions as personal "genius," out of the thin air of a fertile imagination and heroic persistence. "His inventions were calling to him with a sort of siren voice," wrote *Scribner's* in 1879. Moreover, as wizard and natural genius, Edison had no need of formal science, of mathematics and theory; the press played up his superiority to the schools, which on occasion issued scornful pronouncements upon him as a mere "mechanic."

Thus, Edison offered a reassurance that the old routes to personal success were still open, that the mass of inventions and improvements profoundly altering industry and reshaping personal lives truly emerged from a heroic wresting of the secrets of nature for human betterment. The phonograph especially, the inanimate made animate, inspired rhapsodies of technological fantasy. " 'If this can be done,' we ask, 'what is there that cannot be?' " exclaimed the writer in *Scribner's*. "We feel that there may, after all, be a relief for all human ills in the great storehouse of nature," he continued, adding pointedly: "There is an especial appropriateness, perhaps, in its occurring in a time of more than usual discontent."

With his eye to publicity, and no doubt his bemused enjoyment of so much attention, Edison seemed glad to collaborate in the image of the wizard, the wunderkind. In fact, however, Menlo Park and the later laboratories were testing grounds for the full-scale industrial research organizations which would develop within private industries such as General Electric and the American Telephone and Telegraph Company by the turn of the century. Edison hired university-trained scientists among his staff, including Francis R. Upton, a specialist in mathematical physics. Menlo Park was a team operation, the earliest research and development laboratory in America; Edison established the place as an "invention factory," a place where invention might be made to order for private industry. He differed from much of his public by having no illusions on that score. Invention was his business.

Concerning himself with economics as much as technics, Edison viewed his key inventions in light of their commercial feasibility—that is, of competing technologies they might displace. This was especially true of the electric bulb. "The prime desideratum," notes Thomas P. Hughes, "was an incandescent light economically competitive with gas." That competition drove Edison to conceive of "the electric light problem" (in his own words) as part of "a complete system for the distribution of electric light in small units in the same general manner as gas." And he recognized that the lighting system must be part of an

67

even larger "program" which included "the distribution of electric current for heat and power also." This meant, he wrote, "a comprehensive plan, analogous to illumination by gas, covering a network of conductors, all connected together, so that in any given city area the lights could be fed with electricity from several directions, thus eliminating any interruption due to disturbance on any particular section." It meant a structure of central generators, conductors, meters, current regulators, safety devices —and "commercially efficient motors to operate elevators, printing presses, lathes, fans, blowers, etc., etc., by the current generated in central stations and distributed through the network of main conductors installed in city streets." It meant, in short, an entire new system inscribed deeply, underground and overhead, into the life of the city: a system industrial in its character and private in its ownership.

Edison did not "invent" the light bulb; he improved existing models, developing a filament which would glow consistently. And in his quest for a solution to that problem, economic motives played so deep a role they can only with difficulty be separated from the technical procedures themselves. In the end, it is appropriate to say that his skill regarding the lamp proved to be chiefly commercial. Backed by J. P. Morgan, he quickly formed a company, and by 1882 opened the first central power plant in New York, the Pearl Street station, which illuminated eighty-five buildings.

Whether acts of wizardry or genius, or sheer luck, Edison's work belonged to the evolving structure of experimental science and its alliance with industrial capitalism. To stress this obvious fact is not to debunk the myth but to place it in perspective: to see it as a myth which disguises the radical changes occurring in the origins and uses of knowledge in these years. The new relations of science to industrial technology ultimately represented a new relation of human labor to the process of production. Separated by increasingly complex and dense institutions, the shop floor and the research laboratory belonged to the same universe of production. With machines performing more of the work previously performed by people, workers themselves were required to *know* less in order to perform their tasks—to know less because their machines know more. Mechanization entailed, then, the transference of technical knowledge from workers to machines, a process mediated by a new corps of trained engineers. The rise of specialized skills and arcane knowledge corresponded precisely to the obliteration of traditional knowledge among skilled manual laborers. The growing numbers of trained technologists on one hand and unskilled workers on the other were two faces of the same process.

As if called forth by this prime economic motive, Frederick W. Taylor, a foreman at the Midvale Steel Company in Pennsylvania, inaugurated in the 1880's his famous "time-study" experiments, aimed at elimination of waste, inefficiency, and what he called "soldiering" on the part of workers. With his stopwatch— a further encroachment of time on physical movement—Taylor proposed to systematize exactly that process Wells had described as production through destruction: the absolute subordination of "living labor" to the machine. He envisioned a complete renovation of the production process, with standardization of tools and equipment, replanning of factories for greater efficiency, and a "piece-rate" method of payment as incentive for workers. In *The Principles of Scientific Management* (1911), Taylor made explicit the heart of his program: to take possession for management of the "mass of traditional knowledge" once possessed by the workers themselves, "knowledge handed down to them by word of mouth, through the many years in which their trade has been developed from the primitive condition." For Taylor the stopwatch and flowchart were basic instruments whereby management might reduce that knowledge to measurable motions, eradicating their workers' autonomy at one stroke while enhancing their productivity.

Thus, the social distribution of knowledge begins a major shift, a transference (as far as technology and technique are concerned) from bottom to top, in these years of extensive and intensive mechanization. Just as important, and as a symbol of the process, *thought* now appears often in the dumb, mystifying shapes of machines, of standing and moving mechanical objects as incapable of explaining themselves to the unknowing eye as the standing stones of ancient peoples. The momentous event of mechanization, of science and technology coming to perform the labor most significant to the productivity of the system, reproduced itself in ambivalent cultural images of machines and inventors, and in displacements running like waves of shock through the social order.

69

3

CAPITAL AND LABOR

I

"I saw to-day a sight I had never seen before," noted Walt Whitman in February 1879, "and it amazed, and made me serious; three quite good-looking American men, of respectable personal presence, two of them young, carrying chiffonier-bags on their shoulders, and the usual long iron hooks in their hands, plodding along, their eyes cast down, spying for scraps, rags, bones, etc." Included in his notes for a lecture on "the tramp and strike questions," this sight of respectable Americans without work gave testimony to "grim and spectral dangers," long familiar in the Old World but unknown here. "Is the fresh and broad demesne of America," Whitman asked, "destined also to give them foothold and lodgment, permanent domicile?" Growing numbers of strikes and of tramps, of homeless workers stalked by starvation, assaulted the health of the republic. "If the United States, like the countries of the Old World, are also to grow vast crops of poor, desperate, dissatisfied, nomadic, miserably-waged populations, such as we see looming upon us of late years—steadily, even if slowly, eating into them like a cancer of lungs or stomach—then our republican experiment, notwithstanding all its surface-successes, is at heart an unhealthy failure."

Whitman shared his misgivings with large numbers of Americans in these years. The depression of 1873 and the violence of 1877 had struck alarm bells heard everywhere. America seemed once more on the edge of civil disaster. "Sudden as a thunderburst from a clear sky," wrote the journalist J. Dacus in 1877, "the crisis came upon the country. It seemed as if the whole social and political structure was on the very brink of ruin," as thousands of workers, "alleging that they were wronged and oppressed . . . bid defiance to the ordinary instruments of legal authority." Not all citizens, of course, viewed strikers and workers on the tramp with Whitman's sympathy. In a memorable collocation assembled from *The New York Times* of July 1877 by historian Philip Foner, the reader can easily discern the newspaper's point of view of the railroad strikers:

Disaffected elements, roughs, hoodlums, rioters, mob, suspicious-looking individuals, bad characters, thieves, blacklegs, looters, communists, rabble, labor-reform agitators, dangerous class of people, gangs, tramps, drunken section-men, law breakers, threatening crowd, bummers, ruffians, loafers, bullies, vagabonds, cowardly mob, bands of worthless fellows, incendiaries, enemies of society, reckless crowd, malcontents, wretched people, loud-mouthed orators, rapscallions, brigands, robbers, riffraff, terrible felons, idiots.

In short, all but "savage Indians." The dean of the Yale Law School supplied the missing term, however, in "A Paper on Tramps" at an 1877 meeting of the American Social Science Association: "As we utter the word *Tramp*, there arises straightaway before us the spectacle of a lazy, incorrigible, cowardly, utterly depraved savage." In such images of unruly passions and suspicious motives did respectable folk find their fears confirmed: the troubles marked a degeneration of virtue, a loss of those character traits of industry, regularity, and respect for order essential to the republic.

It is noteworthy that the violence of 1877 spurred middle-class organizations of charity and cultural enlightenment in towns and cities across the country. But intimations of disaster, of a cancerous growth attacking the nation's vital organs, did not subside. The 1880's brought even greater numbers of strikes and battles, reaching a crest in what labor historians call the Great Upheaval of 1886, the year of the Knights of Labor's great strike against Jay Gould's railroad in the Southwest, the peak of agitation for an eight-hour day, and the Haymarket riot in Chicago. The perception spread that America was in the grip of alien forces. But exactly who were the aliens became a bone of considerable contention. The vehemence of the *Times*, of journals like *The Nation*, and commentary from respectable middle-class pulpits such as Henry Ward Beecher's in Brooklyn, may have comforted some citizens with the notion that only virtue and discipline were wanted to restore harmony. But for many more, including communities in which small merchants and clergymen joined in support of aggrieved workers, the lack seemed more visible at the top of an increasingly lopsided society. After a harsh attack by police on demonstrating unemployed workers in Tompkins Square in New York in 1876, editor of the New York *Sun* (and later one of the prominent labor journalists of the period) John Swinton wrote angrily that "the power of money has become supreme over everything," securing "for the class who controls it all the special privileges" it required for "complete and absolute domination. This power must be kept in check," he wrote; "it must be broken or it will utterly crush the people."

Of course, "the power of money," class privilege, the dominion of wealth, had seemed potential enemies of "the people" since the early years of the republic, and the language of labor reformers and union leaders in the postwar era rang in accents of antebellum campaigns against monopolies and banks. By the same token, abject poverty, pauperism, the dependency and insecurity of wage-earning, had seemed equally out of place; these were precisely the social evils of Europe it was America's mission to prevent. Now, in the 1870's, these opposite images seemed out of control. During the Grant Administration (1869–77) the new monied power had been involved in scandal, bribery, and corruption reaching even to the Cabinet and the President's circle of intimates: Crédit Mobilier, the Gold Conspiracy, the Whiskey Ring, the notorious Salary Grab. Here the monied classes showed a new brand of arrogance, tampering with the political faith of the people. And a new breed of unscrupulous figures, chiefly financiers, speculators, and railroad promoters, tapping the public purse with apparent impunity, and parading their private wealth and power in lavish mansions and luxurious banquets, offended older business and political groups. With the depression of 1873, and spreading unemployment, poverty, unrest, and strikes in the following years, social contrasts reached a pitch without precedent in American life outside the slave South.

Both extremes seemed alien in the eyes of Americans in several social sectors, especially among that large stratum called the middle class. As that group itself experienced dynamic changes in these years, differentiations of vocation, values, and outlook, perceptions of the social world changed. A premise widely shared in the North before the war, indeed serving as a rallying cry for the Northern cause, held that all labor deserved its just rewards, that personal security and independence was the birthright of free Americans (white males) willing and able to work. Whitman evoked this broad belief and expectation in his remark in the 1870's that the "real culmination" of America lay in the prospective "establishment of millions of comfortable city homesteads and moderate-sized farms, healthy and independent, single separate ownership, fee simple, life in them complete but cheap, within reach of all." This had seemed to be the prevalent aspiration of factory workers, farmers, small merchants, and manufacturers.

Now, Whitman observed, the signs of "exceptional wealth, splendor, countless manufacturers, excess of exports, immense capital and capitalists," represented "a sort of anti-democratic disease and monstrosity." But for some middle-class people on the rise, the immensity of capital and capitalists represented perfectly that ambition of mobility implicit in "single separate ownership." Was not the successful businessman the very model of a "healthy and independent" America? The poor had no one to blame but themselves. Workers, on the other hand, tended to agree with Whitman. Inheritors of the republican rhetoric valuing labor, independence, and free institutions, they tended to view wage labor as another form of slavery, of life-long dependency, and the monied classes as usurpers. The condition of "employee" was not meant to be permanent.

The strength of republican rhetoric, of the prewar consensus regarding "free labor," was such that political battles and ideological campaigns in the Gilded Age took the appearance of struggles over the meaning of the word "America," over the political and cultural authority to define the term and thus to say what reality was and ought to be. The consensus, unstable even at the height of the campaign against slavery and the execution of the war, split asunder in the crisis of the 1870's. New ideological configurations reshaped themselves according to sharply diverse experiences which now divided industrial workers, small farmers, merchants, manufacturers, bankers, and a rapidly growing stratum of lawyers, managers, sales and clerical workers, professional engineers, teachers, and civil servants. Judging from rhetoric alone, the term "America" now seemed the unstable element, the issue in contention. And nowhere more so than in the unrelenting conflict between the two colossal forces of the period, capital and labor.

Like the West and the machine, capital and labor were highly charged, compact with changing and conflicting meanings. Uses of the images by business and workers differed profoundly on one side, but still rang with common meanings on another. Contrast grew increasingly stark and bitter in the eyes of labor, but few labor spokesmen called for an absolute overthrow of capital. Working-class consciousness took forms other than revolutionary action. "We want a system," explained Eugene Debs before his conversion to socialism in the 1890's, "in which the worker shall get what he produces and the capitalist shall produce what he gets." The dominant demands of labor were for fairness and economic justice, and as struggles intensified, a tone of betrayal appeared: had not the laboring man been led to expect a different outcome from his efforts than the prospect of lifelong drudgery and dependence?

The violence of feeling often registered in the speeches and writings of labor spokesmen arose in large part from the dawning sense of discrepancy between political promise and present conditions, between rhetoric and the facts of daily life. On the whole, labor had been drawn to the Republican Party during the Civil War on the basis of that party's espousal of the doctrine of free labor, of the nobility and dignity of productive work. The doctrine was founded on a work ethic which promised personal advancement and security for honest labor, frugal self-management, and disciplined personal character. Were not these virtues precisely the ground of distinction between the free North and the slave South, between the true America and its internal enemies? Embracing all "producing classes," excluding only those who, like speculators, promoters, and bankers, profited from the labors of others, Republicans viewed labor as the only sanctioned means to self-improvement. As Eric Foner writes, "The aspirations of the free labor ideology were thus thoroughly middle-class, for the successful laborer was one who achieved self-employment, and owned his own capital—a business, farm, or shop." With the small enterprise, the shop or farm, still at the basis of the Northern antebellum economy, all producers seemed potential entrepreneurs, and workers "nascent capitalists." "Property is the fruit of labor, property is desirable; is a positive good in the world," taught Abraham Lincoln; "that some would be rich shows that others may become rich." An implicit labor theory of value, that all wealth originates in someone's labor, seemed to assure continuous mobility between the status of laborer and the rank of independent entrepreneur. Drawing on popular sermonizing and storytelling about character reform, temperance, diligence, and self-made men, the free-labor ideology impressed itself deeply on middle-class life.

Its appeal to the majority of workers in the 1850's and 1860's, as the pace of industrialization quickened and factories developed into larger, more demanding institutions, is questionable. But as long as the boundary between wage earner and capitalist seemed relatively passable, as it did in the 1860's, the ideology retained some credibility among workers. Individual workers and labor organizations supported the Republicans during and just after the war years, as the radical wing of the party enacted a program of strengthening the federal government by extending its powers over both civil rights and banking. Support for emancipation, for equality (the Fourteenth Amendment redefining citizenship as a federal rather than a state right), seemed of a piece with the Republican economic program, and as David Montgomery has shown, labor groups looked toward Republican support for their demands, especially the eight-hour day. It became clear even by the end of the 1860's that the economic program would take first priority. Wartime fund-raising measures such as the increase in tariffs on imports and the establishment of direct taxes (including a short-lived income tax), the Legal Tender Act (1862), which increased the money supply by authorizing the issue of fiat paper money by the central government for the first time, and the founding of a National Banking System in 1863 established a key role for the federal government in the making of a unified national system of finance. Instituting the antebellum Whig program of direct government intervention to provide "internal improvements," the Republicans maintained the high tariff to protect manufacturers as well as to provide income for government, supported railroad development by subsidies, land grants, and rights of way, quickened the disposal of the Western public domain into private hands by the Homestead Act, and with its money and banking policies, contributed directly to capital formation, the most urgent need of the rapidly expanding industrial sector.

In pursuit of the twin goals of destroying slavery and enhancing the free labor of Northern industry, the Union government under the Radical Republicans emerged as a genuine national state, complete with powers to issue money, tax individuals and personal property, raise an army by conscription, and confer and protect citizenship and its civil rights. The party would serve as an umbrella for both labor and business interests as long as the free-labor ideology held out the promise that, in David Montgomery's words, something lay "beyond equality," some hope for workers of social and economic, as well as legal, equality. The labor-Republican alliance splintered, however, as disappointment, frustration, and a sense of betrayal grew among workers.

Conditions in the 1870's, the economic crisis in the North and the growing strength of Democratic "Redeemers" in the South, eroded the influence of the Radicals within the Republican Party. The ardent support for the voting and other civil rights of ex-slaves in the South had owed something to moral principle and something to expediency: the Republicans needed black votes for their majority in Congress. Black support lessened dramatically during the 1870's, as business-minded Republicans found willing friends among Southern Democrats. With the balance of commitment shifting from civil rights and equality toward more direct aid to industrial expansion (especially in the underdeveloped South, still reeling from the devastation of the war), Republicans were willing, in 1877, to barter Reconstruction and the federal occupation of the South, with its military protection of blacks, in exchange for the Presidency. Through the Compromise of 1877, the House of Representatives settled the disputed electoral count between Republican Rutherford Hayes and Democrat Samuel Tilden by declaring Hayes the victor by a single vote.

Facilitated in large measure by the intervention of Thomas Scott, president of the Pennsylvania Railroad, the nation's largest corporation at the time, the compromise was designed to forge an alliance between Northern Republicans and friendly Southern Democrats especially interested in federal aid for such regional projects as the completion of the Southern Pacific Railroad. Agreeing to abandon the efforts to swing votes for Tilden, the South gained autonomy for white-controlled state governments and the understanding that it might pursue its policies of racial discrimination without Northern intervention. As C. Vann Woodward has shown, the "politics of reconciliation" did not work smoothly for all parties. The compromise patently failed to bring the South into the new industrial order on a par with other sections. But it did open the region to Northern capital, which kept the South as a loyal "satellite" of the dominant industrial regime. Thus, concluded Woodward, "the South became a bulwark instead of a menace to the new order."

In that new order, it became clear, the ideology of free labor that promised independence and mobility for all honest, diligent laborers had developed into a justification of big business, and further, an implied insult to the cultural status of manual laborers. Surrounded by images of status, success, and wealth, increasingly locked into a wage system which offered small hope of release from toil by independent ownership, and finding the horny-handed laborer increasingly characterized by such epithets as the *Times* employed in 1877, labor spokesmen adopted an angry, defensive tone. William Sylvis, leader of the iron molders in the 1860's, damned "effeminate non-producers" while praising the true "dignity of labor" of industrial workers, "the bone and muscle of the nation, the very pillars of our temple of liberty." "Labor . . . creates everything and does everything, and is the protector and preserver of all," proclaimed the Knights of St. Crispin, or the Sovereigns of Industry, a cooperative league of workingmen based in New England. Without labor, thundered Eugene Debs, "the warehouses would stand empty, factories would be silent, ships and docks would rot, cities would tumble down, and universal ruin would prevail."

Such apocalyptic words reflected the spirit of duress of the times, when heights of production also provoked nightmares of destruction. But the essential fact, as David Montgomery has shown, is that working people saw themselves as the true inheritors of the republican tradition, the genuine upholders of free labor. In their oratory, their defense of labor, and their assault on privilege and the corrupting powers of wealth, labor spokesmen fashioned a figure of the worker drawn from the older "producer class" together with the image of a defender of the republic. The language of republicanism and fervent Americanism has suggested to some that labor remained in these years within the middle-class consensus. And, to be sure, features of individualistic thought appear in the persistence of a simple labor theory of value, on the basis of which each laborer demands a just portion of his product. An examination of rhetorical figures suggests that even the fiercest antagonists in these years often shared a common vocabulary, common assertions of the "dignity of labor," the value of diligence and regular habits, the importance of discipline and "character." Such common imagery reflects the transitional character of the moment, the first disbelieving and disapproving recognition that the wage system had become a permanent fixture of American life. Dominated by craftsmen and seasoned industrial workers, labor organizations early in the period refused to accept this change and still drew on a free-labor rhetoric while proposing cooperatives and collective ownership of factories and businesses. The republican and work-ethic imagery points, then, to deeper issues than battles over hours and wages and work-place control. On another level, struggles between labor and capital raged on the ground of culture, the meaning of the nation itself at stake.

II

Raising an evangelical warning about sundry "perils" facing the nation, the Home Missionary minister Josiah Strong took note in 1886, the year of labor's "Great Upheaval," of "an almost impassable gulf" existing between industrial employees and employers. His widely reprinted popular tract, *Our Country*, warned of a "present crisis" to social peace and the integrity of the Protestant faith and the Anglo-Saxon race. America's mission to settle the West and awaken the world to Christ seemed threatened by unrestricted immigration, rising Romanism, sinful cities, irresponsible wealth, and socialism. The latter peril arose from that impassable gulf created by a factory system which had "developed a dependent class" on one hand, and, on the other, owners with "little personal acquaintance" with their employees and

78

"little personal interest in them." The very impersonality of the system, so unlike the recent past when journeymen and proprietors sat side by side at the workbench, wrote Strong, now "rendered it vastly more difficult to rise from the condition of employee to that of an employer, thus separating the classes more widely."

By the late 1880's, that separation had become palpable in communities throughout the nation. Where workers and owners may once have shared common experiences, of community (in smaller towns and cities), schools, churches, civic groups, now barriers arose: the wealthy left congested residential areas for secluded, clean, and fresh suburban areas; they sent their children to exclusive schools, their wives to expensive resorts and summer homes and on trips abroad, themselves and their families to newly built elegant churches with comfortable pews where they could hear Sunday sermons about the virtue of wealth, the sorrows of poverty. And more and more, as the industrial working class took on a distinctly "foreign" cast with heavy immigration from Catholic and Slavic nations, the wealthy came to seem a homogeneous group: white, Anglo-Saxon, Protestant, and Republican. "The men who were getting to the top," writes Carl Degler, "even in the 1870's—that alleged era of the self-made man —had not been poor farm boys or uneducated immigrant lads starting at the bottom, but instead men who had been given rather exceptional opportunities to make the race to the top." Older propertied elites, such as the Boston Brahmins, easily accommodated their interests to those of the new self-made breed; through alliances of old and new wealth throughout the country, businessmen came more and more to seem a ruling class with cultural norms of its own.

We have to reckon, then, with the fact and the perception of a widening class rift. The context includes the intense rate of technological change, the shift from steam to electrical power, which altered daily relations between workers and management at work places. Technological change also made new demands on individual entrepreneurs, new forms of competition, and new challenges to policy and bookkeeping. Social definitions of basic categories—capital, labor, enterprise, work, ownership—all underwent shifting and sliding alterations in the watershed decades of the 1870's and 1880's. The rapidity of change left in its wake confusion and anger, a loss of bearings, and a gathering of forces. Both the rate of business failure—some contemporary observers spoke of a 95 percent rate in the 1870's and 1880's—and the incidence of strikes—close to 37,000, involving 7 million workers on record between 1881 and 1905—provide dramatic indices of turmoil.

To all appearances, the age belonged to big business, to railroad leaders, industrialists, and financiers like the Harrimans, the Stanfords, the Carnegies and Rockefellers and Swifts and Morgans. These were household names, better known in the press and pulpit than those of labor leaders like William Sylvis, Ira Steward, Uriah Stephens, Terence Powderly. Men of business seemed the epitome of the era, models who served to lure "men of ambition and ability" into the fray of competition, according to H. J. Habakkuk, "not only because of the gains which might be made there—though they were sometimes enormous—but because businessmen, a Rockefeller or a Pierpont Morgan, were leading men of the country." They were also portrayed as models of virtue in "rags to riches" fiction and in the literature of advice and exhortation by preachers like Henry Ward Beecher and Russell Conwell (whose "acres of diamonds" pamphlet sold in the millions) and by articulate businessmen themselves. Speaking to students in a commercial college in 1885, Andrew Carnegie admonished: "You know that there is no genuine, praiseworthy success in life if you are not honest, truthful, fair-dealing."

The warning suggests a region of ambiguity in the very image of success, for the public knew well enough that virtue was the easiest victim in the hard world of competition. Repressed as overt criticism of business in the success literature, that knowledge appeared in the frequent portrayal in popular stories such as those by Horatio Alger of wicked and cruel bankers who threaten widows with foreclosure. In Alger's world, as John Cawelti has noted, industrial enterprises rarely appear; benevolent figures are usually diligent and honest merchants, and successful young men settle for modestly lucrative positions within the firm. Measured against the antebellum work ethic, the robber barons seemed aggrandizers rather than honest and frugal producers. Success literature hid this conflict in melodramatic victories over the unscrupulous capitalist, but could not eliminate it altogether. The popular image of the business world held unresolved tensions: on one hand, it seemed the field of just rewards, on the other, a realm of questionable motives and unbridled appetites.

The image accumulated its ambiguities under circumstances of increasingly unnerving competition, in which rewards flowed more often to sheer power than entrepreneurial skill. In the very celebration of the businessman as the epitome of American individualism, we detect signs of concern that the older individualistic virtues no longer apply, that the ability to mobilize, to concentrate, to *incorporate*, counted for more than thrift and diligence. The enormous role of luck in Alger's tales may contain a covert recognition that the route to success required some magical outside assistance. For it was clear, even in images of robber barons and captains of industry, that business was a kind of warfare, in which all's fair which succeeds.

"They pursued their game of war on each other with zest and without mercy," writes Louis Hacker about the railroad companies in the 1860's and 1870's. The image of warfare filtered into public discourse in accounts of these very doings by speculators like Jay Gould and empire builders like Hill and Huntington. While the spectacle appalled, it also thrilled, and certain Americans leaped to defend such motives and practices as true to the natural order of things. "The race is to the strong," the Episcopal Bishop of Massachusetts, William Lawrence, assured his flock, adding the further guarantee that "Godliness is in league with riches." The celebrity of the English social philosopher Herbert Spencer among business groups and their supporters provided another rich source of imagery. Spencer's "Social Darwinism" seemed to sanction precisely that scene of tumult and conflict, of rising and falling fortunes. "Nature's cure for most social and political diseases is better than man's," argued Nicholas Murray Butler, president of Columbia University. A law of nature, added Yale sociologist William Graham Sumner, the struggle for existence "can no more be done away with than gravitation." "It is here," stated Andrew Carnegie in his efforts to account for his own phenomenal rise to fame and fortune through competition; "we cannot evade it. And while the law may be sometimes hard for the individual, it is best for the race, because it insures the survival of the fittest in every department."

In fact, efforts to evade, to control, to do away with destructive competition, emerged by the 1880's as a cardinal motive of the biggest business interests. Increasingly, the instrument of success proved to be more effective organization, the restructuring of enterprises into corporations in which financing and sales along with production fell under control of a single entity. Within the age of the robber barons, another age and another form took shape, that of the giant corporate body. The age of celebrated individualism harbored the decisive decline of proprietors, family businesses, simple partnerships: the familiar forms of capital. These older forms of commercial and manufacturing enterprise did not wholly disappear, of course, but they were no longer typical and they diminished in importance.

Two interrelated motives lay behind the enormous increase in the use of the device of incorporation in the postbellum years: the desire to control competition and the wish to facilitate access to capital. A chronic shortage of capital before the war, together with prospects for high returns, led many foreigners to invest in American railroad companies. The need expanded significantly with the growth of new industrial enterprises after the war, and government banking, money, and credit policies eased the way for the expansion of intermediary institutions such as banks and insurance companies, to transfer private savings into capital formation. While the supply of circulating money increased significantly through government policies, it did not keep pace with economic growth, because of steadily falling prices during the postwar decades and the significant increase in the national market. As market exchanges became the pervasive form of economic activity (in contrast, for example, to the relative self-sufficiency of family farms earlier in the century), as more and more of economic life came under the rule of the competitive market, the demand for money increased and intensified.

In a period of expanding economic growth and more or less unstable money supply, the advantages of incorporation were manifold, for it permitted a number of people to pool their capital and their efforts under one name, as a single entity. By tradition, the granting of corporate status usually required a special act by the sovereign, or, in the United States after the Revolution, by state legislatures, an act which included provisions regulating the internal organization of the corporate body and its public functions. Chief Justice Marshall gave this view its classic expression in the Dartmouth College case of 1819. "A corporation," he wrote, "is an artificial being, invisible, intangible, and existing only in contemplation of law. Being a mere creature of law, it possesses only those properties which the charter of its creation confers upon it." The status was granted in these early years chiefly to companies providing transport, water supply, insurance, banking. State governments often joined such chartered companies in "mixed enterprises" which subordinated private profit-seeking to public service: the establishment of external economies essential to agriculture, commerce, and industry.

As James Willard Hurst points out, American corporate law developed in a homegrown fashion, in response to the pressures of changing circumstances. After the Civil War, the practice of the special charter requiring a separate act of a legislature gave way to standard general laws and much simpler, more generous, and less regulatory procedures. In many states (New Jersey particularly), incorporation by the 1870's had become more of a right than a privilege, a status virtually for the asking. This democratization of procedure thus made available to business an easy and quick legitimation of what came to seem an indispensable instrument, in Hurst's words, "for mustering and disciplining large amounts of capital and allowing dependable continuity for its use." Freed from encumbrances often attached to special charters, and from the presumption of public service, of any but a profit-making purpose, the corporation swiftly displaced unincorporated forms (individual ownership, partnership) as the most significant organization of business.

The corporation embodied a legally sanctioned fiction, that an association of people constituted a single entity which might hold property, sue and be sued, enter contracts, and continue in existence beyond the lifetime or membership of any of its participants. The association itself was understood as strictly contractual, not necessarily comprised of people acquainted with each other or joined by any common motive other than profit seeking. The law called for a delegation of control and policy making to a board of directors and managers: the power, that is, to issue shares to the public at large with the understanding that shareholders were legally immune from liability for the debts of the corporate entity. Thus, the mass of shareholders, while technically owners of the corporation, willingly abandoned authority

83

over their investment in return for the security of limited liability. Centralized control proved to be an economic asset in its own right, permitting efficiencies of administration, freedom of negotiation, extensions of control among many companies within single industries, and integrating whole industrial steps, from the extraction of raw materials to processing and marketing, within single companies. The corporate form produced a variety of forms only faintly anticipated by entrepreneurs before the war, fostering protean changes of purpose, from running a railroad to spinning textiles, mining coal to making toys. Such ease of change, of purpose, function, even name, altered basic concepts such as ownership; property itself "acquired a new meaning," writes Daniel Boorstin, "a new mystery; a new unintelligibility."

With the corporate device as its chief instrument, business grew increasingly arcane and mysterious, spawning new roles intermediary between capital and labor, in middle management, accounting, legal departments, public relations, advertising, marketing, sales: the entire apparatus of twentieth-century corporate life was developed in these years and clouded the public perception of the typical acts of business. Organization and administration emerged as major virtues, along with obedience and loyalty. At the same time the rhetoric of success continued to hail the self-made man as the paragon of free labor, even as the virtues of that fictive character grew less and less relevant. Thus, incorporation engendered a cultural paradox. While praising the stern virtues of struggle and risk taking, Nicholas Murray Butler could still exclaim: "I weigh my words when I say that in my judgment the limited liability corporation is the greatest single discovery of modern times," far surpassing "even steam and electricity."

Seedtime of a new corporate order, the Gilded Age was dominated by images of personal power, of force, determination, the will to prevail. To be sure, in the early postwar decades the corporate form seemed to provide a stage for strong individuals, a field of struggle on which it was possible to entertain an ideology of social Darwinism even while piecing together structures which aimed to diminish risk and submerge the laissez-faire doctrine in cornered markets and controlled resources. "The growth of a large business," wrote John D. Rockefeller, "is merely a survival of the fittest, the working out of a law of nature and a law of God."

With savings from his partnership in a small produce-commission business in Cleveland, Rockefeller invested in oil during the Civil War, organized a small refining company, and in 1870 incorporated the Standard Oil Company of Ohio. The fierceness of competition in this lucrative trade in one of the essential ingredients for illumination and lubrication led to drastically unstable conditions, secret deals between refiners and railroads for advantageous rebates, and fluctuating prices. It was urgent, Rockefeller explained, for someone to "bring some order out of what was rapidly becoming a state of chaos."

Submitting chaos to order, Rockefeller created in Standard Oil a virtual state of his own. Within a decade he wrested control of about 90 percent of the trade. "It is well understood in commercial circles," noted a congressional investigating committee in 1886, "that the Standard Oil Company brooks no competition; that its settled policy and firm determination is to crush out all who may be rash enough to enter the field against it; that it hesitates at nothing in the accomplishment of this purpose." The more colorful methods included threats, fraud, chicanery, and open violence. But seeing an opportunity to control the entire process, from extraction to marketing, Rockefeller and his lawyers seized on the corporate device, chartering under the permissive New Jersey laws the famous South Improvement Company. Under its charter he joined with a handful of other refiners and several railroad companies in a convenient arrangement whereby member carriers would return generous rebates to member refiners. The successful aim was to eliminate competition and achieve monopoly over wells, refineries, pipelines, railroads, and delivery routes. Under the banner of Standard Oil, Rockefeller (whose name by now symbolized a well-disciplined and adept organization) developed an intricate marketing system, dividing the country into districts and subdistricts, and employing methods from price cutting to coercion against retailers reluctant to accept his products under his terms. The corporation won its victories by superior organization and efficiency in production and sales. About his rivals Rockefeller remarked: "They had not the means to build pipe lines, bulk ships, tank wagons;

they couldn't have their agents all over the country, couldn't manufacture their own acid, bungs, wicks, lamps, do their own cooperage—so many things; it ramified indefinitely."

An "apostle of order," writes the historian Edward C. Kirkland, Rockefeller saw through his own rhetoric to understand that "the incalculable must give way to the rational, strife to cooperation." Often caricatured as a tight-fisted, mean-spirited Baptist, Rockefeller grasped the significance of his endeavors as a phase in the unfolding of a new corporate order. "This movement," he wrote, "was the origin of the whole system of modern economic administration. It has revolutionized the way of doing business all over the world. The time was ripe for it. It had to come, though all we saw at the moment was the need to save ourselves from wasteful conditions . . . The day of combination is here to stay. Individualism has gone, never to return." Standard Oil (the name itself significant) typified the major trend in business, toward integration, standardization, and central administration.

Moreover, while founding corporations, artificial persons with a legal and economic life of their own, the Rockefellers, Harrimans, Hills, and hundreds of their regional and local counterparts also founded family dynasties that employed devices of incorporation, forming themselves into businesslike entities, trusts, foundations, and holding companies serving to keep intact and transferable through inheritance the family's fortune. The same logic that introduced the private corporation into the broad American demesne also produced new monied dynasties: a ruling stratum of inherited wealth, position, and power. Behind Rockefeller's tearless farewell to the classic American individualism and its doctrine of free and virtuous labor, the hand of a new secular Providence performed its deeds.

III

The rate of failure in the postbellum business world suggests how exceptional were the robber barons and their lesser cousins. But those who survived did so on a scale of conspicuous display by which the successful represented themselves as the most prominent and potent figures in the society, princely in their mansions, their banquets, their excursions to pleasure resorts, their philanthropy and admonishments about success, and firm, resolute, sharp-eyed and far-reaching in their actual business. Their power to attract attention, even as objects of criticism and scorn as well as envy, derived as much from the willingness of the press to follow their doings as from the monumental scale of their city homes, their new towering office buildings and railroad terminals, the museums and libraries and civic buildings all inscribed with their preferred style of elegance and power. Such display made perfectly plain who ruled the society.

Portraying itself as success, business thus captured the free-labor ideology, convincing the middle classes that in competitive enterprise lay the route to fulfillment, to the true America. Predominantly Protestants of Anglo-Saxon origins, the leading business families reinforced this claim with cultural homogeneity, an assertion of authority over a native tradition. In cultural as well as economic and legal ownership, America seemed to belong to its entrepreneurs. For Mark Twain it was Hank Morgan, the "Boss," who represented the Yankee; Henry James chose as his leading character in *The American* (1877) a Western millionaire with the appropriate New World name of Christopher Newman. And while such characterizations in fiction, sermons, editorial commentary, often assumed a background of labor, of physical skill as well as entrepreneurial acumen and a desire for self-improvement, the popular image of the industrial worker in the same years underwent a major revision; the worker now appeared as foreign, alien, in need of Americanizing.

A new American working class arose in these years, recruited out of the necessities of economic growth and shaped by the rapidly changing character of both industrial labor and entrepreneurial structure. Wage labor emerged, unequivocally, as the definitive working-class experience, a proletarianization no longer the imagined nightmare of independent artisans and failed entrepreneurs but the typical lot of American workers. Growing even more rapidly than the general population, which almost doubled between 1870 and 1900, the industrial labor force expanded to more than a third of the population by the end of the century. The figures represent a worldwide pattern of industrial and urban growth: a massive movement of rural peoples into factories and cities. In the United States, currents of migration from the countryside mingled with overseas immigration to change the actual composition as well as the public image of the worker: now less likely to be a skilled artisan of English, Welsh, or German background—with pride in craft, experience in trade unions, some degree of economic and cultural security—but more likely an unskilled·laborer with no previous industrial experience. And among the new wage earners, the foreign born or their children counted for a major percentage. Immigrants alone represented a third of the total population increase between 1860 and 1900, and by 1870 one out of every three industrial workers was an immigrant (the proportion would remain constant until the 1920's).

Increasing ethnic diversity and the making of a new industrial working class constituted a single process, introducing cultural difference into American life on an unprecedented scale. "Not every foreigner is a workingman," observed a Chicago clergyman in 1887, but "it may almost be said that every workingman is a foreigner." The remark fell not very short of the mark, since in many of the larger cities, including Chicago, the majority of the population were immigrants and their offspring. Moreover, an aura of a more general cultural foreignness began to attach itself to manual wage labor itself, particularly in light of the growth of salaried white-collar occupations among an increasingly suburban middle class. Often crowded into cramped living spaces, in slum tenements or abandoned middle-class housing in older districts, working-class families tended toward ethnic and racial enclaves where native languages and styles of life prevailed. Work was often dirty, backbreaking, and frustrating. Working women and children seemed at odds with middle-class ideals of home and school. In the popular press, workers found themselves stereotyped as the unwashed, unenlightened masses, swayed by disreputable-looking bomb throwers and associated with brutish caricatures of Irish potato eaters, slow-witted Slovaks, fun-loving Italians. On every count, labor seemed to represent a foreign culture, alien to American values epitomized by successful representatives of capital.

The most dramatic visible symptom of tensions governing working-class life appeared in the growing number of industrial strikes, reaching the tens of thousands in incidence, and involving hundreds of thousands of workers in the peak years of 1877, 1886, 1892–93. A ready weapon in the era before widespread adoption of union contracts and collective bargaining, the strike was often a spontaneous response to local circumstances, a protest against an arbitrary firing by a foreman, an assertion of rights against a change in work rules. The number of striking workers in the 1870's and 1880's far exceeded registered union membership. But strikes were not simply responses to economic and working conditions. They signified more than protest, and although their character differed from case to case—and altered over time—they were an expression of working-class life.

As a working-class event within public life, "strike" represented a defiance of the cardinal norm of everyday life: compliance with the authority of employers. The strike was a rupture, a release, an act of negation by which a sense of positive freedom came to the fore. The word itself ran deep in the history of work, naming a variety of simple, basic acts in the crafts of carpentry, surveying, bricklaying, tanning, farming, shipbuilding, fishing, and sailing. Directly from the nautical meaning of lowering sails or taking down, and more generally unfixing and putting out of use, the term began to appear early in the industrial era in its familiar sense of work stoppage. To strike work or tools was to assert the power of workers over the process of production: to strike was, in short, an act of work, albeit negative. It was, moreover, a collective act, embodying a recognition that the freedom which arose from negation belonged to a common group. Thus, a significant cultural element of virtually all strikes eludes strict calculation: "the rush out of the gates," in David Montgomery's words, "the songs they savored, the symbolic violence, the parades, and the oratory all bore witness to those aspects of the strike which cannot be subjected to statistical correlations."

The 1880's witnessed almost ten thousand strikes and lockouts; close to 700,000 workers went out in 1886 alone, the year of the "Great Upheaval." That decade brought into sharpest focus what from the 1860's had served as labor's leading national issue, the eight-hour day. The 1873 depression had rendered almost wholly ineffective legislation and agreements limiting work hours in the 1860's; ten, twelve, or more hours of work, with irregular seasonal layoffs, were common. The focal event of 1886 was the plan for a national general strike on May 1 to demand an "eight-hour" law. Here was an attempt (by no means the first, but the most dramatic to date) to plan a nationwide strike to mobilize workers into a national movement. The turnout on May 1 was only about 300,000, but the significance of events in Chicago on May 3 overshadowed the issue of the eight-hour day. At the McCormick Harvester Company, four strikers were killed by police. A protest meeeting was called for Haymarket Square; it proceeded peacefully until, as the crowd was dispersing, a bomb was thrown, killing a policeman; in the riot that followed (for which the police had already arrayed their might), seven more police and four civilians lost their lives. "The bomb was a godsend to the enemies of the labor movement," wrote John Swinton. Police rounded up eight known anarchists, charged them with the killings (the actual thrower of the bomb has never been identified), and four were executed in 1887. The event proved a setback for the eight-hour movement, and the onset of a fatal decline in the strength of the Knights of Labor. The Chicago "red scare" flamed across the nation, branding labor with the charge of fomenting anarchy and violence.

What lay behind the readiness to strike, to refuse, to unfix and put down tools, with all the attendant consequences of economic hardship, beating, and arrest? The extremity of economic need is an obvious though incomplete explanation. In part, the strikes were in response to maneuvers by industrialists: wage cuts designed to increase productivity by decreasing costs; an intensified application of advanced machine technology, eliminating many traditional crafts and speeding up the pace of work; a more fevered competition among businesses at a time of increasing consolidation and concentration of economic control. A rough economic profile from the end of the 1880's indicates how close to the margin of poverty many workers were compelled to live. About 45 percent of the industrial laborers barely held on above the $500-per-year poverty line; about 40 percent lived below the line of tolerable existence, surviving in shabby tenements and run-down neighborhoods by dint of income eked out by working wives and children. About a fourth of those below the poverty line lived in actual destitution. A small group of highly skilled workers, about 15 percent, were capable of earning from $800 to $1,100 a year. The common daily pay for unskilled labor remained about $1.50. Moreover, hardships were exacerbated by periods of high unemployment (as much as 16 percent) during the depressions of the mid-1870's and mid-1880's.

This is not to speak of substandard conditions beyond the home, such as schooling, sewer, water, and lighting in working-class neighborhoods. Moreover, conditions at work contributed to a readiness to strike the tools. Hazards to health and to life itself were common in the heavy-metal industries, in textile factories, and in chemical plants. The railroad took a particularly horrible toll: 72,000 employees killed on the tracks between 1890 and 1917, and close to 2 million injured; another 158,000 killed in repair shops and roundhouses. Workmen's compensation did not appear until the 1930's, and railroad disability insurance not until 1947. When we take into account the heat and danger from molten steel at open hearths, the threats of cave-ins and toxic gases in coal mines, the danger to fingers and limbs in all kinds of machines with unguarded moving parts—a picture emerges of mechanized violence inherent in the industrial work place.

Not only did industrial wage earners lack adequate protection against injury or insurance to cover time lost from work, they labored under conditions set by the clock. Measurement of work by units of time was basic to the accounting system of the productive process. Measurement by time represented the transformation of the laborer's efforts, his skills, intelligence, and muscle power, into a salable commodity: his own labor converted into a market value, into wages. The image of machinery as "labor-saving" held a bitter irony for workers: not only did machines threaten life and limb, not only did they increasingly threaten the usefulness of craft skills, but, employed by capital to increase productivity as rapidly as possible, they often increased the amount of physical exertion over time. No wonder the eight-hour movement, to make workers "masters of their own time," won such wholehearted working-class support—and no wonder the movement consistently failed in these years.

Another issue concerned what came to be known as the "union work rule." This complex issue related to agreement with management over such matters as rates of work and pay, tempo of work, and output. At the beginning of the period, a significant degree of autonomy in establishing these conditions lay with skilled craftsmen, workers already experienced in industrial labor. A growing number of strikes in the 1880's and 1890's concerned these matters, as management undertook "efficiency" campaigns to wrest control from skilled workers. By the close of the period, "scientific management" had provided a rationale and a body of methods precisely to transfer work-place control to employers, and in so doing to complete a process inherent in industrialization: the appropriation of inherited craft skills by industrial capital. To protect their own skills and the traditional rights of control over them, industrial artisans displayed what David Montgomery has described as a "spirit of mutuality": "technical knowledge acquired on the job was embedded in a mutualistic ethical code, also acquired on the job, and together these attributes provided skilled workers with considerable autonomy at their work and powers of resistance to the wishes of their employers." Resistance increasingly took the form of "sympathy strikes," which in the 1880's and 1890's represented a growing percentage of all strikes.

While it is rash to infer a unified working-class consciousness from the incidence of strikes and other expressions of work-place dissatisfaction, evidence suggests a pervasive rejection of the concept of wage labor. But workers, members of the larger society whether foreign-born or native, were not immune to cultural influences. The story of the "self-made man" pervaded the popular media and political and clerical rhetoric. While Horatio Alger had depicted the "humble beginnings" of this fictive character as rural, many living testimonies had shifted the setting to fit an urban industrial world. Thus Andrew Carnegie, himself once an immigrant boy: "From the dark cellar running a steam engine at two dollars a week, begrimed with coal dirt, without a trace of the elevating influences of life, I was lifted into paradise, yes, heaven, as it seemed to me, with newspapers, pens, pencils, and sunshine about me . . . I felt that my foot was upon the ladder and that I was bound to climb."

The typical legend of providential success in the new America included a concept whose influence and role in working-class culture has not received the critical attention it deserves, that of "character." The term is implicit in Carnegie's reference to "elevating influences," the usual source of character and respectability, and explicit in such commonplaces of the period as Lincoln's:

92

"If any continue through life in the condition of hired laborer, it is not the fault of the system, but because of either a dependent nature which prefers it, or improvidence, folly, or singular misfortune." Even labor spokesmen frequently voiced protests and demands in a language which evoked a similar notion of character. In its *Address of the National Labor Congress to the Workingmen of the United States* (1866)—a significant early formulation of a national policy for workers—the National Labor Union supported the campaign for a legal eight-hour day by linking it to "the virtue, the intelligence, and the independence of the working classes," essential to "the success of our republican institutions. Any system," the document argued, "social or political, which tends to keep the masses in ignorance, whether by unjust or oppressive laws, or by over-manual labor, is injurious alike to the interests of the state and the individual."

How widespread was working-class acceptance of a normative bourgeois idea of virtue is difficult to say. Certainly, workers' social institutions, fraternal orders, benevolent societies, clubs, and reading groups—as well as communal neighborhood groups centered in church, family, drinking place—presented alternatives to reigning values of acquisitive individualism. Immigrant workers, especially, clung to neighborhood and street life against "Americanizing" pressures of charity groups and social reformers who sought to inculcate new habits of regularity and temperance. Moreover, numerous short-lived cooperative enterprises arose in the 1870's and 1880's, both consumer and producer cooperatives: grocery and general retail stores, newspapers, banks, and factories producing shoes, pianos, soap, brooms, and so on. Taking into account such new patterns of organizing the necessities of life, we can speak, as does David Montgomery, of "a collectivist counterculture in the midst of the growing factory system," a "spirit of mutuality" arising from the very conditions of wage labor.

But, in fact, mutuality did not lead to an effectively unified working class. The "religion of solidarity," which Edward Bellamy tried to promote in the nation as a whole and the Knights of Labor attempted to instill among all "producers," encountered not only the resistance of a dominant culture of individualism and competition but also divisions among workers such as ethnic

93

antagonism, language and religious differences between skilled and unskilled workers.

Ethnic, racial, and sexual discrimination, geographical dispersion; exhausting and often impoverishing working and living conditions; and increasingly staunch and violent opposition from employers, the press, and the government, all hampered the fledgling labor movement in these years, and helped set the conditions for the decline of "reformism"—the principled opposition to the wage system—and the victory of the policy of the American Federation of Labor in the 1890's. The beginnings of intense organization after the Civil War show labor and its supporters among the reform community searching for viable institutional forms: the reform association, the trade union (some already in the late 1860's calling themselves "national"), several abortive labor parties, and sections (small, but vocal and influential) of the International Workingmen's Association (for which Karl Marx was a leading spokesman). Statistical evidence is not fully reliable, but at no point did the trade unions themselves include more than 10 percent of the industrial work force; no union in this period succeeded in recruiting as much as one third of any given trade, and most of the mass-production industries successfully resisted unionization.

While unions did not encompass all the meanings of "labor" in these years, and the unevenness of their growth and their success in particular regions, industries, and communities limited their representativeness, still, the trade union was a uniquely working-class form. It rose to prominence in these years and, better than any other structure, gave expression to common thoughts about common experiences. Of course, the term embraced a range of ideas about strategy and tactics, and historians have described in detail the main lines of division, between "reform" groups such as the "assemblies" of the Knights of Labor and the "trade-unions" among specific crafts, which eventually comprised the American Federation of Labor. The Knights advocated broad unions of skilled and unskilled workers, and included small businessmen among the class of "producers"; they rejected the legitimacy and permanence of wages, and looked toward "the organization of all laborers into one great solidarity, and the direction of their united efforts toward measures that shall, by peaceful processes, evolve the working classes out of their present condition in the wage-system into a cooperative system." Within the Knights, however, ran another current, which preferred struggles for immediate improvements and grew doubtful of an eventual "cooperative commonwealth." Held especially by skilled workers in traditional crafts, this point of view came into ascendancy late in the 1880's and 1890's, as membership in the Knights declined and the strength of the AFL increased. Under Samuel Gompers, the AFL made improved wages the center of its program, giving it priority over long-range reform. "Unions, pure and simple," wrote Gompers, "are the natural organization of wage workers to secure their present and practical improvement and to achieve their final emancipation . . . The way out of the wage system is through higher wages." Excluding "reform" from its tactics, the AFL fashioned the strike and boycott as weapons to set bargaining into motion, to make the "union label" the mark of legitimacy. Thus, the label seemed to signify labor's willingness to accept the wage system in exchange for a secure place within the social order, and under the AFL, "union" and "strike" would often come to seem vehicles of integration rather than agents of insurrection.

The spirit of the 1870's and 1880's belonged to the Knights: their formulation of the labor-capital conflict seemed to exercise the most powerful sway. Moreover, their insistence on "one great solidarity" arose from a state of affairs rife with division and antagonism: not only labor against capital but skilled Protestant workers against unskilled Catholic and Jewish newcomers; whites against blacks and Asians; men against women. Such antagonisms existed in real measure. New immigrants and blacks in the North were used as strikebreakers; often they were targets of violent attack by strikers, and of aggrieved resentment thereafter. Segregated neighborhoods and ethnic and racial competition for jobs abetted such antagonisms. Ethnicity, racial and sexual prejudices, proved in many cases stronger forces than class identification. Discriminatory practices by employers contributed to such antagonisms: blacks assigned the lowest order of work, denied apprenticeships and the opportunity to learn mechanical skills; women, still second-class citizens, earning less pay for equal work, thus seeming to "cheapen" the labor market.

Still, while racist and sexist biases reigned throughout the culture, labor organizations offered an alternative. The National

Labor Union, founded by William H. Sylvis in 1866, admitted women and blacks to full membership, actively campaigned for their support, and advocated "equal pay for equal work." The NLU did not survive the defeat of its Labor Reform Party in the elections of 1872, and the Knights of Labor, founded in 1869 by a tailor, Uriah H. Stephens, emerged as the most potent national organization of workers in the following two decades. It excluded only bankers, lawyers, gamblers, and liquor dealers from its membership of "producers," and, like the NLU, advocated racial, sexual, and ethnic equality. To be sure, women were not accepted as a matter of course; not only patriarchal attitudes about the "weaker" and "fair" sex who belonged "at home" but economic fears that women laborers lowered the price of labor often clouded the egalitarian program of the Knights. Nevertheless, their assemblies included several comprised entirely of women, and others of Southern black workers. In their famous Preamble, the Knights included equal pay for women along with abolition of child labor, an eight-hour day, a graduated income tax, and government ownership of "telegraphs, telephones and railroads" as measures necessary to achieve a cooperative society. In short, in its public statements, the labor movement opposed the various forms of inequality—racial, sexual, and economic— accepted as a matter of course throughout America.

And in doing so, labor thought of itself as upholding nothing so much as the fundamental American traditions of republicanism and equality—indeed, as the most vigorous defenders of that tradition: so far from "foreign" as to be the most authentic voice of America itself. Labor attitudes on social issues embodied an amalgam of values and outlooks derived from sundry cultural sources. Evidence suggests the beginnings at least of a significant coalescence of influences into a distinct labor culture in these years. The most common rhetorical form of labor statements, its speeches and programs, its calls to action and its rallying songs, expressed an unmistakable fusion of republicanism and evangelical Protestantism. One common form was the alternative "declaration of independence," of which dozens appeared in these years, issued on the Fourth of July by unions, farmers' groups, black organizations, women's-rights groups. and socialists. Typically, it opened with the familiar preamble of principles: "We hold these truths to be self-evident"; proceeded into a bill of complaints against monopolies and economic injustice, concluding with a series of resolutions for reform. Furthermore, calls for a "Golden Rule of Christ," for a "new Pentecost," and statements such as George E. McNeill's that "the hope of peaceful solution to the problem of today rests in the Christianizing influence of our free institutions," support Herbert Gutman's argument that workers found in Protestantism a profound "notion of right" for their struggles. It is telling, moreover, that Protestants marched without a qualm under banners proclaiming the names of patron saints of labor, that workers of all creeds accepted the implied medievalism and chivalric code of the *Knights* of Labor without question. Indeed, religious sources of labor culture showed as much in the actual social groupings of workers as in their evangelical rhetoric, in fraternal orders such as the Knights, in countless church groups and benevolent societies, in labor "temples" and the "mummery" of pageants and parades. To be sure, a widespread proliferation of such associations occurred throughout the society in these years: professional societies, sporting clubs, and clubs of hobbyists, of amateur enthusiasts of local history and geography. Workers often participated in these as citizens of their local communities or as sportsmen or stamp collectors. But, in unions and working-class community groups, it was clear that membership implied a commonality of the work experience, and that the secret pledges and oaths and proclamations of solidarity implied a distinct, if unspecific, religious model. Just as important was the wage-earning experience itself, its lessons in collective enterprise. Of course, the work place was also a place of internal hierarchy; master craftsmen and apprentices and helpers were not equal, and under subcontracting arrangements, skilled workers often assumed the role of "boss" toward the unskilled. But on the whole the efforts by craft unions to formulate and uphold regular work rules, to clarify the various work tasks and their functional importance, were grounded in an ethic of cooperation, of mutuality: that is, it flowed from the rhetoric of republican and religious equality. To a certain extent, the movement toward producer cooperatives, a key plank of the Knights, found an impetus in the cooperative arrangements among workers at work. Strikes, too, were occasions of mutuality, and performance of women, blacks, Catholics, and ethnic groups on the picket line provided experiences of unity and equality. Thus, the "religion of solidarity" proclaimed by Edward Bellamy and other Protestant reformers was often a living experience within labor.

We know too little of this evolving labor culture which developed as a conscious alternative to the culture of competitive individualism, of acquisitiveness and segregation. It was short-lived, although its legacy reappears throughout the later history of labor. A residual culture of ethnic identity, religious and re-publican· communitarianism, it was also in some instances fostered by class-conscious radicals. In Chicago, for example, German anarchists not only preached dynamite and self-defense as "propaganda of the deed" but included in their program alternative institutions of everyday life: schools and libraries, reading clubs and mutual-benefit societies, groups of poets and dramatists dedicated to ridicule and mockery of "high" culture. A consciousness of positive cultural difference appeared in the words of George E. McNeill: "We complain that culture busies itself upon immaterial subjects—conning the olden lore, delving for the unrevealed treasures that lie embossed in humanity." Arguing that "civilization is common property," he wrote that "the institutions that enable the many to read and write and speak their native language amply and correctly are communistic institutions, inasmuch as the results are common property, even when the buildings are under private ownership." And he envisioned a process in which, as "the laborer receives more and more for his earnings," as hours decrease and factory buildings are "so improved that labor shall become a blessing instead of a curse, a pleasure instead of a pain," culture itself will undergo radical revision. Instead of the present "poor, ignorant, physically and mentally, and sometimes morally, deformed unskilled worker," the "now-dawning day" will show "a well-built, fully equipped manhood, using the morning hours in the duties and pleasures of the sun-lit home; taking his morning paper in the well-equipped reading-room of the manufactory." The worker will be, then, a man of "civilization." True enough, McNeill still imagines "civilization" as a comfortable middle-class life available to all. But in 1890 the vision implied for labor a "new revolution" which "shall evolve the dude out of existence; the rot of a false-named culture shall be of the past."

Once a shock to the American body politic, the "impassable gulf" between labor and capital came shortly enough to be accepted, tolerated as inevitable. In the 1880's and 1890's, however, the body politic still reeled in shock that America should encompass a gulf of any sort. Was it for this, the Knights of Labor asked in its Preamble, that we took the land, "by physical power, by robbery or fraud," from the Indians? Indian lands were "originally common property." Can we justify "driving the native from the land of his fathers," if their once-sacred possession now "remains in the hands of individual proprietors?" If we committed that act "in the name of civilization, then in that name their possessions should be common property." This rare piece of logic regarding the Indian warfare just subsiding took on added point with the revelations of the census of 1890. Based on its figures, Charles Spahr calculated a range of income distribution which provided one measure of the shape and depth of the gulf. Out of 12 million families, 11 million lived on incomes below $1,200 a year. The average income of this group was $380, far below the accepted poverty line. In the population as a whole, the richest one percent earned more than the total income of the poorest 50 percent, and commanded more wealth than the remaining 99 percent. About half of all American families lived without property.

Statistics measured only the economic dimensions of the gulf. In addition, labor had begun to rear structures of culture at odds with the individualist values of business, of middle-class aspiration. Not that working people were immune to such aspirations, or that a wholly distinct working-class culture established itself in these years as an independent sector of American life. But it was palpable to many labor spokesmen that unions and corporations arose from radically different outlooks, from sharply diverging views of human relations. Both collective entities, both representing consolidations on behalf of economic interest, unions and corporations diverged dramatically in the relation of their members to the organization as a whole. Corporations absolved their investors from liability should the joint enterprise fail. Relations between investors and directors, between the body of owners and the cadre of managers, became increasingly impersonal, indirect, governed by technicalities of law. To be sure, unions, too, would eventually develop internal bureaucracies and a self-perpetuating stratum of leaders. But the predominant meaning of "union" in these years lay in the motto of the Knights of Labor: "An injury to one is the concern of all." Rather than absolving members of liability, unions fostered a sense of mutual responsibility. Members counted on protection, on the willingness of the "all" to come to the aid of the "one."

Such differences in the human relations of unions and corporations arose from differences in the daily experiences of workers and businessmen. Born in competition, corporations formed themselves as superior economic fighting units. They existed solely for the sake of the market, and assumed acquisitiveness as the primary motive of economic behavior. Unions stood on a different ground, at the place of work rather than the marketplace of trade. They assumed equality among their members, a virtually religious communal bond expressed in oaths, emblems, hymns, and, in the case of the Knights, in rites of secrecy. Many unions continued to oppose the wage system as a system of enforced and permanent inequality. They condemned unbridled competition and celebrated productive labor as the source of cultural value as well as economic wealth. Moreover, arising from the "idea of solidarity," as Norman Ware has remarked about the Knights of Labor, the very word "union" echoed with the original principle of the nation itself—E Pluribus Unum—while "incorporation" implied a unity based on unequal members. Thus, in the eyes of unions, the incorporation of America seemed a profound contradiction in terms. In the antithesis between "union" and "corporation," the age indeed witnessed an impassable gulf of troubling proportions, for it remained unsettled on which side lay the true America.

4

MYSTERIES OF THE GREAT CITY

I

The road to salvation in John Bunyan's renowned Christian allegory, *The Pilgrim's Progress* (1678), led from the City of Destruction to the City of Zion, the Celestial City which "stood upon a mighty hill." On his perilous route away from "the place of all evil," the Pilgrim passes through the Town of Carnal-Policy (home of Master Worldly Wiseman), and the Town of Vanity and its infamous Fair where could be found "all such Merchandize sold, as Houses, Lands, Trades, Places, Honours, Preferments, Titles, Countryes, Kingdoms, Lusts, Pleasures and Delights of all sorts." In addition to buying and selling, Vanity Fair provided entertainments of "Jugling, Cheats, Games, Plays, Fools, Apes, Knaves, and Rougues," and the more gruesome sights, "and that for nothing," of "Thefts, Murders, Adulteries, False-swearers, and that of a bloodred colour." The beleaguered Pilgrim finally crosses the Delectable Mountains and reaches a City "builded of Pearls and precious stones," the Celestial City which "shone like the Sun," whose streets "paved with Gold" echoed with the hymns of its white-robed inhabitants.

"I have used similitudes," the English Bunyan declared in his epigraph taken from *Hosea*, and his images of alternative cities, the blood-red city of man and the white, shining city of God, inscribed themselves deep within the Protestant imagination in America. From its publication late in the seventeenth century until the Civil War, *The Pilgrim's Progress* ranked with the Bible as the best-read book in America, a standard catechism and mode

101

of instruction. It was commonplace in respectable families for children to "play" Pilgrim's Progress, to enact event and plot as do the little people in Louisa May Alcott's perennial best-seller, *Little Women* (1868). And although the sales of Bunyan's text, and the unqualified pious response to it, fell off sharply after the war, its similitudes of good and evil cities continued to color perceptions. Bunyan's image of a city "upon a mighty hill," moreover, echoed with one of the most famous and oft-repeated sentences in the history of Protestant American culture—John Winthrop's declaration aboard the *Arabella,* in 1630, just before it touched land at Boston harbor with the first colonists of the Massachusetts Bay Colony, that "wee must consider that wee shall be as a Citty upon a Hill, the eies of all people are upon us." Winthrop's sermon, known as "A Modell of Christian Charity," has been taken as the inaugural document of Protestant America, the text which first articulated the colonists' goal of knitting themselves together as "one body in Christ," as a single corporate entity bound by charity and love, in covenant with God. Under that covenant, in Winthrop's vision, America itself might be a Celestial City, a city of man redeemed by the white city of God.

The vision and hope persisted in Protestant rhetoric, as Sacvan Bercovitch has shown, even into the era of the gilded cities of the late nineteenth century. A double-edged tradition, it bequeathed (with the help of Bunyan) images of Vanity Fair as well as of a city upon a hill, a fabric of images of corruption, sin, and destruction, which colored the secular perceptions of many Americans in these years of the most rapid and thorough and tumultuous urbanization the country had yet experienced.

Josiah Strong in his tract of 1886 painted the city as the "storm center" of "our civilization," its "most serious menace." His portrait is utterly of a City of Destruction: "Here the sway of Mammon is widest . . . Here luxuries are gathered—everything that dazzles the eye, or tempts the appetite . . . Dives and Lazarus are brought face to face; here, in sharp contrast, are the *ennui* of surfeit and the desperation of starvation." Poverty breeds discontent and socialism, he wrote in that year of upheaval, multiplying "the dangerous elements": "Here is heaped the social dynamite; here roughs, gamblers, thieves, robbers, lawless and desperate men of all sorts, congregate; men who are ready on any pretext to raise riots." Strong anticipated a coming Armageddon, an urban apocalypse, unless the Christian forces took heed. Nor were secular perceptions immune from these intimations. "Present tendencies are hurrying modern society toward inevitable catastrophe," wrote Henry George, evoking a picture of "new barbarians" gathering strength "in the squalid quarters of great cities." Against this prospect, George cast his own city upon a hill: a "healthful home" for every city family, "set in its garden," with the mechanical aids of light, heat, telephone, and access to libraries, concerts, theaters, all at hand for an elevated life.

Within the traditional image of the fallen city lay another image, less of moral condemnation and more of fear and anxiety: the image of the city as mystery, as unfathomable darkness and shadow. Best understood as a trope, a figure of speech, mystery had attached itself to the very idea of a city, as opposed to the countryside, from earliest historical times. The biblical Sodom and Gomorrah, the Rome of Petronius and Juvenal, the murderous court intrigues and decadent pleasures of fashionable life portrayed in English Renaissance and Restoration drama, contributed a literary background to Bunyan's similitudes, making it possible for him to allegorize in simple, easily available terms the moral condition of humans by reference to cities. As cities throughout Europe began to expand and change their character with the coming of the industrial revolution, the trope of mystery also changed; more secular, it focused less on sin and more on a new inexplicableness in city crowds and spaces, a new unintelligibility in human relations. "The face of every one / That passes by me is a mystery!" wrote Wordsworth about his experience on "those overflowing streets" of early-nineteenth-century London, and about St. Bartholomew's Fair in that city: "Oh, blank confusion! true epitome / Of what the mighty City is herself." With denser crowds, more intricate, bewildering divisions of space, sharpening contrasts between rich and poor, the nineteenth-century industrializing city seemed a ripe setting for Gothic romance, and Eugène Sue's delvings into the hidden underworld in his *Mysteries of Paris* set a style for lurid city writings, for guidebooks promising to "unveil" the "secrets" of the city. In America before the Civil War, Charles Brockden Brown, Poe, George Lippard, Hawthorne, and Melville all resorted to mystery in their portrayals of the city.

The figure remained undiminished in potency in the postbellum years, in popular and serious fiction, and in public discourse in general. But two significant changes of emphasis occurred. The sheer intensity of growth, in population, in territory, in material shape, resulted in a critical crossing of a line between "city" and "great city," or metropolis. With the rise of the metropolis (New York and Chicago the most typical) came an awareness of new regions of mystery, and new attitudes toward it. Especially in discourses of fiction, social science, and political commentary addressed to middle-class audiences, mystery fused with the sense of immediate menace that Josiah Strong expressed: poverty, crime, threat of insurrection, political corruption, and the physical dangers (adding a mechanical, automatic element to the fear of apocalypse) of exploding gas mains and inflammable electrical wires. Confronting the "choking confusion, scuffling blind bewilderment" of traffic on Broadway, one writer asked, in an article in 1870 on "The Future of New York": "Where is the growth of a city like New York . . . to stop?" Would the city eventually annex the very nation with the same ineluctable force with which it engulfed adjacent towns? The answer lay in the mysterious "Manhattan sphinx."

The great city had enlarged the scope and scale of mystery itself, bursting the conventional biblical and Gothic tropes to form a new figure, a fusion of social, political, and technological peril. Mystery had been raised to the level of spectacle, the daily performances of city life now seemed to more and more commentators to be parades of obscurity, of enigma, of silent sphinxes challenging the puzzled citizen.

The response of middle-class citizens to that challenge represents the new attitude. For this age of the metropolis is also the age of reform, of more concerted, collective efforts on the part of homeowners and property holders, newly aroused to their potential metropolitan powers, to take control of urban reality, to define it, shape, and order it according to an evolving urban ideal, a secular Celestial City of shapely boulevards, healthful parks, comfortable and secure private habitations, and elegant public buildings. The programs of reform faced mystery squarely, determined to replace the blood-red tints of Vanity Fair with the shining gold and whiteness of the City of Zion.

Manifesting a new attitude, reformers set out to cure the city by transforming its mysteries into light. Except for outlying provincial fundamentalism, even evangelical missionary zeal was directed toward saving the city, to help its poor and protect its citizens from the threats of crime, corruption, and disorder. Militant Christian purpose appeared in "crusades" for charitable works among the "other half," the downtrodden and foreign-born, for good government and improved citizenship, for sanitation, street lighting, boulevards, and parks. Such practical works, which occupied Christian and liberal reform groups increasingly after the fright of 1877, drew together values dispersed throughout white Protestant culture. A new, receptive view of the city appeared in popular fiction, for example, a view which also wished to transform mystery into light by acts of the imagination.

Like the Pilgrim's path to salvation, Horatio Alger's road to success also lay through a city, but the Alger hero makes his progress within the place, converting Bunyan's linear allegory through a symbolic landscape into a vertical rise within the city. And in the course of transforming himself, the hero also works a transformation on the reader's sense of the city, disclosing celestial opportunities within Vanity Fair. Alger's secular fables work by magic, by luck, rather than by providence. But in their schematic form they offer narrative underpinnings to a new worldly acceptance of the urban place. A place of chance encounters, the city in Alger's fictions consists of exchanges. In his first novel, *Ragged Dick: Or, Street Life in New York* (1867), as Dick initiates Frank, a newly found friend from the country, into the sights and ways of the city, so Frank initiates Dick into the pleasures of new clothing, proper speech, and a bank account. The exchange, which inaugurates Dick's rise from carefree, hard-boiled bootblack to a man of affairs (in later novels), occurs during an extended tour of Manhattan on which Dick guides Frank, demystifying the system of street numbering, the meaning of sights and sounds ("What does he mean?" asks Frank when he hears a street crier calling "Glass puddin." "Perhaps you'd like some," said Dick, before his friend realizes it is a glazier offering his services), and showing Frank how to negotiate the perils of Broadway traffic, as well as how to recognize the various swindles and cheats awaiting the unwitting country victim. "A feller has to look sharp in this city, or he'll lose his eye-teeth before he knows it," Dick remarks after the boys meet a luckless country chap just fleeced of fifty dollars. Dick turns detective to help the victim regain his cash, and explains to Frank the mechanics of the drop game and other wiles of the city. And in doing so, he teaches that the city is indeed manageable with the right combination of savvy, alertness, and native virtue. Street-wise to the city's crooked ways, Dick instructs Frank that what is visible is not a reliable guide to what is true. With "people thronging the sidewalks" and "shop-windows with their multifarious contents," Frank finds Broadway "an interesting spectacle." A stranger, he views the city vicariously, passively. Dick knows that Wall Street, "not very wide or very long," is "of very great importance," considering "the amount of money involved in the transactions which take place in a single day in this street. Much greater in length, and lined with stores" as it may be, Broadway "stands second to Wall Street in this respect." The narrative wishes to make the invisible visible, to cleanse the city of its mystery by applying proper names to places and actions.

The narrative rends the veil of mystery hiding the city, or makes a spectacle of it, just as it transfigures Dick's street crafts of deciphering the world and fending for himself into bourgeois skills of self-advancement. It is precisely the continuity of identity between Ragged Dick and Richard Hunter, Esq., that represents the fable's instruction in transfiguring Vanity Fair into Celestial City. And in that process a key event lies in the chapter called "A Battle and a Victory," in which Dick, like the Pilgrim slaying the "foul Fiend" Apollyan, lord of the City of Destruction, defeats the sneering Mickey Maguire, who has picked a fight after "surveying Dick's new clothes with a scornful air." Unregenerate Irish immigrant tough, Mickey represents those forces of mystery which require an act of violence to keep them in place, a redemptive act in which Dick, resembling a Western dime-novel hero (looking ahead to *The Virginian*), behaves with "a quiet strength and coolness." It is immediately thereafter that Dick proclaims to "a worthy citizen," the policeman on the scene: "I wish I wasn't a boot-black." The following morning he opens his first savings account at a bank. The exchange of virtues and powers transacted in the novel confirms itself finally in the emergence of Richard Hunter, Esq., benign, helpful to others, but ready to fight dragons, a shining, celestial exemplar in the carnal city.

"In the street-life of the metropolis," Alger concludes his magical tale, "a boy needs to be on the alert, and have all his wits about him." By brilliant intuition, Alger understood that the secular city, properly seen, is the prime instrument of bourgeois success. Not to be abandoned to the cheats of Vanity Fair and thugs like Mickey Maguire, the city must be recovered, recaptured as the city upon a hill. Alger supplied an instructive narrative, a fictive analogue to campaigns for reform, crusades to cast out darkness, to replace mystery with light and reason.

A middle-class version of the city emerged and became widespread in these years; it took on tangible shapes in new neighborhoods, public buildings, redesigned downtown regions, and parks. The version included an explanation of evil: city bosses raised to power by an alliance of scheming speculators and ignorant immigrant voters, blindly loyal to political chieftains. Redemption lay in a revived sense of responsible citizenship among middling property holders and city homesteaders, who in their good sense would turn to men of intelligence and specialized training, "experts," to reform city government and restore order and harmony to city streets. "Deliberate analysis" is what is needed for "The City of the Future," wrote O. B. Bunce, editor of *Appleton's*, in 1878; a "definite design" is required in place of the "caprices" of self-interested individuals. "The greatest enemy," wrote *The American Architect and Building News* in the same year, is "private 'enterprise.'" The fate of the city, of "distribution of people in towns, their means of transit, their thoroughfares, parks, places of recreation, regions of business and residence," is too weighty to be "left to the mercy of accident." Such matters deserve to be in the hands of "distinct officers, commissioners, conservators," an elite corps "beyond the reach of party influence . . . specially trained to watch over the growth, development, and improvement of town." If the future of the city were to lie in the direction of Zion, then trained intelligence must take control.

Among the figures offering "deliberate analysis," none spoke with greater authority and precision than Frederick Law Olmsted, premier landscape architect and city designer of the era. Olmsted's accomplishments earn him the rank of major artist: not only Central Park but scores of other city parks, entire communities such as the suburb of Riverside near Chicago, college campuses, the grounds for state capitols, hospitals and railroad stations, conservation designs for Yosemite and Niagara Falls, private estates such as Biltmore in North Carolina, and, finally, in his last great project, the grounds for the World's Columbian Exposition. Olmsted undertook a mission to teach the metropolis about itself, to clarify its parts, its outcroppings as well as its dense centers: to teach it especially to recognize its spaces as sites of meaning. In the language of cultivated reform, he argued for an enlightened point of view. Hoping that "property owners" would be "wise enough to act as a body in reference to their common interests"—the interests of civic peace as well as personal profit—Olmsted pointedly addressed the "well-educated, orderly, industrious and well-to-do citizens" who owned a stake in the city's society, who held the future in their hands. He appealed to this group, in short, as *residents* as well as entrepreneurs, as sharing significant interests with all those "who are struggling to maintain an honorable independence" in their own "decent, wholesome, tidy dwellings."

Olmsted's great message addressed the city as a habitation, a structure and instrument for daily living. He rested his argument for "design" on a historical phenomenon: the splitting of the city into places of work (though he referred most often to "business" or "commerce") and of residence. The argument for the park, for a middle ground, was based on this split, this bifurcation which would govern the shape and uses of the park: the "two great classifications of commercial and domestic." In proposing his designs, Olmsted often took the stance of historian, attempting to clarify in words what his parks would clarify in space: the shape and significance of the fractured urban world. Apart from their function as places of "recreation," his parks would serve as nodal points, setting into perspective the new relations between "commercial" and "domestic."

Olmsted conceived of the disfigurement of cities as arising from their underlying economic purpose: "the extensive intercourse between people possessing one class of the resources of wealth and prosperity and those possessing other classes." The great city was a marketplace, a site of trade and consumption. And its inhabitants engaged with each other on the basis of property, of what each "possessed." This view of the city took for granted the ownership of exchangeable property—goods or money—and the possession, as well, of *landed* property, of individual homesteads as the location of life outside the market. Olmsted assumed a world divided between exchangeable and permanent property, between the downtown market and the home, explaining that the separation of realms arose from improvements in communications and transport: downtown market regions grew inhospitable to any life beyond that of trade. Compaction had concentrated homes and shops and industries in the same dense areas, on the same narrow streets, bringing "stagnation of air and excessive deprivation of sunlight," disease, pestilence, plague. Such revenges of nature were, in fact, still visited upon American cities in the 1870's and 1880's, and with cholera and yellow fever a real threat, it was clear that the "old-fashioned" notion of a functioning city based on a gridiron street plan must give way to more sanitary and sanative practices. Disease, moreover, raised only one of the "special problems" resulting from town growth. "Disorders and treasonable tumults" also may follow, he wrote in 1868, with the memory of the 1863 Draft Riots in New York still fresh, for a growing population adds "to the number of its idle, thriftless, criminal and dangerous classes."

With those "dangerous classes" always in mind, Olmsted conceived his parks as prime features of a system of order and security, apparently noncoercive means of control and stability. His argument for the park presumed the private home, presumed it as the basis of citizenship, of commitment to "order and system." It presumed the home to lie elsewhere than downtown—in an outlying or suburban region such as he himself had designed in Riverside, as a model town—to be a richly foliaged space with all modern services and conveniences, a fresh-air suburb with curvilinear roads in place of streets. The city park presumed not only a significant distance between commercial and domestic areas but sharp contrast between downtown and residential streets. That contrast served as a leading reason for Olmsted's parks, a major argument for the necessity of parks, and a chief motive for his design of open spaces in the form of picturesque pastoral retreats.

"We want a ground," Olmsted wrote in his best-known essay, "Public Parks and the Enlargement of Towns" (1870), "to which people may easily go after their day's work is done, and where they may stroll for an hour, seeing, hearing, and feeling nothing of the bustle and jar of the streets . . . We want the greatest possible contrast with the restraining and confining conditions of the town, which compel us to walk circumspectly, watchfully, jealously, which compel us to look closely upon others without sympathy." The park would serve as an anodyne to the pressures of the street, the exhausting effort to avoid collision, the constant calculation of motives and intentions. The street is an impersonal reflection of the impersonal marketplace, he writes, a hardening experience, in which people brush against thousands of their fellowmen daily, "and yet have no experience of anything in common with them." The park will provide precisely the opportunity for commonness, for free intercourse within "a simple, broad, open space of greensward" with "depth of wood and enough about it . . . to completely shut out the city from our landscapes." Here people would assemble "with an evident glee in the prospect of coming together, all classes largely represented, with a common purpose, not at all intellectual, competitive with none, disposing to jealousy and spiritual or intellectual pride toward none, each individual adding by his mere presence to the pleasure of all others, all helping to the greater happiness of each."

The image evokes nothing less than Winthrop's city upon a hill, a picture of the city-in-the-park as a corporate body joined in secular love and harmony, free from "all manner of vile things." What Olmsted understood as "vile" about streets, however, was not only the hard impersonality of commercial transaction; it also included the distinct ways of life of working-class neighborhoods, the styles and games of street life which he perceived as threatening difference. Addressing a Boston audience in 1870, he urged his listeners to "go into one of those red cross streets any fine evening next summer, and ask how it is with their residents?" People sitting on doorsteps, on curbstones, mothers "anxiously regarding their children who are dodging about at their play, among the noisy wheels on the pavement": is such a street fit for true neighborliness?

Consider how often you see young men in knots of perhaps half a dozen in lounging attitudes rudely obstructing the sidewalks, chiefly led in their little conversation by the suggestions given to their minds by what or whom they see passing in the street, men, women, or children, whom

110

they do not know, and for whom they have no respect or sympathy. There is nothing among them or about them which is adopted to bring into play a spark of admiration, of delicacy, manliness, or tenderness. You see them presently descend in search of physical comfort to a brilliantly lighted basement, where they find others of their sort, see, hear, smell, drink and eat all manner of vile things.

Contrast this scene, he urged, with that of a "tea-table with neighbors and wives and mothers and children, and all things clean and wholesome, softening and refining."

Embodied in the concept of the park, then, lay a motive to eradicate the communal culture of working-class and immigrant streets, to erase that culture's offensive and disturbing foreignness, and replace it with middle-class norms of hearth and tea table. The motive was not aesthetic or philanthropic alone, for such streets represented a political menace as well. Here the boss found his strength, and more menacing, here were brewed the makings of an independent and incendiary politics in the form of strikes, manifestations, riots. One explicit aim of the park was to remove the political threat of the street. Citing Jeremy Bentham's influential essay on "The Means of Preventing Crimes," Olmsted explained that "any innocent amusement," such as viewing "congregated human life" in an "open landscape," or chancing upon "scattered dainty cows and flocks of black-faced sheep" in a meadow artfully hidden in the recesses of a city park, tends "to weaken the dangerous inclinations" of the dangerous classes. He offered the park as an influence favorable to "courtesy, self-control, and temperance."

A benign coercion, Olmsted's park presented itself as a practical pedagogy: on one side, all pastoral picture, composed views, nature artfully framed as spectacle, and on the other, firm regulation, clear rules, sufficient police. Disturbed by the slovenly treatment of the park, its corrupt supervision under Boss Tweed's regime, Olmsted conducted a pamphlet campaign to insist on the necessity, to fulfill the ideal ambitions of the park, of rules and regulations, of a disciplined corps of park keepers. He also insisted that control be invested in a park board of appointed (not elected) specialists and respected citizens; such a group could be counted on to perform its duties in the manner of "a board of directors of a commercial corporation." Behind pastoral harmony, its Jeffersonian hope for a public space free of class distinction and division, lay the ordering hand of corporate organization, the values of system and hierarchy. Olmsted betrayed no sign of awareness of this apparent contradiction of ends and means. Against the rule of bosses and ruthless speculators, of the forces of mystery, the Jeffersonian ideal of cultivated intelligence in service to the Republic now implied the stewardship of a qualified elite. Set in a planned landscape detached from time, a zone free of the temporal demands of commerce (though governed by strict opening and closing hours), the vision of harmony now implied not a reformed social order but a therapy. A city upon a hill within the city of destruction, a celestial place amid Vanity Fair, the park implied a scenario of recovered inner balance on one hand, and firm, elite supervision through corporate forms on the other.

II

An intricate symbol of mystery, the great city proved to be a source of mystification, the very place where incorporation, pervading the spheres of everyday life, disguised itself in continued spectacles such as Central Park. To anxious reformers and their constituents, the causes of growth, of greatness, remained baffling, beyond control. Calling for a restoration of goodness, cleanliness, light, they found the "other half" and its teeming streets unfathomable and threatening. More parks, better street lamps, a firm hand against the Mickey Maguires: these campaigns against mystery failed to comprehend the city as a social force whose fusion of factory, marketplace, and home in a process of incorporation reshaped the entire society and its culture. That process altered relations, defied inherited values, transformed instruments of perception and communication, even as it transformed the perceptible social world.

In a common observation, the rise of the city implied the decline of the countryside. In 1899, the demographer Adna Weber would find it "astonishing," in his pioneering work in "social statistics," *The Growth of Cities in the Nineteenth Century*, that "the development of cities ... should outstrip that of the rural districts which they serve." That cities should serve rural districts had

112

already become a quaint notion a generation earlier. The Unitarian minister David Wasson observed with alarm in 1874, in a *North American Review* essay titled "The Modern Type of Oppression," that "the country is now but a suburb of the city," its "simple manners, moderate desires, and autonomous life . . . as good as disappeared." Even on the distant prairies, Olmsted had noted in 1870, clothing, furniture, food, conversation already displayed "intimacy . . . with the town. . . . The railway time-table hangs with the almanac."

The perception implied a serious crisis in definition. "It is not altogether easy to define the distinguishing characteristics of a city," admitted Weber. It had become an entity without clear demarcation, a form without precedent. Its rise and the doom of the countryside were one and the same, simultaneous and contingent on each other. Throughout the world, industrial urbanization had created "metropolis" and "colony" at one stroke. Wherever the imperial metropolis arose, a stricken countryside lay prostrate in its streets, its demise and impoverishment essential to the city's very greatness.

The term "metropolis" signified a commanding position within a region which included hinterland. New economic, social, and political relations between the center and its outlying districts manifest themselves in the postwar decades as rise and fall, prosperity and impoverishment. The revision of physical spaces produced in the great city a reflective image, a simulacrum of unseen economic and social relations. Cities expanded not by absolute increases in population alone but also by thickening regional networks of transport and communication. Internally, each region replicated the relations between "advanced" and "backward" which characterized the entire national system of urban regions—smaller cities, such as Bridgeport, Trenton, Fall River, Evanston, remaining relatively backward, less diverse and dense than nearby metropolises. Often, mill cities or government centers, subordinate places, performed clear-cut specialized functions within their regions. Distinctly cities, yet hardly metropolitan, they served as vehicles of urban influence on large numbers of people: intermediary places, in some ways trapped by their specializations in limbo between the cosmopolitanism of the big city and the provincialism of the small town. They were confined to hinterland status by the same process which brought regional watersheds, farmers' markets, milk sheds, and rural trade within the metropolitan orbit.

Along with the entire regional countryside, these small islands of urbanism also provided outlets for the overflow of goods from larger cities. If, by 1900, about nine tenths of all manufacturing took place within cities, the need for markets close at hand dictated corporate decisions in locating warehouses, terminals, grain elevators, chain stores. The need for uninterrupted flow from the raw to the processed placed a premium on velocity and proximity. Thus, cities colonized their regions, sending out (by the 1890's) electrified mass transit to hold suburban dormitory communities and industrial satellite towns within their orbit. Newspapers developed regional zones in the very years (the 1880's and 1890's) when advertising became their chief source of revenue.

In the 1880's, as much as 40 percent of the population of rural townships seemed to disappear. Images of bustling, frenetic cities arose against a background of abandoned farmhouses and deserted villages, and many Americans pondered the change with regret and lament. But these emptied places and impoverished regions were as much icons of incorporation as factories, railroads, and department stores. It was not that progress had passed them by. The emptying itself represented a kind of integration. Not only does an impoverished countryside provide fresh supplies of unskilled, cheap labor, but it keeps in reserve a standing supply of local labor for factories escaping from regions of higher pay, unions, and competition. Backward regions also represented easy markets for mass-produced goods. No place was so backward as to be out of reach of a railroad head and telegraph office, transmission belts which fed goods and information to country stores at rural crossroads. In the South and Midwest, such stores spearheaded an invasion of city-made goods. They were also significant nodal points in an evolving structure of distribution, a corps of traveling "drummers," of advertisers and managers at city headquarters monitoring sales, credit, stock turnover. The lessons learned by manufacturers in the most efficient modes of rural distribution just after the war paved the way for the great mail-order and chain-store invasion of the countryside in the later 1880's and 1890's, the heyday of Sears Roebuck, Montgomery Ward, and Woolworth's.

The countryside found a place fashioned for it within the urban system: it became an impoverished zone, a market colony, a cheap source of food, labor, and certain raw materials. Its function was precisely to remain a backwater, to remain dependent. The classic instance was, of course, the defeated South. To speak of metropolis, then, is to speak not only of individual cities but of a national system, a coordination of urban regions linked by rail and telegraph, creating a network of producing and consuming goods. The great city remains incomprehensible without a view of its position within such a system.

Even before the Civil War, American cities had begun to experience major change: railroad tracks cutting across streets, bridges, and viaducts, bringing heavier traffic. The decades following the war witnessed a major acceleration, striking many contemporaries as a radical departure. In these years, American society decisively crossed the threshold of modern urban culture, swiftly outpacing its European counterparts, whose cities had borne the brunt of industrialization a generation earlier. Even under the shattering thrust of railroads, factories, and masses of rural immigrants, European cities had, on the whole, retained a residue of earlier stages; medieval structures survived as "old towns," marking a center as a visible memory of an older, more coherent and unified social order. Just prior to industrialization, in the Baroque era, European capitals had enlarged their scale and the magnificence of their public buildings, re-creating the older central spaces into theatrical areas for the display of royal and imperial power, the city-as-commune already surrendering to the city-as-spectacle. In the nineteenth century arose the great public museums and concert halls, the widening of streets into grand boulevards (as in Paris), the planting of public gardens and parks. The planned residential squares of London appealed especially to Americans, like Olmsted, seeking alternatives to the quite different path taken in their native cities.

With the exception of Washington, conceived from the outset as a ceremonial city in the style of the Baroque, American cities had almost universally adopted the "grid" as their basic scheme, a scheme which blocked out spaces as parcels of property to be filled in at the will of the owner. Public regulation—of building heights, for example—proved rare until the zoning laws adopted in many cities by the early twentieth century. Dividing space into private packages for sale, for development or speculation, the grid proclaimed a rule of profit, delineating the city as "real estate" rather than as communal space. And with eyes keen for rising values, city governments, in collaboration with boards of trade and chambers of commerce, opened their spaces to unrestricted industrial expansion, enticing factories, warehouses, freight yards, and great retail stores with subsidies, low taxes, free "externals," in the form of transportation, railroad links, water supply, police and fire protection. Acting on the speculative principle encouraged by the grid layout of space, bankers, merchants, and manufacturers, and their political allies, provided the impetus and economic means for filling in those spaces with uncoordinated but profitable enterprises.

Even before the onset of industrialization, sheer growth measured by rise in commercial value of land provided the index to urban prosperity. The most astonishing instance of growth, and a rapid transition from commercial to industrial predominance, was Chicago. From a small trading post at the juncture of water and land routes inland in 1831, it had become the dominant trade center of its region by the Civil War, survived a great fire that destroyed its downtown in 1871, reached a population of half a million by 1880, and three times that number by 1900. By the turn of the century, both New York and Chicago—the former the country's major port and financial center and one of the world's largest markets, and the latter the country's midland empire of basic industries in food and metal and transportation —had overspread old spaces, flowed into newly annexed regions, and formed giant metropolitan areas with uncertain boundaries.

All told, the apparatus set in place in these years—the systems of transportation, communication, production, and distribution —imposed itself as the instrument of corporate business: the making and selling of goods. The corporate mode inscribed itself in a continental system. Its principle was coordination, and its method subordination of individual units (factories, offices, retail counters—and whole cities) to metropolitan headquarters. Not rationalization alone, not the production-distribution nexus, but

116

the principle of hierarchy governed the development. Sam Bass Warner suggests that the large-scale factories might serve as "apt metaphors for the new metropolis itself": the Akron rubber factory, the cash-register plant at Dayton, the steel works at Homestead. They evolved out of a need for consolidation to assure more rapid and increased processing of raw materials into goods. "To assure a very large and regular output" was the declared goal of Alexander Lyman Holley, chief engineer in the design of Carnegie's several steel plants in Pittsburgh. The Bessemer process and its improvements required a restructuring of work space, an enlargement of scale and concentration of parts. While it is size that strikes and awes the eye, it is the internal relation of parts, which permits speed of handling and "the saving of rehandling," that matters. Holley's account is unmistakably clear about the concepts guiding his designs at Pittsburgh: "As the cheap transportation of supplies of products in process of manufacture, and of products to market, is a feature of first importance, these works were laid out, not with a view of making the buildings artistically parallel with the existing roads or with each other, but of laying down convenient railroads with easy curves; the buildings were made to fit the transportation." The same might have been said about the evolving shapes of most American cities: buildings and their inhabitants subordinate to the forms of corporate industry.

Cities did not expand and change mindlessly, by mere entropy. If they lacked democratic planning, they submitted to corporate planning—which is to say, to the overlapping, planned evolution of many private competitive enterprises. The visible forms make this clear: the power of organized wealth, answerable only to the limits of the possible. The message was plain in the imperial façades that dressed the new railroad stations, courthouses, warehouses, department stores, office buildings, and mansions of the rich: façades which in their eclectic composition of classical, Gothic, and Renaissance styles suggested a new cultural imperialism, a confidence of appropriation. It was plain, as well, in the stark divisions of land use, the increasingly divisive "sector-and-ring" patterns (Chicago is a clear example) that segregated spaces by function (commercial, industrial, and political downtown; surrounding and outlying residential neighborhoods) and by class and income. Residences set aside from areas devoted to

117

making and buying (the work of producing and of selling; the work of shopping), and visible poverty set aside from visible affluence, with marked-off degrees between them: thus, the city reflected and reinforced the hierarchies within the corporate structure itself.

The message was perhaps most plain, most vivid, in the process whereby these decisions, which put buildings and people in their proper places, were inflicted upon the body of the city. It displayed the same pattern David Wells observed in the formation of working capital: "the absolute destruction of what once had been wealth . . . the breaking up and destruction of the old machinery, and its replacement by new." The main principle was rising land value that followed from greater, more concentrated use of downtown areas; as land rose in value, greater profits accrued to greater improvements. Old buildings gave way to new. The cycle of construction, destruction, construction, was furious. In Chicago, the fire of 1871 gave it a natural spur, and immensely greater private wealth arose from the rebuilding alone. The destruction-construction cycle was effected by municipal governments, in the laying of underground water and sewer pipes, gas lines, cables and electric wires (usually overhead) for mass transit and street lighting, elevated tracks for steam engines —services usually financed by city bonds but developed and owned by private utility and transit companies. Newer residential areas of the more affluent were often serviced first; run-down areas near the city center, the quarters of the poorest workers and recent immigrants, made do with primitive facilities for sanitation. Open gutters and cesspools remained common in working-class neighborhoods near polluting factories. The cycle of inner urban construction thus followed the pattern of uneven and contradictory development manifest across the nation, between cities and countryside, and among kinds of cities.

The sight of upheaval was commonplace: old landmarks destroyed, new structures of a different kind hoisted in their place; a new scale of tall building obliterating older buildings; neighborhoods changing their face as well as their ethnic and social character, as homes formerly of the rich became sites of multiple flats and crowded rooms. Surely the many faces of the city belonged to a single body. But unity seemed dispersed in a multiplicity of appearances, and especially in appearances which

118

disguised—department stores dressed in a garment more appropriate to Italian Renaissance palaces, or railroad stations presented as cathedrals. Commercial and public buildings became spectacles of style in these years of "picturesque eclecticism." Many of the fashionable architects were trained in its arts of disguise at the fountainhead of academic styles, the Academy of Beaux-Arts in Paris.

In fact, the number of buildings designed by architects rather than construction engineers like Holley was quite small. A commission to design a commercial or public building offered a fairly rare opportunity to make an impression on the expanding city, to leave a mark and perhaps influence the larger shape of things. Although the eclecticism rampant in these years earned the contempt of Louis Sullivan and others in the "Chicago School" seeking nontraditional solutions for the new, tall commercial building in the late 1880's and early 1890's, the picturesque did at least represent a gesture toward something more than mere engineering, mere naked construction. Still, its practical effect was to dress new structures bearing modern functions in old garb, confusing their identity with spectacle. To put a complex matter in simple terms: while engineers designed inner space in response to new functional needs, architects took as their problem the design of appropriate "fronts" out of the standard vocabulary of styles and motifs, whether Gothic or Moorish, Baroque or Romanesque. Buildings thus appealed to the eye, as visual treats, festooned with historical associations. Using a language which consisted of classical orders or broken arches or elaborate cornices or textured stone, architects drew pictures on their buildings, allusive pictures calling up memories of other buildings, of stylistic movements as a whole. Thus, "architecture" came to stand for educated and tasteful *picturing*, and in its academic practices it reared buildings which furthered the sense of discontinuity in everyday life: discontinuity and fracture between what façades and interiors implied, between allusions of visible design and invisible organizations of life performed in the building. And as buildings stretched upward, too high to be taken in by the eye all at once, their inner work as corporate headquarters or clearing houses of arcane transactions receded from view, from intelligibility, and from criticism. Even the most rationally designed skyscrapers still presented themselves as statements of implacable power, and even forms designed to demystify the interior organization of space only further mystified the larger organization of life.

Height and size as gratuitous statements of power appeared in their most pure form in the relatively useless towers of railroad stations, in the elegantly picturesque designs of New York's Grand Central, Boston's Park Square Station, and Chicago's Illinois Central. These massive downtown structures, usually identifying the center of the city, served multiple functions, combining hotels, train sheds, and office space with spacious vestibules, vast concourses with ticket offices, baggage rooms, and restaurants. In most cases, they represented collaborations: engineers designed the shed, platforms, and tunnels, the places of the work of railroading, hidden from view behind an architect's stylish front and monumental public spaces. Their multiple functions represented travel, interconnection, coordination, the spatial form of placelessness, of being neither here nor there, but on the way.

For a period, Gothic styles prevailed: "Railway terminals and hotels are to the nineteenth century what monasteries and cathedrals were to the thirteenth," wrote *Building News* in 1875, in justification of the prevailing cathedral style. But the appropriateness of the cathedral struck the critical Louis Sullivan in another, ironic light. About the Illinois Central, its eclectic marbles and mosaics and its richly elegant waiting room located *above* the tracks, he wrote: "Its lucidity is like unto the Stygian murk ... A unique spot on earth—holy in inequity, where, to go in you go out, and to go out you go in; where to go up you go down, and to go down—you go up." The magnificence of the waiting room and the elaborate if misplaced staircase had its point, Sullivan implies, for it makes epic confusion of what by its character is already confused: the relations between space and time, the concept itself of "place." For the railroad stations inserted at the heart of cities an emblem of the immense fact that "distance" had become a matter of time rather than space, that (after 1883) all times were now one. Like a giant clock seated in the city's midst, the terminal represented regulation, system, obedience to schedule. By necessity, its spaces were provisional: not habitations or places of continuous labor but sites of comings and goings. In its housing of multiple structures keyed to each other, the terminal

120

stood as a virtual model of the new form of the urban: not so much a distinctive "place" as a place for movement, for transactions made against an infallible clock. The "murk" Sullivan perceived in the ecclesiastical and palatial styles of these newfangled houses exuded from the very character of the enclosure: not only did "style" obscure the clarity of combined functions within the place, but those functions represented the loss of an older idea of the city as a settled place, of departure and arrival as genuine adventure.

III

Technology provided the visible instruments of change, but the character of urban transformation (not only in places designated as cities but throughout the society) lay not in mechanization alone but in its context: expansion of the marketplace. "Self-provisioning practices of the home," in Harry Braverman's words, persisted until the end of the century, many city working-class families still keeping small vegetable gardens and even some livestock, pigs and goats being not uncommon sights along New York's upper East River as late as the 1890's. Home processing of foods, purchased in bulk, was still common: preserving, canning, pickling were among the tasks of wives and mothers, along with the making of women's and children's clothing, the finishing of sheets and curtains. Fewer than half of 7,000 working-class families surveyed by the U.S. Bureau of Labor between 1889 and 1892 purchased bread, buying huge quantities of flour, instead, for home-baked loafs. But the trend toward the manufactured was patently powerful. The crowding of working-class quarters in cities made it all the more difficult, as Braverman notes, "to carry on the old life." And the new life, based on the destruction of "social artifice," now depended increasingly on what was marketed. As the domestic making of goods receded, city dwellers became more and more enmeshed in the market, more and more dependent on buying and selling, selling their labor in order to buy their sustenance; the network of personal relations, of family, friends, neighbors, comes to count for less in the maintenance of life than the impersonal transactions and abstract structures of the marketplace.

It was in these decades, late in the nineteenth century, that the

121

city became the site of the universal market. Great cities developed in these years as the most thoroughly transformed, most completely commodified regions of the country, land and housing themselves subject to the most severe control of market values and practices.

The logic of market relations eluded those liberal reformers who called for a restored Jeffersonian estate of responsible citizenship on the part of property holders, many of whom held only precariously to their status in a fluctuating economy. That logic proved difficult to grasp for all city consumers, owners and tenants alike, precisely because of its changing forms in everyday life, of the mysteries it generated (how goods were made, for example, or how they appeared neatly packaged on store shelves), of the spectacles of consumption it produced. Of course, the market met resistances. Especially among immigrant and slum households, family itself was a shelter, and the street culture Olmsted found so vile provided a protective shield of community life. On the whole, neighborhoods remained vibrant, city dwellers often identifying themselves as much by neighborhood and block as by city, and the street games of children and youths embodied residual forms of autonomy and freedom. But at one level, often unconscious, the very persistence of such forms and activities represented resistance to the emerging culture of the marketplace, of incorporation.

The most common, if most subtle, implication of transformed human relations appeared in the steady emergence of new modes of *experience*. In technologies of communication, vicarious experience began to erode direct physical experience of the world. Viewing and looking at representations, words and images, city people found themselves addressed more often as passive spectators than as active participants, consumers of images and sensations produced by others: the very principle of composition embodied by Olmsted in the design of Central Park. Steam-powered printing presses, improved methods of lithography and photoengraving, and, in the 1890's, the halftone method of mechanically reproducing photographs in newspapers, periodicals, and books, led to an unprecedented quantity of visual data. A great proliferation of newspapers and journals appeared between 1870 and 1890: existing big-city newspapers multiplied circulation several times over; the 1880's saw the beginnings of such new journals

122

as *Cosmopolitan,* the *Ladies' Home Journal, McClure's,* and *Munsey's Magazine.* This upsurge of information in media answered to needs created by growing physical distances among sections of cities, by enlarged city size and scale, and by social distinctions in the population. This was the first age of modern mass-spectator sports, of professional and collegiate games witnessed in stadiums by thousands of seated onlookers. And perhaps the very paradigm of changes in scale, in the management of illusion, in roles prepared for seated audiences, lay in the traveling circus, grown into a gigantic "three ring" enterprise in these years, so large and complex, writes Neil Harris, that the administration of its movements "was often likened to military mobilization." "Intimacy was lost," writes Harris about the differences between P. T. Barnum's earlier art of humbug and the evolving forms of the 1870's. Instead of interacting with performers, audiences were now "passive prisoners of their own excitement and bewilderment." Pageantry and broad pantomime replaced the clever repartee and jostling of the earlier mode. In theatrical production, machinery of illusion took over, lavish scenic effects becoming the keynote of impresarios like Augustin Daly and Steele MacKaye. "The thrust toward the spectacular had taken over mass entertainment," Harris concludes.

New styles of journalism displayed similar tendencies. Appearing in a burst across the country in the 1880's and 1890's, the great city dailies displaced older "journals of opinion," which had catered chiefly to commercial and political interests. Such were Horace Greeley's New York *Tribune* and James Gordon Bennett's New York *Herald:* vehicles for an informed "burgher." To be sure, these established papers themselves grew increasingly concerned with circulation, with competition from more sensational tabloids and the "penny press," and, by the Civil War, had already employed the telegraph and on-the-scene correspondents to report battlefield and trans-Atlantic news. Telegraphic news companies such as the Associated Press, faster printing presses, and new inventions such as the telephone, typewriter, mechanical typesetters, and photoengraving machines enhanced capacity for swift gathering and disseminating of news. The spread of artificial illumination on streets and in homes, by means of gas, kerosene, and electricity, dramatically increased the practice, after 1870, of publishing evening newspapers in the afternoon, especially to catch homebound shoppers and workers and downtown evening crowds. The big city dailies devised new techniques: the "interview" with celebrities; the globe-hopping reporter; multiple editions during the day—as many as nine or ten—each with a different, more "timely" banner headline; the use of bold type, colored ink, and, eventually, halftone photographs and Sunday color supplements. The new metropolitan dailies proffered a new concept of "news" itself: "anything that will make people talk," in the words of Charles A. Dana of the New York *Sun*, which specialized in the "human interest" story. Once a Brook Farm radical and later a conservative critic of Gilded Age politics, Dana represented a relatively restrained and reformist outlook; the "new journalism" was better represented by Joseph Pulitzer of the New York *World*, who urged his reporters to concentrate on "what is original, distinctive, dramatic, romantic . . . odd, apt to be talked about." It was a literary concept, suggested Robert Park, an urban form of village gossip, designed to make the lives of distant others seem near and "human." The large dailies invaded regions served by a thriving foreign-language press, a labor press, and a religious press, and sought to win readers by offering to newcomers especially, in Park's words, "a window looking out into the larger world outside the narrow circle of the immigrant community." The dailies invented a language of mass intelligibility, using bold headlines, artful clichés, and halftone photographs (especially in the Sunday paper, inaugurated in these years) to win readers.

It was not simply economic competition for the unique which drove the dailies in their quest for the dramatic and the sensational. If news itself came to mean whatever captured attention, what might shock readers into an experience of the unique, the source of the change was as much cultural as economic. Monopolized by telegraphic press services, the older kind of news, a record of a significant event, now arrived at the offices of the dailies in packaged form. The telegraphic system, observed a writer in 1870, has "made all the leading papers so nearly alike as to their news that one does not differ in that respect materially from the others." The conditions themselves of gathering what had been thought of as news, then, made the world seem the same regardless of the name of the newspaper. The apparently unique, the shocking, the "new," provided a way of making history seem

124

immediate and personal just at a moment when its individuality and unpredictability had seemed to disappear. Thus, the dailies dramatized a paradox of metropolitan life itself: the more knowable the world came to seem as *information*, the more remote and opaque it came to seem as *experience*. The more people needed newspapers for a sense of the world, the less did newspapers seem able to satisfy that need by yesterday's means, and the greater the need for shock and sensation, for spectacle.

Yet, in providing surrogate experience, the newspaper only deepened the separations it seemed to overcome—deepened them by giving them a precise form: the form of reading and looking. Each individual paper, a replica of hundreds of thousands of others, served as a private opening to a world identical to that of one's companion on a streetcar, a companion likely to remain as distant, remote, and strange as the day's "news" comes to seem familiar, personal, and real. And yet the physical form itself of the familiar, the personal, the unique, made the represented experience seem unreal. News represented in the typographical form of columns of print serves, suggested the German critic Walter Benjamin in the twentieth century, "to isolate what happens from the realm in which it could affect the experience of the reader." Unlike the printed page of a novel, the newspaper page declares itself without mistake as good only for a day, for this reading only: as if today's history of the world has nothing in common with yesterday's or tomorrow's, except the repetition of the typographical form. Thus, by isolating information from experience, the daily newspaper deadens memory while it makes "reality" banal. The big-city press, then, crystallized the cultural predicament Olmsted discovered in the commercial street: the condition of isolation and nervous calculation. Assuming separation in the very act of seeming to dissolve it, in their daily recurrence the newspapers expressed concretely this estrangement of a consciousness no longer capable of free intimacy with its own material life. The form in which it projected its readers' assumed wish to overcome distance concealed its own devices for confirming distance, deepening mystery, and presenting the world as a spectacle for consumption. Surrogate or vicarious familiarity served only to reinforce strangeness.

Among the services provided by the daily press to a readership for whom everyday life seemed more and more deprived of genuine adventure, vicarious adventure stood high. Exploration of forbidden and menacing spaces emerged in the 1890's as a leading mode of the dailies, making spectacles of "the nether side of New York" or "the other half." The reporter appeared now often as a performer, one who had ventured into alien streets and habitations, perhaps in disguise, and returned with a tale, a personal story of the dark underside of the city. Jacob Riis was just such a figure; his spectacular revelations of tenement life appeared first in Dana's *Sun*, for which he labored as "star" crusading reporter. The personal reporter who placed himself, his name, his signature (thereby earning for himself the role of "celebrity" in the culture ruled by the press), between the reader and a unique, threatening experience came into prominence in this decade precisely as an explorer of the "other half." Such was Stephen Crane's role during his newspaper days early in the 1890's, many of his "Bowery Tales" appearing first as newspaper stories of wanderings through districts of wretchedness. Crane wished to subvert the conventional view of the "other" as a merely pathetic, disreputable drunkard and pauper, exactly the typical view which prevailed in the press, laced with appeals to "charity," and, in Riis's writings, to middle-class worries over safety and security. The "other half " existed in the press as the city's social mystery—"the eternal mystery of social conditions," Crane remarked with irony—raised to spectacle.

The first halftone photograph ever reproduced in a New York paper was a picture of "Shantytown" in the *Daily Graphic* (whose nameplate featured a camera, telegraph wires, and the sun) in 1880. By the end of the century, photographs were commonplace. At the same time, the amount of space given over to advertisements increased phenomenally. The newspaper, we must remember, consisted of several "departments," such as news, feature-story, editorial, and commercial advertisement. We must remember, too, that while the city dailies gave millions an opportunity for private, vicarious spectacles, it unified all those privacies—first by making the world seem familiar to them in an identical way (filtering experience into simple images), and second by placing them all in the identical condition, as customers, consumers of the paper's "reality," and eventually of the paper's advertised goods. How the dailies represented the "other," and especially "the other half," belonged to the same process by

126

which they presented goods for consumption. The connection was neither explicit nor obvious, but it was effective. For the advertisement came increasingly to signify precisely how "we" differ from the "other half." The advertisement thus gave the reader a location, a definite place and point of reference, teaching readers how to think of themselves as occupying the same urban space, sharing the same corpus, with social "misery."

The lesson addressed itself to inhabitants of comfortable private homes: "families cuddle the joys of the fireside," as Crane described the implicit newspaper scenario in a poem, "when spurred by tales of dire lone agony." Riis assumed as much in his "guided tour" of places known mysteriously as "Bottle Alley," "Bandit's Roost," and "Hell's Kitchen." His device was touristic, a journey by rail into a strange country:

Leaving the Elevated Railroad where it dives under the Brooklyn Bridge at Franklin Square, scarce a dozen steps will take you where we wish to go . . . with its rush and roar echoing yet in our ears we have turned the corner from prosperity to poverty. We stand upon the domain of the tenement . . . enough of them everywhere. Suppose we look into one? . . . Be a little careful, please! The hall is dark and you might stumble over the children pitching pennies there . . . Here where the hall turns and dives into utter darkness is a step and another, another, a flight of stairs. You can feel your way, if you cannot see it.

Riis's purpose is to make you see it, see and touch it, as a personal event—though artfully distanced and mediated by his own picturing. Accompanied by photographs, his stories and books represented the slum as the antithesis of the home, a breeding ground of menacing ignorance and discontent. By word and picture, Riis portrayed the slum as an offense to all notions of the clean, the sanitary, and the civilized. The portrait appealed to middle-class conscience and to charity, arousing anger against unregulated slumlords, pity for the Italian and Jewish and Chinese and black aliens under their greedy thumb, and satisfaction among the middle classes for their own good fortune. For the social conscience Riis evoked through his spectacles of poverty served also to confirm the high value of the clean, well-equipped, privately owned home as the norm of American life.

Riis and other reformers assumed that foreign inhabitants of the slums also viewed themselves as helpless victims, degraded by filth and crime, harboring resentment against the day they might unleash their wrath. The "more fortunate classes," George E. Waring had written in 1878, were obliged to serve as "official guardians" of "those who are utterly powerless to help themselves." Sanitation engineer and associate of Olmsted's on the Central Park project, Waring wrote about the "tenement house class": "As a rule they will live like pigs, and die like sheep, unless they are compelled to live decently and are prevented by the strong protection of authority against evils over which they have no control." He made these comments in support of a competition sponsored by the *Plumber and Sanitation Engineer* for a "model House for Working People," a contest among architects which resulted in the "dumb-bell" tenement, which offered fireproof stairways, a toilet for every two families, and a central court. In 1891, Riis estimated that nearly half the city's population lived in the 39,000 tenements packed in the lower end of the island, many without water or indoor toilets. Certain areas on the Lower East Side in the 1890's were calculated to be the densest regions of human habitation on earth. The figures suggest how many people Waring, Riis, and their readers imagined to be helpless, in need of official guardianship. And Adna Weber's estimate in 1899 that in American cities with populations exceeding 100,000 no more than 23 percent owned their homes, the figure declining to 6 percent in New York, tells even more strikingly how small a group of propertied citizens the reformers addressed. The discrepancy between an overwhelming majority of tenants and a tiny number of homeowners indicated the dimensions of the social rift at the center of urban society.

Housing in American cities, warned Lewis W. Leeds, also writing on sanitation in 1878, threatened to divide "society into classes more decisively and more objectionably than obtains in any of the old countries." The "fine house," the "healthy house," have become marks of invidious social distinction, setting apart the "rich and strong" from the "laboring classes." Housing for the "laboring classes," notes Leeds, deserves primary attention, for "the first thing required in the formation of any town is labor, and the constant and daily want forever after is labor." The remark casts into useful perspective the spectacle of contrast performed in the press, between "home" and "slum." For the

128

very foundation upon which home rested was distance and exemption from labor. Possession of a home came to imply transcendence of labor; a place and a time free of the demands of the regulating clock.

Of course, the home, like commuter coaches arriving and departing at the terminal, in truth regulated itself by the clock. And "domesticity" itself meant (though the word disguised the fact) a kind of labor: what else was the home, the sphere of women, but the site of woman's labor? To be sure, domestic labor of the housewife enjoyed a status in the daily and periodical press associated with freedom; it was a duty freely performed, to make a nest where conjugal love and maternal care would nurture, secure, and protect the family from the "outside." The image enjoyed the broadest acceptance, even in face of the fact that most of the rapidly growing number of women in the work force outside the home labored as servants, performing other people's domestic duties. Indeed, the image of the domestic sphere, with its hearth, its parlor table, its warm kitchen and loyal wife-mother, served as the centerpiece of a cluster of images representing the norm of American life. To be sure, the popular image gave tacit recognition to the work within the home. Harriet Beecher Stowe, for example, addressed her popular *House and Home Papers* (1872) to the "lady who does her own work" (implying that women without servants might still hold the rank of "lady," still think of themselves as respectable). In 1869, she had helped her sister Catherine Beecher revise an earlier handbook on "domestic economy," now retitled *The American Woman's Home*, which argued against the keeping of servants and for an equitable sharing of duties within the family. Still, the lady of the house found herself more and more in the role of *housewife*, a term with heartwarming associations.

With the rise of food and clothing industries, domestic labor came to consist chiefly of budgeting and shopping rather than making. From place of labor for self-support, the home had become the place of consumption. How to be a "lady who does her own work" came very quickly after the Civil War to mean how to be a lady who shops; indeed, who sustains herself as "lady" by wise and efficient shopping. And here we encounter another of the paradoxes which seemed so mysteriously to govern city life. Just as the private home emerged as a pervasive image of freedom, of refuge, so that freedom seemed more and more linked to goods produced elsewhere: goods representing (even if represented otherwise in advertising) that market from which the home seemed a refuge. Mass-produced goods brought into the home a dependency on the very economy whose inner form Olmsted found in the isolated inwardness of the street. Less visible, and often buried beneath that same street, were mechanical intrusions into homes: gas and water lines, plumbing, electricity. Home and flat came under control of an intricate apparatus, in most cities owned by private interests that exacted utility fees for services. The introduction of electricity for private use in the 1880's—what Reyner Banham describes as "the greatest environmental revolution in human history since the domestication of fire"—tightened the system decisively. Increasingly, the private home owed its security and comfort to external systems. And such systems took control of the city environment exactly at a time when privacy took the shape of refuge and haven.

IV

Of all city spectacles, none surpassed the giant department store, the emporium of consumption born and nurtured in these years. Here the citizen met a new world of goods: not goods alone, but a *world* of goods, constructed and shaped by the store into objects of desire. Here the very word "consumption" came to life. From its earlier senses of destruction (as by fire or disease), of squandering, wasting, using up, by the 1890's consumption had won acceptance as a term designating such goods as food and clothing, "all those desirable things which directly satisfy human needs and desires." Department stores emerged as places retailing goods, specializing in cultivating both their desirability and their consumability: the ease with which they are used up. They specialized, that is, not only in selling multiple lines of consumer goods but in the presentation, the advertisement, of such goods as desirable, as necessary. In department stores, buyers of goods learned new roles for themselves, apprehended themselves as *consumers*, something different from mere users of goods. The store itself conveyed that difference, taught it in the physical and spatial features it developed; it also taught consumption through an auxiliary institution it helped raise to vast powers in these

130

years: advertising. Thus, the department store stood as a prime urban artifact of the age, a place of learning as well as buying: a pedagogy of modernity. From meager beginnings before the Civil War—when only a few city merchants included more than one line of goods in the same establishment—the true department store, with its variety of factory-made goods offered for sale under the same roof, arose in the 1870's and 1880's, pushing aside the small specialty shop as the major form of downtown retailing. Unlike the vast mail-order and chain-store empires mushrooming across the countryside, Woolworth's "five and ten cent stores," Montgomery Ward, Sears, and the Great Atlantic and Pacific Tea Company, the downtown department store confined itself to one location. Imported from Parisian arcades in the 1860's, the pattern of dividing goods and spaces for their display and sale into "departments" took hold, and older "dry-goods" stores like Macy's and Lord & Taylor expanded and subdivided to include a greater variety of goods, from ready-made clothing to mass-produced furniture. By the end of the 1880's, such names as A. T. Stewart and Macy of New York, Marshall Field of Chicago, Wanamaker of Philadelphia, Jordan Marsh of Boston had become virtually synonymous with the names of their cities.

The most exhilarating prospects of the great city were revealed in the brilliance of such places, called up by the magic of such names alone. Lavishly designed palaces of consumption, department stores tempted their customers (presumed to be shoppers entering from the street, requiring spectacular distraction to win their attention) with monumental neoclassical fronts, ornamental doorways, large window displays, and, inside, often a central courtyard with tinted leaded-glass skylights, a rotunda with upper floors visible as galleries (a form of eye-catching and mind-soothing appeal introduced in America by A. T. Stewart in his new store of the 1860's); floors, columns, and sweeping staircases of marble; plush carpets, chandeliers, fixtures of richly polished wood and fine glass. To shop here was no idle matter, no merely perfunctory transaction. Here goods showed themselves as more than mere goods, mere objects of use; displayed under sparkling lights, in artful arrangements, they spoke a language of value beyond the practical. Department stores experimented (especially after the shift from gas to electric lights late in the 1880's) in presenting goods as if they represented something other than

131

themselves, some touch of class, of status, of prestige. The aim, of course, hardly differed from that of merchants in all times and places, to make their goods as irresistible as possible. But the scale of the department store, the range of daily existence it embraced in its many "departments," and the intensity of its efforts to enhance the symbolic value of its goods bestowed on merchandise alone a new power in everyday life. Here the quotidian, the commonplace things of existence—clothing, furnishings—seemed magical and glamorous: not only a new world of goods but the world itself newly imagined as consisting of goods and their consumption.

As much as the school, and much like the factory, the department store served its customers as an educational institution. Proffering infinite charm at cheap prices, it sold along with its goods a lesson in modern living. The departments taught the social location of goods: trousers as "men's clothing," silks as "women's wear," reclining chairs as "parlor furniture." It systematized, conveniently, the world of goods into discrete names, each with its niche, and in visible spatial relation to all others. Like the mail-order catalogue, the department store organized the world as consumable objects, each serving a household role. The store *represented* the world, and represented it chiefly in the form of an ideal home inhabited by ideal role-playing characters. Expanded to include personal items like stationery, jewelry, perfumes, cosmetics, and patent medicines, along with kitchen appliances and household tools, department stores taught families what they needed, taught symbolic as well as practical functions of things. The lessons inhered in the design of things themselves, their packaging and advertisement, their place and manner of presentation, the entire gestalt assuming a continuous act of learning and using, along with buying. The new stores minimized the appearance of trade on behalf of the pleasures of the goods. Fixed prices, along with charge accounts, made the economic transaction, the exchange of money for goods, as efficient, as unobtrusive as possible.

What lay behind this apparently sudden rise, virtually complete and already "modern" by the 1880's, of new methods of marketing, of buying and selling, of the new prominence of manufactured goods? To say simply that the improved productive system provided more goods for daily use than ever before

132

does not suffice. Economy alone cannot account for department stores considered as an urban institution, a place of learning as well as of buying and selling. Instead, these places created a unique fusion of economic and cultural values; they were staging grounds for the making and confirming of new relations between goods and people. In the department store, in the links it formed between home and factory, between goods and their values, and in the spectacle it made of itself, we find another source of mystery within the great city.

The store served at once as education, an explication of phonographs and typewriters, packaged soaps and detergents, ready-made clothing and furniture, and at the same time as bafflement, an obfuscation of those very lessons. For in the very act of disclosing links between goods and private use, it disguised links between goods and factories, the origins of goods within a particular mode of production. The form itself of the early stores betrayed the calculation within the spectacle: a complex machinery of accounting and coordination, of stockkeeping and purchase order, of hierarchy and control, that lay behind the glittering façade, the ceremonial entrances, the bright interiors, all suggesting a kind of magical appearance of goods as if from nowhere. The front deployed all available technology to further its illusions: electric lights, telephone lines between departments, pneumatic tubes, passenger elevators. Such devices provided a technical underpinning, the overt manifestations of a backstage system holding the entire structure of separate departments in place. At the same time, the visibility of certain components of the system—the cash register at each department, for example—reminded the customer of what seemed the only final truth behind the performance, that these arrayed goods belonged to the store until purchase marked a transfer of ownership. The spectacle diminished but did not eliminate the presence of the market; instead, it used its physical resources to make a spectacle of the place as a mere switching point for goods, a stage where the ownership of goods changed hands.

Department stores embodied physical systems and also social systems. In their astonishing size, competing with the new railroad terminals as monumental enclosures serving multiple purposes, they accustomed people to an unprecedented scale in downtown buildings, to solving the mystifying problems of movement and passage among its aisles of differing goods, its several floors holding distinct departments, its maze-like patterns of purchase and display. And the relation to the factory was omnipresent, organic, and reciprocal. Behind the monumental fronts and beneath the surface elegance lay a design almost strictly analogous to that emerging in the larger factories under the influence of electricity, a design of specialized spaces and functions. Even as early as the 1870's, the newer stores provided acres of floor space; by the end of the century, Macy's and Marshall Field's occupied new buildings, each with more than a million square feet of floor space. The stores employed small armies of sales and stock and office workers, predominantly women; by the late 1890's, Macy's counted more than 3,000 persons on its payroll, and Marshall Field's more than doubled that figure within a few years. In scale of enterprise and of space converted to profitable use, the department stores resembled the largest factories. Like the factory, the multiple-product store came in the 1880's to count less on economies of scale and more on velocity, on efficiency of movement of goods from distribution point to warehouse to store: from stock to counter to sale. Just as increasingly rapid flow of materials governed the design of factories, so rapid "stock-turn" or "turn-over" governed the internal system of the store, its pressures on salespeople to meet quotas, on department managers to specialize in specific lines, to employ more seductive means of display and advertisement. Department stores, because of economic necessity, installed the principles of productivity at the very heart of the city.

The factory lay as a hidden presence within the store, both forms subject to mounting competitive pressures. Reciprocity between them tightened in the 1880's and 1890's, particularly as, in Alfred Chandler's words, "the new mass production industries became capital-intensive and management-intensive." A number of results flowed from this development. With greater fixed costs, corporations felt a greater need "to keep their machinery of workers and managerial staff fully employed," leading to greater efforts at control of marketing and distribution as well as of raw materials. Moreover, more efficient machinery and management drastically reduced the ratio of labor to capital, leading to further efforts to integrate distribution with production within single industries. Department stores expanded in response to these changes within the economy, their departmentalization reflecting new bureaucratic structures within industrial enterprises. Furthermore, this changing ratio of labor to capital, the inflation of the corps of management and its office forces, initiated a slow but determined shift in the work force away from production proper to "services" in the spheres of distribution and exchange, where greater specialization and a fine-meshed division of labor also began to appear. Increasingly the realm of women workers, the category of "clerical" in the 1900 census showed a threefold increase in size since 1870, embracing a range of jobs such as bookkeepers, cashiers, bill collectors, stenographers, typists, secretaries, telephone operators. And as "clerical" came to imply an aspiration to remain permanently above the rank of industrial worker, the department store and its magical world of goods found in the same development a mass of new customers anxious to exchange their incomes for the assurance promised by goods of immunity from poverty, insecurity, the increasingly degraded status of the manual worker.

The department store found its function, then, in dispensing images along with goods, and in this task the store counted increasingly on another new institution of the great city, the advertising industry. Equal to "the school and the church in the magnitude of its social influence," according to David Potter in *People of Plenty* (1954), advertising arose at that "critical point" when "society shifts from production to consumption." The shift, just underway in these decades of vastly enhanced capacity in the consumer-goods industries, required that culture be "reoriented," in Potter's word, to stress consumption, to train people in new needs and new kinds of behavior. The advertisement serves, moreover, not only to instill desires for goods but also to disguise the character of consumption, to make it seem an act different from a merely functional, life-enhancing use of an object. Advertisement endowed goods with a language of their own, a language of promise radically new in the history of man-made things. If the advertisement aimed to make consumption of a particular product habitual, it also aimed to make habitual the identification of products with something else, with ideas, feelings, status.

Advertising arose as a functional institution, linked to the great shifts in the spheres of production and distribution, to new technologies of communication, to the growing empires of the big-city press, and to the rise of the department store. The giant store itself, remarked Robert Park in the 1920's, was virtually "a creation of the Sunday newspapers" and their enlarged space devoted to advertisements. In these years, the advertisement became an integral element within an evolving system. Until the 1880's, newspaper advertisements had served local merchants chiefly; their mode was verbal, informative, and brief, an item on a page crowded with sundry brief items and notices. With few exceptions, such as patent-medicine ads, they eschewed the rhetoric of persuasion. Even through the 1860's and 1870's, newspaper ads were rarely more than four column-inches in size, and typographical regularity remained the norm. In the following decade of enhanced production and incorporation, everything changed at once. The new magazines set the pace; by the end of the decade, they carried half- and full-page copy prepared now not by merchants but by new "advertising agencies," such as N. W. Ayer and Sons, founded in 1869, and J. Walter Thompson, founded in 1878. The change was accompanied by an unanticipated graphic and typographical freedom, including the use of color. The rise of the large department stores in the 1870's had initiated the change in style as well as scale. Between 1870 and 1900, the volume of advertising multiplied more than tenfold, from 50 to 542 millions of dollars per year. Such an increase indicated not only an absolute expansion but a decisive change in the function of advertising, its role in both production and distribution of goods being, in Chandler's words, "still another ancillary distribution institution." Basing their widening influence on the patronage of the mass retailers, the advertising agencies took another step toward their position of extraordinary power when, in the 1880's and 1890's, large corporate manufacturers shifted to direct advertising of their products for a national market. Producers of cigarettes, soaps, breakfast cereals, canned soups, fountain pens, typewriters, launched the first campaigns to identify their products, to stir up demand for their particular brand name. Now responsibility for the pattern of advertising belonged less to the agency creating the advertisement and more to a specialized task force in the sales office, which decided on brand names and the location and volume of advertisement.

Thus, mass-produced goods for daily use, "consumer's goods" rather than "luxury goods," established the pattern of mass advertising.

The older function simply to inform had swiftly given way to a mode in which information as such now fused with a message about the product, together with a message about the potential consumer, that he or she *required* the product in order to satisfy a need incited and articulated by the advertisement itself. Advertisements now presented themselves often as small dramas, in word and picture, offering along with their message a vicarious experience of the satisfaction promised by the product. They offered, that is, a spectacle, in which reading and seeing provided access to a presumed and promised reality. In some cases the drama turned on a testimonial:

If cleanliness is next to Godliness, soap must be considered as a means of Grace, and a clergyman who recommends moral things should be willing to recommend soap. I am told that my commendation of Pear's Soap has opened for it a large sale in the United States. I am willing to stand by every word in favor of it that I ever uttered. A man must be fastidious indeed who is not satisfied with it.

Henry Ward Beecher

In this little passage, which appeared in 1888, the basic mode of the advertisement is already present, already achieved, already performing its work of fusing a message about a product with a message about the customer. The work takes the form of an apparently simple syllogism, expressed openly in the first sentence: an appeal to the logical links among "Grace," "soap," and "clergyman." Who would deny the linkage, especially when cleanliness, sanitation, fresh air, so urgently preoccupied precisely the city people who would recognize the authority of Henry Ward Beecher, minister of the comfortable congregation of the Plymouth Church in Brooklyn? The advertisement thus establishes its own authority to make "Pear's" identical to soap (and to its associations with grace). The best-known preacher of the age pledges his word.

Although amusing (surely the reader is meant to recognize a touch of tongue-in-cheek humor in Beecher's "fastidious"), at bottom the advertisement serves a single goal: to link a desirable good with a brand name; to direct desire not to the good alone but to a particular brand. Commercial trademarks and brand names came into their own in the Gilded Age, proliferating especially as the consumer-goods industries so rapidly expanded their productive powers and corporate structures in these years. The mark or name is a peculiar kind of expression, originating not as a spontaneous act of naming on the part of people discovering a new object in their midst but as an act from above, the manufacturer's act, sanctioned and protected by the law of copyright: a fiction underwritten by laws protecting what came to be known as "intellectual property," the brand name. Such new words which bounded into the public domain in these years as Kodak, Chiclet, Uneeda Biscuit have no status whatsoever as words, as coins of human exchange, outside the boundaries of the advertisement. The aim of the ad is to extend those boundaries, to make "Kodak" equivalent with "camera," that is, to reconceive the product entirely within a language of market exchange.

The vicarious drama of the advertisement presents itself as a mimesis, a guide to reality. Its inherent principle, then, is obfuscation, confusion of realms, bewilderment of identification. The question of honesty or accuracy is irrelevant. Insofar as the advertisement inserts a name of ownership between the usable object and the potential user—insofar as it wishes to transform the potential user into a *customer*—it inevitably misguides its audience about the true character of the product.

The advertisement is a construction, like a work of art, in which a good stands forth, displays itself as an object for use (it makes no difference whether its claims for beauty or health are true or not), an object with a distinct name that passes as a true name of qualities. It is, however, no more than a name of ownership, the object for use also an object for sale. The advertisement is unique among artworks in that its cardinal premise is falsehood, deceit, its purpose being to conceal the connection between labor and its product in order to persuade consumers to purchase *this* brand. The advertisement suggests the fictive powers of that product, its ability to stand for what it is not. In the advertisement, the good performs its work imaginatively, symbolically, and its character as a commodity is manifest in the fictive drama precisely to the degree that it is suppressed and negated. The advertisement gives to the product of labor a life, an animation, that can only serve to intensify the fiction of its independence from living labor. Like the patterns of space evolving in the city itself, the advertisement separated the realms of production and consumption, hiding their connections. For the advertisement addresses, above all, people who also labor; it addresses them as "consumers," as if the two acts belonged to different people. In fact, the particular styles developed in these years addressed an audience presumed to be (and presumed to see itself as such) already "middle class" in its tastes, outlook, and expectations. The denial of the labor of its audience is thus of prime importance to the mode of the advertisement, a corollary to its denial of the labor represented in its goods.

The city became the site of these baffling transactions: the place where people assembled to labor in production and consume in consumption, to consume, that is, the products of their own labor returned to them in advertised commodities as something mysteriously without origin. "A commodity is therefore a mysterious thing," writes Marx in one of his famous passages, "because in it the social character of men's labor appears to them as an objective character stamped upon the product of that labor." By animating commodities, giving them voice and motion, advertising performed the symbolic process Marx discerned. In the world of the ad, social relations assume "the fantastic form of a relation between things."

As the most visible social expression of the relations between capital and labor, the great city came to embody the reciprocal relations between production and consumption in their most acute form. Consumption emerged as the hidden purpose of cities: consumption crystallized in advertising as a perpetuation of the corporate form of private ownership of production. In the end, the paradoxes of Vanity Fair, its spectacles of mystery in street and park, in home and store, in regions fragmented and set against each other, arose from the increasingly arcane practices of buying and selling.

5

THE POLITICS OF CULTURE

I

In "What Makes a Life Significant?" William James recalls a "happy week" at the famous Chautauqua grounds in upstate New York. Founded in 1874 as an annual summer retreat for Methodist Sunday-school teachers and church workers, by the 1890's the Chautauqua assembly had supplemented its summer classes with home-study and correspondence courses. Under the educational direction of William Rainey Harper, later president of the University of Chicago, Chautauqua became synonymous with American self-education, an outgrowth of the antebellum lyceum movements through which distinguished lecturers had brought culture and learning into remote cities and towns. For James, visiting Chautauqua in 1896 (he published his essay in 1899), the place had become a "sacred enclosure," its atmosphere infused with success. "Sobriety and industry, intelligence and goodness, orderliness and ideality, prosperity and cheerfulness, pervade the air . . . Beautifully laid out in the forest and drained, and equipped with means for satisfying all the necessary lower and most of the superfluous higher wants to man," the town included a college, a chorus of seven hundred voices, athletic fields, schools, religious services, daily lectures, "no zymotic diseases, no poverty, no drunkenness, no crime, no police," and "perpetually running soda-water fountains." Founded on the principle of enlightenment for the common man, Chautauqua had become a "middle-class paradise." "You have culture, you have kindness," James observed, "you have cheapness, you have

140

equality, you have the best fruits of what mankind has fought and bled and striven for under the name of civilization for centuries."

Obviously, the "happy week" displeased the famous Harvard psychologist and philosopher, its "foretaste of what human society might be . . . with no suffering and no dark corners," turning sour for him. Why? Had not Chautauqua managed to achieve just what James's friends among intellectuals and reformers of the 1880's so desperately desired, a worldly Celestial City? Rejecting this very vision precisely because of its insulation from suffering, from adventure and risk, from those dangers which make life significant, James reflected in this essay, as in his other writings of the 1890's, a new turn in that decade, a "reorientation," as John Higham has put it, in values and ideals. In its very success, middle-class culture had come to seem stifling, enervating, effeminate, devoid of opportunities for manly heroism. The same nagging and nervous discontent which drove Roosevelt, Wister, and Remington to the West, Henry Adams to medieval France and the South Seas, and the offspring of Northern elite families into cults of arts and crafts, militarism, and Orientalism, drove James away from Chautauqua, "wishing for heroism and the spectacle of human nature on the rack."

He finds that spectacle, as he leaves the vicinity of the assembly, in an unexpected place: through the window of the speeding train, in a flashing glimpse of "a workman doing something on the dizzy edge of a sky-scaling iron construction." What is unexpected is the discovery of "great fields of heroism lying round about me . . . in the daily lives of the laboring classes," in physical work, in cattle yards and mines, on vessels and lumber rafts, "wherever a scythe, an axe, a pick, or a shovel is wielded." The scales falling from his eyes, James realizes at once that heroism need not be confined to the romance of battle. His soul fills with "a wave of sympathy with the common life of common men."

Recounting this extraordinary moment, James urges the students in his audience to resist that endemic blindness to the "lives of the other half," that American condition by which "everybody remains outside everybody else's sight." His new insight attacks the very basis of the Chautauqua ideal: if we wish to "redeem life from insignificance," he writes, "culture and refinement all alone are not enough." Instead, we must stiffen "our own ideals" with the tonic of the common laborer's "sterner stuff of manly virtue."

141

By such an infusion of masculinity into the predominantly feminine precincts of refinement, the entire society will "pass toward some newer and better equilibrium." In that process, indeed, the unrefined laboring masses also stand to benefit through "some sort of fusion, some chemical combination" with the "ideal aspirations" of culture. Just as "we" must learn to see that our comfortable lives depend on "their patient hearts and enduring backs and shoulders," so they, especially the ignorant immigrants among them, must open their eyes to the higher things about them. With "one-half of our fellow-country-men . . . entirely blind to the internal significance of the lives of the other half," we live in treacherous disunity. By joining the culture of art, refinement, formal education with the daily heroism of unwashed but patient and enduring labor, James thus envisions a restored and renewed body politic, a fusion of higher and lower through a revitalized culture: Chautauqua invigorated with the life of the street, field, and factory.

Similar images of a whole restored through culture had preoccupied a wide range of Americans in the previous three decades. Indeed, the idea of self-cultivation represented by Chautauqua had seemed the very promise of social unity and harmony. And, to be sure, it succeeded, as James observed, but at the cost of insulating itself from the daily realities of great numbers of unprivileged fellow citizens. The presiding concept of culture, James explained, restricted the applicability of the Chautauqua idea, thus fostering further exclusions, blindness, disharmonies, rather than the unity so desperately wanted. The intellectual and aesthetic realms of "sweetness and light" (in Matthew Arnold's famous words) must open themselves to physical labor, to risk and adventure, if America were to achieve genuine social harmony. James's critique, then, expresses dissatisfaction with a notion of culture as *mere* sweetness and light; he accepts the value of "ideal aspirations" but wishes to bring even the lower orders within their domain by an exchange of virtues. Thus, through an expanded concept of culture, might Americans of all social classes become visible and real to each other.

Both Chautauqua and James's criticism of its limitations belong to a current of thinking in the Gilded Age which viewed culture as a hopeful social and political force. By culture, most thinkers in the period meant nonutilitarian activities and goods:

the arts, religion, personal refinement, formal higher education. In effect, the word implied *leisure:* those energies which did not go into the making of a living. Imprecise and vague, the term nevertheless named definite aspirations to rise above the mundane, to enrich one's life by cultivation of nonmaterial enjoyments. Sometimes called genteel or high or elite, this notion of culture differs considerably, giving rise to frequent confusion, from the notion more common today (and throughout this book) of culture as the "way of life" of a society or group. Thus, while James saw culture and labor as unfortunately separate from each other, we might just as well speak of the culture of labor, referring thereby to values and habits, to structures of thinking, feeling, and acting shared by the community of labor. This broader definition of culture embraces the arts and intellectual experiences, but is not confined to them. While genteel or elite notions of culture are normative, setting special value on certain styles of art or patterns of behavior, the broader definition is descriptive, referring to the entire complex realm within a society in which values and outlooks take shape and guide behavior. The culture of the Gilded Age, we might then say, contained a particular idea of culture as a privileged domain of refinement, aesthetic sensibility, and higher learning.

The Chautauqua James saw had been produced, refined, and set in place during the Gilded Age as a virtually official middle-class image of America. It was, moreover, a deliberate and conscious alternative to two extremes, the lavish and conspicuous squandering of wealth among the very rich, and the squalor of the very poor. The extremes represented menace, peril to the original idea of a republic of freeholding independent property holders. Culture would offer a middle ground, and insofar as it was based on education (the purpose on which Chautauqua rested), it offered a democratizing influence, accessible to all those willing to raise themselves to the status of American. Culture and refinement, then, conveyed a political message, a vision of a harmonious body politic under the rule of reason, light, and sweet, cheerful emotion.

This vision of a middle-class paradise drew on several sources and models. Founded on a newly fashioned creed of art and learning in the service of Protestant virtue, it came to represent an official American version of reality. And although that outlook

143

crystallized in almost direct response to the turmoil and impassable gulfs accompanying industrial incorporation—the new immigrant work force, the doom of the countryside and rise of the great city, the mechanization of daily life, the invasion of the marketplace into human relations, the corruption and scandal of a political universe dominated by great wealth—it sealed itself off from these realities. The emergent idea of the cultured life made it increasingly difficult, as James recognized, for its devotees even to *see* the rest of the world, let alone see it critically. Stock notions of the "other half " were implanted in the evolving middle-class consensus, notions which served the negative purpose of proclaiming what the true America was not, what it must exclude or eradicate in order to preserve itself. Thus, incorporation spawned a normative ideal of culture which served as protection against other realities.

Advocates and guardians of culture performed a major role in these years, setting in place what remain the key official institutions: large private universities, municipal museums and concert halls, immense central public libraries. In a mere decade, an entire apparatus appeared, an infrastructure which monumentalized the presence of culture, of high art and learning, within the society: the Metropolitan Museum of Art in New York and the Boston Museum of Fine Arts in 1870, the Philadelphia Museum of Art in 1876, the Art Institute of Chicago in 1879. Open to the public, such institutions seemed to their advocates and supporters democratic enterprises, serving to diffuse knowledge, taste, and refinement. What they in fact diffused, however, was a set of corollaries to the idea of culture. Organized by the urban elite, dominated by ladies of high society, staffed by professionally trained personnel, housing classic works of European art donated by wealthy private collectors, the museums subliminally associated art with wealth, and the power to donate and administer with social station and training. Their architecture reinforced the message: magnificent palaces with neoclassical fronts, marble columns, sweeping staircases, frescoed ceilings, and stained-glass windows. The splendor of the museums conveyed an idea of art as public magnificence, available in hushed corridors through a corresponding act of munificence by private wealth. European and classical masterpieces epitomized the highest, purest art. Thus, museums established as a physical fact the notion that culture filtered downward from a distant past, from overseas, from the sacred founts of wealth and private power. By the same token, private universities emerged bearing the names of their donors as monuments to the philanthropy of private wealth: Cornell, Johns Hopkins, Vanderbilt, and Stanford Universities, the Carnegie Institute of Technology, and the University of Chicago (founded by a gift from John D. Rockefeller), all appearing between the late 1860's and the early 1890's.

A complex of factors lay behind these developments; they included the recent accumulation of an economic surplus large enough to fund such nonprofit enterprises. The new significance of knowledge, of the social as well as the physical sciences, contributed to the rise of private elite universities and the professionalization of graduate study. No doubt, personal motives were important: the wish for a conspicuous display of philanthropy on the part of wealthy donors, and for status on the part of the gentry, for whom the custodianship of culture provided desirable opportunities for *noblesse oblige*. Also, associated with leisure, culture seemed increasingly the sphere of women, of ladies of charity as well as schoolteachers and librarians; indeed, cultivation was already the touchstone of femininity. The rise to power of culture was at once the rise of a powerful idea of the feminine, of woman's role: the dispensing of values nonmaterial, nonaggressive, nonexploitative. As culture came to seem the repository of elevating thoughts and cleansing emotions, it seemed all the more as if the rough world of masculine enterprise had called into being its redemptive opposite.

New social roles developed for culture. Changes in social structure, the polarization of rich and poor, and the growth of a salaried middle class anxious about its own status opened the opportunity—indeed, created the necessity—for the healing properties identified with high culture. When narrowly defined as art, polite cultivation and manners, genteel styles of speech and dress, culture seemed antithetical to the rough and tumble of everyday life, to the quotidian and the practical, yet available through the ministrations of women as a refining and redeeming anodyne. Women represented "the beauty principle," the influential minister and theologian Horace Bushnell wrote in 1869; it was complementary to the "force principle" represented by men. The terms appear in his tract against voting rights for women,

Women's Suffrage: The Reform Against Nature, which argued that participation in the civil realm would corrupt the feminine character, their "indoor faculty, *covert*, as the law would say, and complementary, mistress and dispenser of the enjoyabilities." In her *The American Woman's Home*, published the same year, Catharine Beecher agreed that women should rule the domestic sphere, stay away from the ballot box, and devote themselves to the "great mission" of "self-denial." In her influential *Treatise on Domestic Economy* of 1841, of which the 1869 book was a revision in collaboration with her sister Harriet Beecher Stowe, she had urged American women to take up their "exalted privilege" to "renovate degraded man, and 'clothe all climes with beauty.'"

For Bushnell and Beecher, culture performed its work chiefly in the home, the domestic sphere protected from the corrupting powers of the competitive marketplace and the political arena by the nurturing powers of women. The notion exercised great appeal, reflected in the outburst of popular manuals and treatises such as Beecher's and Stowe's on domestic arrangements, on furnishings, choice of wallpapers, design of rooms; of mass-produced miniature plaster sculpture such as John Roger's genre scenes of country life and family happiness; and a corresponding rise in concern with child rearing. Early implantation of culture lay as a motive behind the founding of kindergartens in these decades. The growing literature of domesticity must be counted along with the founding of museums and concert halls, the creation of public parks, and the spread of public schools, as part of a concerted middle-class effort to find in culture both pleasure and instruction, Bushnell's "enjoyabilities" and Beecher's lessons in the virtue of sacrifice and domestic harmony.

This feminization of culture, its location within the precincts of the home, implied that view of culture William James found so stifling at Chautauqua, a view of aesthetic experience as merely receptive, passive, spectatorial. Writing about the design of parks in 1870, Olmsted had evoked that very theory, describing, as he put it, two capacities latent in all people, the "exertive" and the "receptive." One kind of park design might well "stimulate" exertion, games and sports, for example. Another, related to "music and the fine arts generally," will "cause us to receive pleasure without conscious exertion." A place designed for games and sports would encourage that very competitiveness and reminder of physical labor he wished to expunge from the zone of the park. Sports and games would invite rowdy working-class youths and disrupt the tranquillity of promenade and contemplation. The receptive faculties, he continued, can further be divided into two types, the "gregarious" and the "neighborly." By allowing people to congregate in peace and quiet, the public park will satisfy the first need. The second is more difficult to describe, and Olmsted reaches for an illustration "in a familiar domestic gathering, where the prattle of the children mingles with the easy conversation of the more sedate, the bodily requirements satisfied with good cheer, fresh air, agreeable light, moderate temperature, snug shelter, and decorations adapted to please the eye." The domestic scene thus induces "a pleasurable wakefulness of mind without stimulating exertion." It induces that very condition Bushnell described, in which the "masculine force" sinks "into the bigger self that he calls his home . . . sheltered in the womanly peace he has protected, for the gentler and more dear protection of his own stormy life."

Feminization thus implied that art and culture were sinking into, a losing of oneself in a larger emotion, a "bigger self." It was this apparent selflessness of the experience of art which emerged as a common motif in numerous commentaries about the social utility and necessity of culture. Culture was represented increasingly as the antidote to unruly feeling, to rebellious impulses, and especially to such impulses showing themselves with more frequency, as the years went on, among the lower orders. The conjunction of culture with wealth and property on one hand, with surrender, self-denial, and subordination to something larger on the other, gave it a cardinal place among instruments of social control and reform. Moreover, by offering a middle ground presumably secure from aggressions of the marketplace, culture would offer an alternative to class hostility. It would disarm potential revolution, and embrace all classes.

Throughout the period, writers made explicit the political uses of culture. For the art critic James Jackson Jarves in the late 1860's, museums, galleries, churches, universities, and parks served as "moral physical reformers." He cited Central Park itself as "a great free school for the people . . . a magnetic charm of decent behavior, giving salutary lessons in order, discipline, comeliness, culminating in mutual good will." A decade later, after the turmoil of the 1870's, the Unitarian minister Jonathan Baxter Harrison adopted a more embattled tone. His observations and tours of factory towns in New England convinced him that America was "in the earlier stages of a war on property, and upon everything that satisfied what are called the higher wants of life." Raising the alarm in *Certain Dangerous Tendencies in American Life* (1880), he recounted his firsthand investigations in a New England mill town, where he found among workers "distrust, suspicion, and hostility regarding all who do not belong to their class."

Harrison undertook to learn as much as he could about the culture of mill workers: "I saw their food and their methods of preparing it, examined the books and papers which they read, and listened to their accounts of their own life and work and experience." He found the New York "story papers" and their serialized tales devoured by factory youths "vapid, silly, turgid, and incoherent." He found "older operatives, especially foreigners," deeply engaged in the reading of a labor newspaper just then carrying "a very long serial story of the overthrow of the republic in 1880" by revolutionary workers. In such literary offerings and in the "declaration of principles" printed weekly, "the tone and spirit of the paper are indescribably bitter, and expressive of intense hostility against the possessors of property and culture." In the evenings, younger workers of both sexes divert themselves in one or another of the many saloons and music halls in the town, listening to ballad singers and a striking, suave black performer of spirituals and minstrels. Sexual behavior, he is pleased to say, seems in good order, "more pure and free" than most moralists think, which proves the happy point that "toil represses passion." Factory workers have "little leisure for vicious thoughts, for nourishing mischievous and profligate desires." Thus, the minister concludes on the question of the hours of labor that the more the better; all men need more than eight hours of work a day "in order to keep down and utilize the forces of the animal nature and passions." Otherwise, "society would rot in measureless and fatal animalism." On this count, the culture of industrialism is to be applauded.

But social hostility is not so easily repressed. Harrison proposes that the mill owners take responsibility, in their own interest, to provide "suitable reading matter" for their hands, uniting with "cultivated people" in the town to publish low-priced, elevating newspapers for the working people. On a national scale, "those who believe in culture, in property, and in order" must take steps to found "the necessary agencies for the diffusion of a new culture." The sheer cultural differences of workers, native-born and foreign-born alike, represent the dangerous tendency. "We do not know as much about them as we should," writes Harrison, striking a chord James, too, would echo: "It is not safe or wise to allow so large a class to be so far alien and separate from the influences and spirit of our national life."

While Harrison does not make explicit the theme of feminization, a theory of pacification through culture runs through his warnings and his proposals. We find the concept repeated in the press and in sermons throughout the period: fear, on one hand, of the cultural degradation and alienation produced by industrial life and immigration, and, on the other, reinforcement of an image of the cultured home as middle ground, a domestic island of virtue and stability. Tenders of machines, observed the Boston Brahmin industrialist Edward Atkinson in 1876, risk "becoming a machine, well-oiled and cared for, but incapable of independent life." In the past, labor itself was the basis of culture, calling "upon all the faculties." The routinization of mechanical labor has radically altered the relations: "the culture and refinements of today come from leisure and opportunity more than from the development of men in the necessary work of their lives." Deprived of the very "capability of enjoyment," those who toil at machines seek only "bad and sensational books" and the excitement of cheap amusements. Labor's new proletarian culture has created a new condition, requiring for workers "instruction in what constitutes the true use of leisure." Work will remain, he implies, a realm of unredeemed exertion.

With cultural proletarianization looming as threat and menace, the cultivated home grew stronger and laid greater claim as the official image of America. "The laborer ought to be ashamed of himself," admonished Henry Ward Beecher on the appropriate date of July 4, 1876, "who in 20 years does not own the ground on which his house stands . . . who has not in that house provided carpets for the rooms, who has not his China plates, who has not his chromos, who has not some books nestling on the shelf." The image descended from above. "Just a plain, roomy house," wrote

Mark Twain and Charles Dudley Warner about the habitation of the good Squire Oliver Montague in *The Gilded Age* (1874), bastion of the "middle ground" in that novel of scoundrels and schemers.

Every room had its book-cases or book-shelves, and was more or less a library; upon every table was liable to be a litter of new books, fresh periodicals and daily newspapers. There were plants in the sunny windows and some choice engravings on the walls, with bits of color in oil or watercolors; the piano was sure to be open and strewn with music; and there were photographs and little souvenirs here and there of foreign travel.

The authors may well have had in view their own splendid homes in the literary community of Nook Farm in Hartford, with every room "more or less a library." But, as Beecher happily explained, the same (or its image) could be reproduced for all Americans, especially by what James Parton in *Triumphs of Enterprise, Ingenuity, and Public Spirit* (1874) called "Oil Paintings by Machinery." Chromolithography, argued Parton, perhaps the most popular biographer and essayist of the decade, perfectly suited "the special work of America at the present moment," when floods of immigrants from Europe's under-classes "as well as the emancipated slaves of the South" awaited conversion "into thinking, knowing, skillful, tasteful American citizens."

Parton's shrewd linkage of machinery with culture, of the devices of mechanical reproduction and the potential for mass diffusion of the tangible signs of culture, points to the social changes which made the cultivated middle-class home so urgent and essential an image. Mechanization made possible the mass production of culture in the form of consumable objects. The same process which fragmented labor into minute mechanical tasks, which brought into the cities new masses of people experiencing wage labor for the first time, thus destroyed old forms of labor and community, old cultures of work and shared pleasures, replaced the larger extended family with the nuclear family as the basic domestic unit. As old cultures dissolved, a new culture of mechanically produced goods and values arose in their place; the same process which produced insecurities at the same moment pandered new images of security in home and consumption, in goods inscribed with culture.

The logic of the process remained obscure for most observers, preoccupied as they were by signs of a frightful gulf, a "growing gap," in the economist Simon Patten's words, between the standards of life of the laboring and the employing classes. In his essay of 1889, "The Consumption of Wealth," he presents the first serious effort to understand "abundance" as a new economic reality, viewing the cultural gap with as much misgiving as others. He understood clearly, however, that a solution lay in consumption: not in reordering social relations but in providing more opportunities for the lower classes to consume a greater variety of goods. "Opposition between the interests of different men," he wrote, "can be reduced only by the growth of new pleasures which they can enjoy in common." The problem was ready-made to be solved by mechanical reproduction, a standardization of goods and the pleasures they bestowed.

Patten based his original and prophetic argument on a stunning explication of the logic of consumption. Aiming his barbs against the prevailing image of an "economic man desiring only material wealth," Patten (like Freud) assumed a pleasure-seeking human impulse. Men work not only to relieve the pain of hunger but to gain the pleasure of satisfying their desires. He argued that "repeated gratification" developed new capacities and new needs; appetites develop into tastes, calling for a greater variety of pleasurable experiences. The true measure of a standard of life is thus not the absolute quantity of available goods but "the mental state of a man after the order of his consumption has been changed so as to allow a greater variety."

How, then, might the menacing gap between low and high standards of living be closed? The crux of the class difference is that goods appealing to older, more primitive appetites remain cheap, while more refined goods remain expensive, out of reach of those "newer classes of immigrants" who "seek to remain European in their living ... Drinking, smoking, and other amusements which tend to the wrong direction are much cheapened; while music, art, and education have become in their higher forms more costly." Let us then reverse the priorities, making culture cheaper and mere amusements and vices more expensive. Let us shorten the hours of labor by law, and make accessible cheaper education to raise the working-class level of taste. This will lead to greater consumption of a greater variety of goods on

151

the part of the lower classes, and thus a greater "harmony with their environment." A new middle culture of shared refinement, Patten contends, will not only help maintain social peace but also stimulate even greater production of consumer goods.

In the language of social science, then, Patten repeats the familiar refrain that culture bridges the impassable gulf, the growing gaps in American life. Again he assumes lower classes to be in a lower cultural condition, clinging to old ways only out of stubborn habit. But it is a point of interest and significance that an argument similar to Patten's had already taken root among labor reformers. Jonathan Baxter Harrison had reported in 1880 a conversation with a labor editor who advocated a six-hour workday, arguing that the best means of improving the condition of workers was through a "multiplication of their wants; that is, they should be taught to live more and more expensively." Demanding more, they would compel employers to meet their needs with higher wages. Harrison's friend seemed to be representing the arguments of Ira Steward, self-educated machinist and theorist of the eight-hour movement. "Men who labor excessively are robbed of all ambition to ask for anything more than will satisfy their bodily necessities," wrote Steward in 1865, "while those who labor moderately have time to cultivate tastes and create wants in addition to mere physical comforts." The similarity of argument makes it likely that Patten was familiar with Steward's views, perhaps in their systematic presentation by George Gunton in *Wealth and Progress* (1887), after Steward's death in 1883. But more important is the place of culture—culture conceived as high art, the higher, nonmaterial experiences—in their respective arguments, for the coincidence on this count indicates the power of the concept. Steward, like Patten, advocated a reduction of the hours of labor for the sake of allowing workers to develop their faculties, their "wants, habits, and character," on the basis of which they consume goods. "Frequent contact with an increasing variety of social influences" will thereby increase "their natural capacity to consume wealth." Steward describes the process in terms almost exactly like Patten's: by repeated satisfactions, desires "grow into tastes, and tastes into absolute wants, which ultimately become a part of the fixed character or 'second nature.'"

Thus, the concept of a higher culture guiding consumption

and leading to a society of equals appeals to a bourgeois economist fearful of the degrading effects of immigrant laborers and a
working-class theorist of the major workers' movement of the
era, for the eight-hour day. And for both, culture and America
shared an exceptional identity. "American conditions," wrote
Patten, are especially favorable if only because "the processes of
invention have cheapened the process of reproducing pictures
and brought the beautiful within reach of all." Even advertisements, he points out, reproduce scenes of beauty, filling "the
homes of the poorest people" everywhere with "beautiful objects" at no cost. "And when their taste is improved by contact
with these objects, others more suited to their new condition can
be obtained at a slight increase of cost." Putting it more succinctly, Steward declared: "In America every man is king in
theory, and will be eventually, and in the good time coming every
man will be a capitalist."

II

"Two enemies, unknown before, have risen like spirits of darkness on our social and political horizon"—wrote Francis Parkman in "The Failure of Universal Suffrage" (*North American
Review*, 1878)—"an ignorant proletariat and a half-taught
plutocracy." The eminent historian of more heroic days of conquest and settlement in the New World assured his readers, who
needed no such assurance, that culture befriended neither the
"dangerous classes" nor "vulgar wealth." He called for an alliance of the educated, the cultivated, even the "literary feller"—
all who "find their exercise in the higher fields of thought and
action"—to beat back the menace of "greedy and irresponsible
crowds," the "barbarism . . . ready to overwhelm us." Attacking
the failures of suffrage, Parkman called for a crusade against the
dangers of democracy itself.

"Wherever men of cultivation looked," writes Richard Hofstadter, "they found themselves facing hostile forces and an alien
mentality." "Frustrated aristocrats" and "genteel reformers,"
many of these figures felt themselves out of place in the age,
uncomfortable with both the new businessmen and the new
politicians, and horrified by the new urban masses, swarming
immigrant laborers or paupers and vulgar, success-minded mem-

153

bers of the rising middle class. Some sought roles in politics, joining forces even with labor reformers in the Liberal Republican Party in 1872, later dropping away even further from their primary loyalty to the Republican Party, as Mugwump supporters of Democrat Grover Cleveland in 1884. Others found roles as reformers, advocates of charity, social work, cultural enlightenment. The best-known were teachers and editors: the Harvard art historian Charles Eliot Norton; the editor of *The Nation*, E. L. Godkin; literary editors of the major respectable journals, including George William Curtis of *Harper's Weekly*, and Richard Watson Gilder of the *Century;* poets, playwrights, and critics like Thomas Bailey Aldrich, Bayard Taylor, and Edmund Clarence Stedman. Their ranks included revered literary figures of the recent past, New Englanders who survived into the Gilded Age as notable remnants of a better age: James Russell Lowell, Parkman himself, and, most revered of all, Ralph Waldo Emerson. Destined for the greatest fame among the younger group of alienated and displaced intellectuals was Henry Adams: once editor of the prestigious *North American Review*, historian and teacher at Harvard, novelist and man of letters, jaundiced commentator on the politics and morals of an age he despaired to influence.

Without much say in the affairs of the times, these figures, differing considerably among themselves, have exerted an influence of great magnitude on the intellectual life of the nation since. It is their characterization of the age as "gilded" which has guided historians; many of their documents, such as Godkin's essays and, especially, Henry Adams's *Education of Henry Adams*, have informed the perceptions and attitudes of students. More important, their conception of the marginal role of cultivated intelligence within modern society would become in the twentieth century a common perception among many American academic intellectuals. For they were the first group of writers and thinkers, chiefly literary and political, to view themselves as alienated, and to describe and judge their times against the measure of their own alienation. In doing so, they were led by the force of their perceived circumstances toward cultural criticism, a new kind of writing in which these conservative writers seized on the emerging popular and political culture.

"Of all the civilized nations," complained Charles Eliot Norton bluntly, America was "the most deficient in the higher culture of the mind, and not only in the culture but also in the conditions on which this culture mainly depends." Only "the *Nation* & Harvard & Yale College" stood as "barriers against the invasion of modern barbarism and vulgarity." Deeply Anglophiliac, many of these intellectuals judged the deficiencies of America against the more accommodating world of England, where Oxford and Cambridge remained centers of traditional culture and intellectuals might find respected roles as civil servants. On the whole, they responded with enthusiasm to the writings of John Ruskin and Matthew Arnold, both sharply critical of the culture of industrial society, the decline in appreciation of beauty and of religious values, the erosion of the authority of intelligence. Arnold had written of America, after his visits in the 1880's, that the country seemed given over to practical-minded values and a religion of the heart, that it was lacking "distinction," a judgment which raised some patriotic objections but on the whole met with approval from genteel critics. Known as the "apostle of culture" since his *Culture and Anarchy*, published in 1867 in response to fears that the Reform Bill of that year would unleash anarchy in England, Arnold found an eager audience among American intellectuals. His formulation of culture as the "pursuit of our total perfection," our "best selves," found frequent echoes in American writings, as did his remark that perfection might be pursued "by means of getting to know, on all matters which most concern us, the best which has been thought and said in the world." He urged his American friends and followers to work for public education and a general cultural enlightenment. "A higher, larger civilization, a finer lucidity, is what is needed," he wrote in "A Word About America" in 1888, and suggested that cultivated Americans stop "hopping backwards and forwards over the Atlantic," stay home "and do their best to make the administration, the tribunals, the theatre, the arts" into "visible ideals" for the purging and ennobling of "public sentiment." He urged they become an "apostolate" of civilization.

A similar call had been sounded in 1867 by Emerson. He addressed the Phi Beta Kappa Society at Harvard in that year on the theme of "The Progress of Culture," thirty years after his previous Harvard address before the same society on "The American Scholar." In the earlier lecture he had called, like a young titan, for a radical break with the culture of Europe: "We have listened too long to the courtly muses of Europe." Rejecting "the great, the remote, the romantic," he embraced "the common . . . the familiar, the low," and envisioned an American culture developing through a "gradual domestication of the idea of Culture." Now, more in harmony with Arnold and the changed tenor of the times than with his earlier vision, he invested his faith in "the power of minorities," in the "few superior and attractive men," and called for a "knighthood of virtue" which would, like Arnold's apostolate, "calm and guide" a "barbarous age." Less militant than Parkman in his disdain for the new forces already visible in the postwar years, Emerson nonetheless gave heart to an attitude emerging since Appomattox that inheritors of New England culture and politics now represented a minority of virtue, intelligence, and cultivation, a saving remnant with a mission to preserve civility in public life. Another notable from the New England past, James Russell Lowell, in his "Ode for the Centennial" in 1876, gave crisp expression to a version of America by now official among the intellectual elite:

> *Murmur of many voices in the air*
> *Denounces as degenerate,*
> *Unfaithful guardians of a noble fate,*
> *And prompts indifference or despair;*
> *Is this the country that we dreamed in youth,*
> *Where wisdom and not numbers should have weight,*
> *Seed-field of simpler manners, braver truth,*
> *Where shams could cease to dominate*
> *In household, church, and state?*
> *Is this Atlantis?*

Elsewhere, surveying the ethnic composition of his new "Atlantis" in an essay on politics, Lowell joined Parkman in questioning whether the older culture could survive the new America: would not "equality . . . prove dangerous when interpreted and applied politically by millions of newcomers alien to our traditions"? Was not equality, wrote the old abolitionist, now the most dangerous enemy of the nation, its traditions, and culture itself?

Encouraged by the murmurings of their respected elders, the younger patrician intellectuals in the postwar decades fashioned a broad point of view, a frame of mind which, as Stow Persons has suggested, contained in embryonic form a theory of "mass society," a society in which both the civil and political realms required expert administration and discipline, the rule of men of culture and special training. The theory did not cohere into any particular program for abolishing political democracy; it appeared instead by implication in the form of expression most common to Emerson's knighthood, the critical essay. Nor was their criticism reserved alone for bloated plutocrats and ignorant masses. In "Chromo-Civilization," for example, Godkin excoriated the "pseudo-culture" of that "large body of slenderly equipped persons" who mistake a "smattering" of knowledge and "a desire to see and own pictures" for real culture. A holy anger driving his sentences, Godkin wrote:

A large body of persons has arisen, under the influence of the common schools, magazines, newspapers, and the rapid acquisition of wealth, who are not only engaged in enjoying themselves after their fashion, but who firmly believe that they have reached, in the matter of social, mental, and moral culture, all that is attainable or desirable by anybody, and who, therefore, tackle all the problems of the day—men's, women's, and children's rights and duties, marriage, education, suffrage, life, death, and immortality—with supreme indifference to what anybody else thinks or has ever thought, and have their own trumpery prophets, prophetesses, heroes and heroines, poets, orators, scholars and philosophers, whom they worship with a kind of barbaric fervor. The result is a kind of mental and moral chaos, in which many of the fundamental rules of living, which have been worked out painfully by thousands of years of bitter human experience, seem in imminent risk of disappearing totally.

Real culture, instead, is a result of discipline, of self-denial, "the breaking-in of the powers to the services of the will." It results from obedience to something superior: "the art of doing easily what you don't like to do," as if at the behest of a noble mother.

Among the articulate, well-placed editors and teachers of the age, a notion arose of culture embodying a hierarchy of values corresponding to a social hierarchy of stations or classes. The notion of respecting one's "betters," of "knowing one's place," filtered almost inconspicuously into public discourse, especially in respectable journals. In his lectures on sociology at Yale, William Graham Sumner gave the notion of cultural and social hier-

THE INCORPORATION OF AMERICA

archy perhaps the solidest theoretical foundation in the period. Classifying "societal value" on a curved scale, Sumner portrayed the social world as a range of values descending from "genius" through "talent" to "mediocrity" (identified with "the masses," or middle groups), to "unskilled and illiterate proletariat," to the bottom line of the "defective, dependent, and delinquent." It was clear where the power to rule should lie.

No wonder, then, that Whitman, writing in 1871 in "Democratic Vistas," should exclaim that with "the word Culture . . . we find ourselves abruptly in close quarters with the enemy." Early in the postwar career of the concept, Whitman detected its antidemocratic bias. "As now taught, accepted and carried out," the word propagates invidious distinction and class privilege, "certain portions of the people set off from the rest by a line drawn—they not as privileged as others, but degraded, humiliated, made of no account." Sniffing out the "mass society" implications of "the word Culture," he also observed that the "merely educated classes," those with "taste, intelligence and culture (so-called)" find the masses an "affront." But the deepest affront lay in the implied identification of America itself with a privileged culture distributed and administered with condescension from above, as if from a celestial source. Instead, he insisted on an antebellum egalitarian dogma, that America and democracy are "convertible terms," and called for a "radical change of category, in the distribution of precedence," a "programme of culture" based on equality, on a "native expression-spirit, getting into form." His theory had the sanction of a tradition now losing its appeal among the upper reaches of a society more and more divided into distinct levels yet still alive anu articulate among labor and farm groups. Whitman saw the establishment of political equality in the American Revolution: "the great word Solidarity has arisen." Now the country awaited the step beyond equality toward a culture of solidarity, "not for classes, but for universal man . . . Democracy can never prove itself beyond cavil," he wrote, "until it founds and luxuriantly grows its own forms of art, poems, schools, theology, displacing all that exists, or that has been produced anywhere in the past, under opposite influence." In short, America awaits, for its final realization, a revolution in culture.

Whitman shares with the patricians a jeremiad-like scorn of

158

the contemporary scene; like them he condemns and scorns the manners, morals, and politics of the Grant era. He is even more fierce than the Nortons and Godkins, less polite in saying that "these savage, wolfish parties alarm me," that business had become "this all-devouring modern word." He views the American scene with "severe eyes," like a "physician diagnosing some deep disease," and makes out "a sort of dry and flat Sahara," a wasteland "crowded with petty grotesques, malformations, phantoms, playing meaningless antics." He finds the spectacle "appalling," "flippancy and vulgarity, low cunning, infidelity" everywhere. He also grants that political democracy has its shortcomings. Yet it remains the best safeguard against further corruption and erosion. And furthermore, if we recognize that it serves only as a means to the end of allowing man, "properly train'd in sanest, highest freedom," to become "a law, and a series of laws, unto himself," then attacks on universal suffrage like Parkman's (or Thomas Carlyle's, which Whitman takes up explicitly) appear as retrograde solutions. Instead of less democracy, more is wanted. But in his explanation of the more Whitman's argument founders into the vagueness of metaphysics and nostalgia.

Against the implicit "mass theory" of "the word Culture," Whitman raises a Hegelian formula of a dialectical rapport between the "self " and the "mass." "The two are contradictory," he writes, "but our task is to reconcile them." Reconciliation takes place, however, not through a program of action, of communal experience, but through an image to be provided by democratic poets and artists of a "high average," the creation by writers of "a basic model or portrait of personality for general use," a transcendent type of "personality" which will delineate "the democratic ethology of the future." Drawing up into itself the characteristics of "the People," especially working people—"the facts of farms and jackplanes and engineers, and of the broad range of women also of the middle and working strata"—Whitman's "average," however, loses all specificity. It becomes "universal man," while the world still consists very much of particular men and women in fast solidifying social groups. The "high average" of "Democratic Vistas" rapidly loses touch with the very history whose negative face Whitman observes in such minute detail.

The loss of touch, the historical marginality of Whitman's

program, is all the more apparent when he turns his attention to the social conditions under which his program might succeed. He would take for granted, he explained, a "general good order" in society, an even "more universal ownership of property, general homesteads, general comfort—a vast, intertwining reticulation of wealth." As the social ground for his culture of "universal man," he assumed, that is, an antebellum, free-labor vision of independent producers, "middling property owners," "men and women with occupations, well-off, owners of houses and acres, and with cash in the bank." In 1871, Whitman had as yet no glimmer of what would come to him with a shock in a few years: images of a ruptured society, permanent class divisions. And the middling groups which did arise in the Gilded Age took their cultural bearings from their own insecurities in a changing world, their determination to distinguish themselves through education and cultivation from the masses. Chautauqua would proclaim their democratic vista: culture and refinement coming to represent aspiration, desire for a "better" material life.

"Democratic Vistas" failed in its day to provide a genuine alternative program. It may have struck responsive chords among young artists with radical ideals, the painter Thomas Eakins and, most prominently, the architect Louis Sullivan. But it made no notable impression on the people who had real alternatives. Ethnic, racial, and regional diversity do not figure in Whitman's vista, although his vision of the "high average" would in theory embrace them. His vision of America would need the corrective of Randolph Bourne's image of a "Trans-national America" early in the twentieth century. Moreover, Whitman seemed not to recognize that an alternative to "the word Culture" might arise in conjunction with a political movement created out of economic and social protest, such as the People's Party of the 1890's. Short-lived and doomed, Populism would nevertheless propose a marriage of democratic politics and culture which might well have fit Whitman's program, had he better grasped the new conditions of postbellum society.

Those conditions included developments which eluded the Godkins and Adamses as well as Whitman, new levels and forms of stratification, a segmenting of the society into professional groupings, into new distinct subcultures of vocation and gender, of race and ethnic language. The entire social world came to resemble a chart of separate categories and systems of integration. As "the word Culture" came more and more to represent an outlook congruent with this process, it became all the more difficult to see its forms, visible monuments of culture rendering social divisions and lines of control all but invisible.

III

To be sure, high culture—the culture of the intellectual, the artist, the writer, the thinker—made little direct impression on popular life, where older cultural ways held on against mass newspapers, advertising, story-paper romances. As Jonathan Baxter Harrison lamented, the cultivated lived in ignorance of the "other half"; the details of home and work and community, of preparing food, keeping warm, passing time after work, holding forth and keeping busy in mill and plant and shop, joining others in clubs, church, and labor meetings, burial and fraternal societies—all of which made up the daily life from which gentility stood apart. The rise in the 1890's of social work, of settlement houses, of literary adventures like Harrison's, seeking truth by expedition on the other half's own forbidden terrain, represented reactions against the genteel barriers to firsthand knowledge. By the turn of the century, the fictions of Stephen Crane, Frank Norris, Theodore Dreiser, Upton Sinclair, and the documentary narratives of Jacob Riis, Walter Wyckoff (an intellectual who traveled in disguise as a tramp), and Jack London had made vivid and credible for eager readers the details of social entrapment and cultural difference. In the Gilded Age, however, the realm of the popular would remain in cultured circles the realm of social mystery, of foreign ways and unimaginable consciousness.

It remained especially in the realm of politics, and in the minds of genteel reformers, the very ground of corruption. Here, in the imagination of reform, the twin specters of immoral wealth and ignorant foreign masses met in unholy alliance—met particularly in the figure of the political "boss," the antichrist of reform. A gang of scrofulous and vulturous praetorians, their master a hulking, bearded Nero, their followers a horde of ape-like Irishmen with ragged clothes and battered top hats: so Thomas Nast portrayed the Tammany machine and Boss Tweed. Political car-

161

toonist for *Harper's Weekly*, ardent advocate of the Radical Republican cause, defender of the party's claim to a monopoly of virtue and patriotism, devoted admirer of Grant, Nast propelled the loathed Tweed into immortal fame through caricature. During his vitriolic campaign against Tweed in the early 1870's, Nast's cartoons depicted a political world as seen through faithful Republican eyes: the Tammany machine a tiger devouring the fallen Republic in a Roman arena, at the pleasure of tunic-garbed bosses licking their chops over the "spoils"; the low-browed, beetle-eyed, unshaved Irishman a slave chained to a post of rum and whiskey, induced to leave the old country by false promises, branded "Democrat" upon arrival, put to work as ditchdigger on "boodle" projects, driven to the polls on election day to stuff the ballot boxes. The other half, in this version of political reality, joined bloody hands with the unregenerate Confederacy and the scheming Fifth Avenue capitalist over the prostrate body of the black freedman, an alliance in wickedness and self-interest which remained the Republican stereotype of the Democrat through the 1860's, 1870's, and 1880's. "Nast," said Mark Twain after the reelection of Grant in 1872 against the Democrats and the renegade Liberal Republican Horace Greeley, "you more than any other man have won a prodigious victory for Grant—I mean, rather, for Civilization and Progress."

Mark Twain would shortly wonder about these terms in *The Gilded Age* (1873), but the identification of "civilization" with Republicanism ran deep among Northern elites, even those who bolted to Greeley or who later turned to Cleveland. Mugwumpism itself was an assertion of virtue, a painful turn from the Grand Old Party, which seemed to have lost its soul, especially in the Compromise of 1877, to party hacks and unmitigated greed. In the increasingly bitter, outraged, and mordant comments by Godkin, Adams, and others, culture stood aghast at the spectacle of party politics, of the "spoils system" which distributed the offices of power to the party faithful, regardless of qualifications. The language of political criticism abounded in imagery of rampant animals, creatures low on the scale of evolution. "Where did the public good enter at all into this maze of personal intrigue," wonders Henry Adams's appalled heroine of his novel *Democracy* (1880), "this wilderness of stunted natures where no straight road was to be found, but only the torturous and aimless track of beasts and things that crawl?" The image calls up the frontier, savages in the underbrush, while "straight road" recalls the civilized eighteenth-century New England village where, as in the Virginia of George Washington (slavery apart), reason once dominated nature.

For genteel intellectuals with a taste for battle, defense of civilization took the form of campaigns for civil-service reform, the effort to defeat the spoils system, the rule of party machines and bosses, by removing government positions from patronage, opening them to competitive examination. The crusade aimed to replace the "scum" (as Adams put it) of Washington with properly educated men of intelligence, principle, and genuine loyalty to the republic. True democracy, civil-service reformers like Carl Schurz and George William Curtis went on to say, required absolute probity in government, and that required a corps of dedicated civil servants. The reformers who believed in the rule of the majority stressed the value of university training and family tradition, urging, despite the apparent purpose of their objectives, rule by a cultured elite. For purposes of polity, they argued, issues of state should be removed from politics, from the whimsy of voters and the wickedness of "coarse, selfish, unprincipled" politicians. Over and again, Godkin insisted in *The Nation* that issues such as tariff regulation and monetary policy were too important for merely political decision. Many of them advocates of free trade and sound money, opposing both big business and Greenback agrarians, civil-service reformers looked eventually to government by commission, by experts immune from the vagaries of electoral politics.

Not surprisingly, reformers and genteel intellectuals who stood above party battles invited the scorn of the regulars, a scorn couched frequently in images fusing anger at feminizing culture with sexual innuendo, the manly braggadocio of the stalwart: "political hermaphrodite," "miss-Nancys," "man-milliners." Nonpartisans were a "third sex," "the neuter gender not popular either in nature or society." In the images of both sides, reform above parties and loyalty within parties, the issue seemed to join culture versus politics, the realm of the feminine against the realm of the aggressive masculine. But this apparent bifurcation by sex and culture only obscured the more significant underlying development: high culture—the culture of the intellectual world

—becoming more political in its motives, and politics more cultural in its methods and consequences. In fact, the political implications of "the word Culture" and the cultural policies of the major parties converged to create a single political universe devoted to a single aim: the rule of business goals and methods in government.

For uncontested in the running battles between genteel reformers and party politicians was a figure of speech common to both, that politics and business served each other. Reformers proposed nonpartisan civil servants in order to place government on the "plain principles of business administration." "We shall never govern a great city well or rightly comprehend it," wrote a reform lawyer in 1873, "until we consider its administration as involving a large amount of business done by businessmen, rather than a large mass of politics to be managed by partisans." Moreover, the "plain principles" of business by the 1880's had come to rest less in the old practices of individual cutthroat competition, and more in the new structures of corporate organization, of decision from above by boards of directors. With its program for a governance by experts and the removal of economic policy from electoral decision, civil-service reformers taught the parties a lesson in professionalization, in centralization. In this light, the crusade for civil-service reform proved less an antagonistic assault on the party system than an effort to purify, to systematize, to eliminate the waste and inefficiency of the spoils system.

The idea of business as a model of efficiency followed from the appropriation by businessmen of the free-labor rhetoric of the Radical Republicans, and from the increasingly decisive role played within the two major parties of businessmen themselves: New York's Tom Platt, a banker and president of a lumber company; Michigan's Zachariah Chandler, also a lumber magnate; Chauncey Depew, both railroad counsel and senator. "Leading and substantial citizens," in Theodore Roosevelt's words, filled the upper echelons of leadership in both parties: manufacturers, railroad and insurance executives, corporate managers. The hold of business on the top ranks of the parties increased in the course of the Gilded Age, arriving, with the victory of Benjamin Harrison over Grover Cleveland in 1888, at a state of affairs in the Senate in which, in William Allen White's account, "a United States senator . . . represented principalities and powers in business." In the "Millionaire's Club," which the Senate came to be called in the late 1880's, elected officials represented railroad and insurance companies, coal and iron and cotton interests, and their performance proved true to form, passing higher tariffs, higher premiums to government bondholders, and higher subsidies to contractors.

Apart from several notable acts aiming at regulation of civil rights (the Civil Rights Act of 1875), at government organization (the Pendleton Act, placing a number of positions under civil-service rules in 1883), and at regulation of business (the Interstate Commerce Act of 1887 and the Sherman Anti-Trust Act of 1890, interpreted by the courts initially in favor of corporations against labor unions), the work of government during the Gilded Age seemed concerned mostly with tariffs and money policy, with support for private business interests. Weak Presidents and relatively inactive Congresses gave rise to the perception that government did little. "The government does not govern," noted Henry Adams in 1870. "Congress is inefficient, and shows itself more and more incompetent . . . while the executive is . . . practically deprived of its necessary strengths by the jealousy of the Legislatures." Another observer wrote about state governments: "Legislatures have ceased to create or concentrate public sentiment; they have become clearing houses for the adjustment of claims." Government seemed more and more to follow the lead of business interests, less and less to govern in its own right. Yet at the same time it expanded its functions, widening its role within public life, establishing new departments (Agriculture, Justice, State, and Post Office) and new programs (Bureaus of Statistics, of Education, of Weather, and Commissioners of Immigration, Fish and Fisheries, and numerous new congressional committees). Public expenditure increased severalfold. The size of the federal bureaucracy doubled between 1871 and 1881, while the number of positions covered by the Pendleton Act rose from more than 13,500 in 1884 to more than 94,500 in 1900. Similar expansion in the number of new laws occurred at the state and municipal levels; rewriting of state constitutions was common in the period. With its new federal powers established during the Civil War and confirmed by the Union victory, the central government strengthened its hold over civil society in the very years

165

it remained relatively inactive in shaping the emerging society.

Absence of substantive issues between the postwar parties marked the political universe evolving in these years into what historians call the "third party system," lasting from the realignment which had elected Lincoln in 1860 to the Republican sweep of 1896. Moreover, the recession of divisive issues paralleled a new and extraordinary intensification of national-party loyalty and a correspondingly high voter turnout, as high as 78.5 percent in Presidential elections, and 62.8 percent in off years, between 1876 and 1896. Although the Republicans won every Presidential election but two from the Civil War to 1896 (Grover Cleveland winning twice, in 1884 and 1892), most elections were very close, and the strength of the parties, especially after the end of Reconstruction and the occupation of the South in 1877, was roughly equal. In this situation, writes Robert Marcus, "the closeness of elections, high turnout, and party regularity . . . seemed to be mutually reinforcing phenomena." Regularity or loyalty, or the appeal to party labels and slogans, thus served in lieu of substantive issues as means of mobilizing voters. This is not to say that the political combats were wholly devoid of issues; third-party movements advocating radical change appeared throughout the period, injecting issues the major parties could not ignore.

These ranged from agrarian demands for less deflationary money policies and labor demands for a legal eight-hour day, from calls among embattled Grangers for regulation of transport and grain-elevator rates to antimonopoly platforms for nationalization of railroad and telegraph companies. Third parties regularly agitated the political universe with genuine issues of governance and polity, challenging not only the major parties but the prevailing laissez-faire philosophy regarding government. The principles of the labor-reform newspaper popular among New England mill workers, in Jonathan Baxter Harrison's account of 1880, included government ownership of land, mines, railroads, and highways, demonetization of gold and silver in favor of government-issued greenbacks, a graduated income tax, controlled ground rents, the abolition of interest, and legal eight-hour day. Deciding on "independent political action," the central labor union of New York in 1886 chose Henry George as its candidate for mayor on a platform of positive government intervention in economic life. "We declare," the platform announced, "the true purpose of government to be the maintenance of that sacred right of property which gives to everyone opportunity to employ his labor and security that he shall enjoy its fruits." Wealth belongs "to society at large," the George campaign held. He proposed that the "enormous value" represented by New York real estate "should not go to the enrichment of individuals and corporations, but should be taken in taxation and applied to the improvement and beautifying of the city, to the promotion of the health, comfort, education, and recreation of its people, and to the providing of means of transit commensurate with the needs of a great metropolis."

With support from a significant stratum of nonworkers, doctors, lawyers, teachers, clergymen, and "working employers," the George campaign became a genuine threat to the Democratic machine in New York and to the party system itself. In an unusual display of unity, labor leaders ranging from the trade-unionist Samuel Gompers to the General Master Workman of the Knights of Labor, Terence Powderly, to socialist Daniel DeLeon joined forces behind George. In the face of the threat, Democratic Party regulars persuaded Abram Hewitt to bear their banner. A leader of the anti-Tweed forces in the early 1870's, son-in-law of the revered Peter Cooper, and himself a wealthy industrialist, a gentry politician of unblemished reputation—he had served as Samuel Tilden's campaign manager in 1877, had written on "The Mutual Relations of Capital and Labor," and as a congressman had earned Henry Adams's friendship and respect as "the most useful public man in Washington" —Hewitt swallowed his distaste of the machine and accepted, even welcoming, "death in such a cause" as defeating "these enemies of civilization and social order," the "social danger" of "Socialism, Anarchy and Nihilism."

Hewitt's response bears out Walter Dean Burnham's observation that the party system in these decades aimed to "insulate" business groups from "mass pressures" which might disrupt their industrializing policies. Hewitt launched a frankly ideological campaign, virtually ignoring his Republican opponent, the twenty-eight-year-old aristocrat Theodore Roosevelt, and directed his attack against the very notion of a *labor* party. "A new issue has been suddenly sprung upon this community," he proclaimed in his letter of acceptance. "An attempt is being made to organize one class of our citizens against all other classes." The raising of class issues, he pointed out, represents "a radical departure from the existing methods of free government by political parties composed of citizens in every walk of life." Each party being a coalition including capital and labor, between whom "there never is and never can be any antagonism," the system represented the unity of social classes for the high purpose of efficient government. The working classes, "as they are called," have their legitimate trade unions through which they might submit their "grievances" to "public judgment." Moreover, "self-help is the remedy for all the evils of which men complain. I have had to help myself from the earliest year I can remember, and every struggling young man who chooses to follow the same rule, who will help himself and not become dependent upon public or private charity, can achieve a measure of success that will satisfy every independent citizen."

Hewitt entered the fray, then, with no platform but the defeat of Henry George and his threat to the two-party system, as well as the menace of the radical platform to the rule of private property and corporate wealth. He won the support of "liberal reformers" like Godkin, Curtis, and Schurz. The country demanded a submergence of class issues into a "bigger self" of social harmony. Capital and labor, Hewitt reminded his supporters, are "natural and inseparable allies." It took, however, last-minute back-room deals between seasoned party bosses, Croker of Tammany and Platt of the Republican machine, to swing enough Republican votes away from Roosevelt to defeat the George menace by about twenty thousand votes.

In response to real issues, the major parties resorted to the idea of loyalty, loyalty in the form of voting the straight party ticket. And it was in national campaigns for votes that the major parties performed one of their most significant acts in the governance of the American polity: the conversion of politics into mass spectacle, into cultural event. This, too, served the underlying goal of each party, to maintain viability for its financial supporters. Distinguished by tone and style, by characteristic constituencies, the parties constructed themselves for each election as local and state coalitions, each represented at the top by businessmen or their spokesmen and allies. A cadre of professional or "machine" politicians ran the show, serving as administrators and conduits for campaign funds, rarely running for office themselves but supporting the policies of their donors. The truly "controlling force in American life is not in its politics, but in commerce," the critic John Jay Chapman observed in 1899, in *Causes and Consequences;* he added that the party madness fostered by the Civil War left the machinery of government "in a particularly purchasable state . . . Political power had by the war been condensed and packaged for delivery, and in the natural course of things the political trademarks began to find their way into the coffers of the capitalist."

Those trademarks emerged as the emblems of electoral spectacles, the battles staged by Democrats and Republicans across the country over access to the public purse, the right to fill public positions with faithful party workers, and the power to enact laws on behalf of their paying clients. By the 1870's and 1880's, the parties had consolidated themselves in massive corporate-like structures with chains of command, systems of obedience and deference, and a military rhetoric of campaigns, parades, and banners, "stalwarts" and "half-breeds," the spoils of victory. "The smell of saltpeter, the snorts of horses, the shouts of men, the red and white ripple of the flags that went careening by the smoke and flame"—thus Brand Whitlock described a political parade in 1902, finding in it "some strange suggestion of the war our political contests typify, in spirit and symbol at least." The military metaphor was only partly in jest; for Tammany Hall boss Richard Croker it represented the serious inner meaning of political combat: "Chess is war, business is war; the rivalry of students and athletes is war. Everything is war in which men strive for mastery and power as against other men, and this is one of the essential conditions of progress." Party rhetoric and visible behavior conveyed a picture of the social world as a battleground. Moreover, individuals were helpless creatures unless incorporated into a larger fighting unit, a sheltering "party" under protection of a "leader." The power of Tammany Hall, wrote one of its leaders, lay in its devices, including social services to the poor as well as outright graft and vote buying; it lay in "the completeness of its organization and the thoroughness of its discipline . . . The organization works with the precision of a well-regulated machine."

The national parties learned in these years what recent historians call "cultural politics," adjusting their appeals (their style of merchandising) to ethnic, racial, religious, and sectional difference. Party managers learned to trim and shape their platforms to constituencies composed of these differences, to exploit and harden them into virtual uniforms of identity. Thus, while Republicans continued even in 1896 to "wave the bloody shirt," recalling Civil War memories and the odor of treason attaching to Democrats, the Southern Democratic Party continued as the "party of the fathers," evoking sectional and racial loyalty. Party platforms and campaign techniques addressed particular cultural issues, creating enemies in "negative reference groups," appealing to "high" (ritual) Protestant fears of Scotch–Irish Catholic influences on school boards, or "low" ("pietistic") Protestant anxieties about the drinking habits of German Lutherans. Ethnicity, sectionalism, urban-suburban-rural distinctions: the party system raised tribalism to political salience, exploiting such differences by making them issues of loyalty and defining political interest in the imagery of group identity. Yankee, Southerner, white, black, Presbyterian, Catholic, Jew, city, rural: a political terrain composed of such labels familiar in twentieth-century politics had its origins in the Gilded Age party system.

But more important than such appeals to ethnic and religious identity was the fact that parties retained the appearance of genuine grass-roots organizations. In the cities, they were bound to local neighborhood clubs: Tammany Hall, for example, which evolved from the Society of St. Tammany late in the eighteenth century into the main organ of the Democratic Party in New York City. Neighborhood political clubs offered help to the poor in difficult times, extended hospitality to new immigrants, found jobs for the unemployed (even if makeshift jobs on the public payroll). The party machines moved in two directions at once: toward closer ties of obligation and fealty to neighborhood block and ward, and toward centralization of municipal power within the cadre of chiefs or bosses. The machines were able to perform essential urban functions, such as getting streets paved and streetcars into new neighborhoods; they filled vacuums of power, frequently the result of legal authority over city financing resting with state governments controlled by rural representatives. City machines prided themselves as public benefactors. As Tweed put it: "This population is too hopelessly split up into races and factions to govern it under universal suffrage, except by the bribery of patronage and corruption." And their cultural functions seemed equally essential. Based on the principle that political power originates in personal loyalty—an atavistic notion at odds with the Jeffersonian ideal of an informed citizenry acting for the public good—the machines consisted of a dense network of ward leaders and precinct captains who cultivated personal relations with the voters in their domain, speaking their language, learning their daily needs, assuring them that the ward club and party were ready to help: "None of your justice and law," wrote one city boss, "but help." The clubs held social affairs, kept afterhours saloons. Buffers between immigrants and a hostile city, models for mobility (many bosses were of poor immigrant origins), the machines grounded loyalty not in political ideas but in cultural need.

Getting out the vote was the principal visible goal of party activity. The parties pioneered in techniques of mass persuasion. If their real though unstated aim was to make themselves effective as vehicles through which businessmen might win access to state power, then the open, public goal was to win straight-party votes, to discourage ticket-splitting. If their real politics consisted in packaging themselves for sale to private interests, the public face of the parties also wore the look of merchandise. Election campaigns became sales campaigns, with party symbols (the donkey and elephant invented by cartoonist Thomas Nast in the 1870's took hold immediately) and names of candidates widely distributed on playing cards, posters, buttons, and other novelties. Of course, persuasion often took the form of cash for votes, and the line between getting out the vote and simply inventing it was often too blurred for close scrutiny. But these overt forms of corruption, which aroused the contempt of reformers, disclosed the secret of the system: that politics itself had become a business, and like all businesses, justified its means by its overriding end of private profit. "So many offices depend upon the result of the election," wrote an Iowa politician, "that electioneering is made a business, and politics reduced to a trade."

The boss represented the visible integration of politics and economics, the incorporation of mass politics into corporate society. Visible more as a type than as an actual person, he functioned to keep the transaction between public officials and private interests behind closed doors, out of sight, disguised by the formalism and "warfare" of the campaign. In this he served as a prime vehicle, and for those who saw him, as a visible symbol of the change in political life. He represented a new social phenomenon, a modern turn in civil life: the appearance in significant numbers, enough to count as a critical mass, of *professional* politicians, of those "servants of power" who, in Max Weber's distinction, live "off" politics as a permanent source of income, rather than "for" it as a personal commitment. Weber describes the social character of such a figure as "economically 'dispensable,' " relieved of normal economic concerns. He is the "propertyless politician" who devotes himself to party ends with the understanding that a new social precondition has come into existence: "that regular and reliable income will accrue to those who manage politics." Neither an office seeker nor an administrator, his goals were entirely defined by "victory" and the booty that follows. His skills were techniques of deference and domination.

Party funds accumulated from regular contributions of members and corporate clients, from tribute levied on the salaries of government officeholders beholden to the party machine, and from extralegal sources, bribes, and graft. In this structure, notes Weber, the American machine boss served a critical function; he was "indispensable as the direct recipient of the money of great financial magnates, who would not entrust their money for election purposes to a paid party official, or to anyone else giving public account of his affairs." Through him, to put the matter somewhat differently, part of the surplus wealth from the realm of production found its way as unearned income into the pockets of "professionals" whose labor was to drain political life of political significance, to watch over and manage the disappearance of real power from public view.

Conventional politics became less significant as a vehicle of debate over issues of economic control and social improvement. The party system removed politics from the street, and vested it in the back room. This is not to say that the parties were not responsive to their supporters. But their services in the end reinforced the central illusion of the system: that party allegiance represented authentic participation in political society, in the sharing of power and the making of policy. As Chapman neatly put it, the parties controlled the masses by "bribery and terror-ism," but in the "form of a very plausible appeal to the individual on the ground of self-interest." Like advertising, the party system produced an illusion which disguised its character, its alienation of political power from the very producers of the wealth that supported the system. To say that the parties were sites of cul-tural, rather than genuinely political, behavior is not to say that they were politically feeble or irrelevant, but that their politics lay in displacing economic and social issues by appealing to cul-tural issues, in fostering among voters an imaginary sense of participation and control, while at once denying them the sub-stance of politics. Mass politics substituted cultural difference for ideological difference, made culture seem to be ideology itself. And thereby the major party system exercised its own control, further integrating the daily lives of Americans into the larger corporate system.

IV

Assembled in Omaha on July 4, 1892, the People's Party pro-claimed the aptness of the date: "the one hundred and sixteenth anniversary of the Declaration of Independence." The Populists inaugurated their first national convention on a thundering note of affirmation, identifying their "declaration of principles" with that of the nation's founders. "Filled with the spirit of the grand general and chieftain who established our independence," the convention declared its resolution "to restore the Government of the Republic to the hands of the 'plain people' with whose class it originated. We assert our purposes to be identical with the purposes of the National Constitution, to form a more perfect Union and establish justice . . . We declare that this Republic can only endure as a free government while built upon the love of the whole people for each other and for the nation." Thus the Popu-list movement, born in the agrarian unrest of the previous decade but gathering to itself radical criticisms of industrial capitalism reaching back to the antimonopoly campaigns of the Jacksonian era, laid formal claim to contested ground: it, not "capitalists, corporations, national banks, rings, trusts," represented the gen-uine America, the still-unrealized ethos of "the people."

173

The event was no idle ritual or game. The People's Party in 1892 emerged from an authentic mass movement of farmers in the South, Southwest, and (to a lesser degree) the Middle West. Impetus for a national political party arose directly from the ranks of the National Farmers' Alliance and Industrial Union, out of the dawning recognition (especially in the worsening economic situation of the early 1890's) that only political power over the apparatus of government would enable farmers and all "producers" to break the economic stranglehold of the railroads, banks, and industrial corporations. The Alliance provided the extraordinary spirit of hope and possibility which manifests itself in the Omaha preamble, while several generations of radical social and economic thought, the programs of labor reform as well as farmers' groups, of urban as well as agrarian dissent, found expression in the 1892 platform. The People's Party provided a visible form on the national stage for an agitation which had been welling unevenly across the nation. The party emerged as a synthesis, a coalition, but as it turned out in its debacle in the 1896 election, a quite fragile association of forces. The last and greatest of several third-party movements after the Civil War, the People's Party failed in its high ambitions to define "America" according to its lights. But Populism has remained a haunting figure in American life, not least for signaling the deep connections between the realms of culture and politics. For in the end Populism succumbed to a more powerful alliance between cultural value and political practices than it was able to sustain.

Composed in evangelical accents by Ignatius Donnelly, the Omaha preamble rang with echoes of revivalism, of backwoods democracy and grass-roots outrage. It trembled with apocalyptic apprehensions.

A vast conspiracy against mankind has been organized on two continents, and it is rapidly taking possession of the world. If not met and overthrown at once, it forebodes terrible social convulsions, the destruction of civilization, or the establishment of an absolute despotism.

Many twentieth-century historians and intellectuals have fallen on such passages as evidence of a simplistic satanism, a sign of the movement's confused, retrograde character. To be sure, many

174

Populist spokesmen clothed themselves in the garb of righteous evangels. But their idea of conspiracy drew from the movement's roots in native radicalism, in a secular rhetoric of "equal rights" and "anti-monopoly." "Conspiracy" in 1892 evoked at least a generation of political experience: free-trade opposition to high tariffs, Granger campaigns against railroad monopolies, Greenback condemnation of the "Crime of '73" when "gold bugs" plotted to impose the "gold standard," and enduring campaigns for labor reform, the eight-hour day, Prohibition, women's rights. The several abortive third-party efforts since the Civil War on behalf of these causes all aimed in some measure against a "conspiracy" of the few against the many. By "conspiracy," then, Populism called Satan by his modern name: monopolies and corporations, and their mundane methods of doing business, especially the business of buying votes, bribing officials, and scheming with the major parties.

That revivalism was a major source of Populist rhetoric cannot be denied. It was an element in the collective experiences of the Alliance: the rallies, wagon trains, encampments, stump speakers, and lecturers which for a few intense years from the late 1880's to the early 1890's had given the farmers' movement the momentum of a mass expression. But the Omaha platform did not confine itself to rhetorical solutions. It aimed at no less than a total revision of the conventional picture of American life: to distinguish true issues from the "sham" of such staged performances as the "battle over the tariff" by which the national parties distracted attention from the hard times of daily existence. As a political platform, the Omaha document made two primary assertions: (1) that the chief political issues of the day concerned economic ownership and exchange; and (2) that the aim of political action should be to expand the powers of government over economic life. Asserting the highest end of government to be elimination of "oppression, injustice, and poverty," the platform focused on three obviously urgent concerns for farmers: money, land, and transportation. In regard to each, it called for a radical overturning of existing arrangements: an end to private banks, to speculative land monopolies and "alien ownership," and to private ownership of means of transportation and communication. It called for a flexible national currency and banking system adjusted to credit needs of producers (modeled

175

on the Alliance "Sub-Treasury Plan"), in place of the high interest rates (and constant threat of mortgage foreclosures) of private banks; for government ownership of railroads, telegraph and telephone systems; for a return to the government of "all land now held by railroads and other corporations in excess of their actual needs." In addition, the platform called for a graduated income tax, a Postal Savings Bank, the abolition of private antilabor armies (the "Pinkerton system"), the election of senators by direct vote, the initiative and referendum, and firm opposition to "any subsidy or national aid to any private corporation for any purpose." In short, the Omaha platform proposed a coherent program of economic change by means of government action. Certainly not a socialist platform—it did not call for state ownership of the means of production, of factories and raw materials —it nevertheless pits collective ownership and control against private ownership of those sectors of the economy having to do with exchange, especially money and transportation. But even more pointed than its specific proposals was its insistence on government responsibility for the economic well-being of the nation, for the "people," the true producers of wealth: "Wealth belongs to him who creates it; and every dollar taken from industry without an equivalent is robbery."

The chief political goal of the platform was to win reliable democratic controls over corporate capitalism. Still, the underlying "producer's philosophy" seemed an attack more on the scale of capitalism, on the "greed" of the already rich and powerful, than on the fundamental relations of production: the wage system. Thus, viewing the Populists chiefly as *employing* farmers" rather than the *employed* farmers of the country districts or the mechanics and laborers of the industrial centers," Samuel Gompers argued in 1892 that an "amalgamation of the wage-worker's organization with the People's Party" was "impossible, because it is unnatural." The plank calling for a "Perpetual Labor Union"—"that the union of the labor forces of the United States this day consummated shall be permanent and perpetual; may its spirit enter into all hearts for the salvation of the Republic, and the uplifting of mankind"—thus failed to win large-scale labor support. Its rhetoric more harmonious with the foundering Knights of Labor than with the more limited trade-union objectives of the rising American Federation of Labor, the platform made its appeal for farmer-labor unity on grounds already obsolete in the eyes of the skilled craft workers demanding shorter hours, higher pay, and job security.

The failure of Populism in its goal of forging a national mass movement of "producers" raises questions about the political wisdom of the platform, whether its creators understood well enough the new realities of the urban, corporate society it wished to change; whether, that is, it did not raise an outmoded hope, for a "producer's commonwealth," into a utopian program. More important than its precise political program in 1892 (whether wise or foolish, effective or stumbling) was its deeper agenda, its implicit revision of the prevailing view of politics. For the significance of Populism lies less in its political failure than in its cultural expression. The Omaha platform wished to make its revision in the name of the "outcries of a plundered people," to give voice to voices excluded from the major agencies of representation: the big-city press, the national periodicals, and especially the major parties. In this sense, apart from the indecisive collectivism of the platform, Omaha challenged the power of a version of reality: a challenge to the *culture* of conventional politics. In its platform, Populism established itself as an opposing culture, an alternative view not only of "politics" and "economics" but of the world as such. In its diction, in the style and tone of its language, the platform bespeaks a world seen and understood by "the people," as against a sham world of the national parties. It assumed, of course, that its roots in the Alliance and in the dozens of radical reform groups that also flocked to Omaha granted it authority to speak on behalf of "the people"—an assumption severely shattered by the victory of the conventional in the Republican landslide of 1896.

Still, that assumption had some basis in the fact that Populism had brought together those growing numbers of distressed citizens who had aligned themselves with third-party movements throughout the previous two decades. The size of the dissident vote, never large enough to win a national election, had risen steadily, from just over one percent in 1876 to 11 percent in 1892. "Minor parties regularly captured a significant share of the popular vote," writes Peter H. Argersinger, "and received at least 20 percent in one or more elections from 1874 to 1892 in more than half of the non-Southern states." Often they held a balance of power, "at least once in every state but Vermont" between 1878 and 1892. But their challenge lay at a level deeper than numbers of votes alone. Invariably, they scorned the very notion of "party" and loyalty, and conventional politics. "A very lamentable evil is the education of the people into the belief that a permanent political party is a great good," proclaimed the Prohibition Party (one of the most durable of the dissident coalitions of the period) in 1869. This is not to say that the third parties saw themselves as merely symbolic; they sought office and entered into fusion alliances with major parties when feasible. But they presented themselves less as parties than as movements, as crusades. "Ours is not a political party," declared a North Dakota Populist. "It is more, for in it are crystallized sentiments and measures for the benefit of the whole people." The People's Party itself implied an end to parties, an upwelling of the people in a direct political expression.

And it is in this, in its efforts to give expression to the people as a political entity outside the party system, that Populism must be seen as undertaking a *cultural* campaign of great magnitude: a campaign short-lived but far-reaching in its extrapolitical ambitions. Those ambitions show most forcefully in what Lawrence Goodwyn calls the "movement culture" of the Farmers' Alliance: not only the forms of collective manifestation, such as the wagon trains gathering from all points of the countryside to save a cooperative venture from failure, or the open-air rallies where Southern farmers declared their determination to defy the patterns of deference and racism on which the authority of the "party of the fathers" rested, but also the painfully constructed alternative institutions, the lecture system, the far-flung National Reform Press Association, and the cooperative themselves. Goodwyn portrays a movement in which people learned to act independently on their own behalf, to think critically about their common predicament. There is no denying the evidence of ferment in the Southwestern countryside and small towns. According to one writer, "People commenced to think who had never thought before, and people talked who had seldom spoken." The image suggests an awakening of language, of reading and speaking, of new and radical powers discovered in words. Indeed, among the institutions bred by Populism, none surpassed in importance the Alliance lecture circuit and the far-flung National

Reform Press Association (bringing together dozens of radical newspapers which could count only on their readership for support). Lecturers and journalists breathed new life into the standard words of political discourse, words such as "democracy," "the people," "America."

Populism projected an unmistakable cultural ferment, a ferment in which cultural practices and political ideas mixed in a campaign to restore America to original meanings. Political calls for government ownership, against the grain of inherited Jeffersonian notions of limited government and of laissez-faire to which many independent farmers clung, implied a kind of cultural earthquake. The tremors, however, failed in the end to collapse the walls separating farmers and workers, whites and blacks, country and city. While it survived in splinters and fragments, as a political movement Populism could not resist the assaults of the major party system, rigged election laws, physical intimidation, and the pressures in 1896 to fuse with the Democratic Party in support of William Jennings Bryan and his deceptive "free silver" platform. And one among many explanations for its short-lived glory lies in the overlapping elements of culture and politics in its fundamental assumptions.

Considering itself in a struggle for the true America, Populism inevitably absorbed certain long-standing unresolved ambiguities within the word "America" itself. Is America a *nation*, a body joined by shared cultural values and experiences? Or is it a political state, an apparatus for governance in which laws serve to protect classes rather than universal interests in the society? Of course, the same ambiguity exists in all modern nation-states. The peculiarities of its founding, its assumption that the act which constituted the political state, the very Constitution, also constituted and originated the nation as a whole body. America seemed to promise a fusion of the civil and the political, of the personal lives of people with their status as free citizens. The vesting of political authority in "the people" seemed to fulfill that hope of Enlightenment thinkers like Rousseau and Jefferson that the private person might view his own private interests, for the first time in history, as identical with those of the whole society, of the *nation*, his needs and desires and efforts at enjoyment perfectly consistent with his rights as a citizen. This identity of interest, with its assumption that all citizens share membership

179

in an organic body known as the nation or "the people," was the hope of utopia within the American polity.

The meaning of that utopia lay at the base of political and social controversy throughout the nineteenth century. Was the true America best represented by its most successful citizens, those for whom laws protected the private means of enjoyment —private property and contract—and permitted accumulation of private wealth? Or did utopian "America" demand for its realization a new social order, the abolition of private property, the emergence of the nation as a collective body of shared wealth as well as culture? Experimental utopian communities before the Civil War attempted to put into practice this implicit America: a corporate body fusing the personal and the social in communal polity. The utopia remained effective in conventional society and politics as well, assimilated into the rhetoric of politics which continued to assume that "one nation, indivisible" meant a total identity of private interests with those of the political state. With universal white manhood suffrage achieved under Jackson, and especially with the victory of Union over Secession in the Civil War, the presumed identity of nation and state, of "the people" and their government, deepened into a commonplace orthodoxy of both political and cultural thought.

Thus, America originated and evolved as a nation unique among nations: simultaneously an ideal of a restored harmony between the civil and the political, the private and the public, and a set of political institutions embodying that ideal. Americans of all persuasions rarely opposed the state as such, for to do so, as abolitionists and the slave power both discovered, was to place themselves perilously outside the nation, to declare themselves antagonists to the corporate entity of America itself. Constituted in the name of "the people," the republican state seemed one with the nation, the society, the culture. Not the state itself, but those who temporarily occupied its sacred corridors and residences, placed themselves in contention in the normal political processes. Questions of power and policy, in Gilded Age politics, receded in favor of contentions over "America," over which party best represented its original virtue, its continuing utopia.

To be sure, increasing numbers of Americans, especially in the tense struggles of the 1880's and early 1890's, experienced the state firsthand as a power clearly antagonistic to their interests,

180

not only as laws favoring monopolies but as armed force prepared to shoot and kill in defense of property. Small revolutionary parties emerged but failed to make state power, its legitimacy and aims, a national political issue. Populism eschewed revolution, but the very intensity of its commitment to the utopian element in "America" held a germ of revolutionary thought. The Populists confronted a political world in which the state had secured its own powerful, independent existence as an entity within the body politic. A good many frustrated radicals began to wonder whether the original America could be restored without overturning the seats of power, a seizure of control by "the people." The cultural impetus drove toward utopian revolution. Yet the same cultural premises also defined republican forms as the only political means for the freeing of the nation from obstructive selfish interests. Thus the fatal attraction of an alliance with the Democratic Party. In the end, Populism would founder in the ill-assorted mixture of culture and politics at the core of its vision, a failure which mirrored the confused relations between those realms of discourse and practice within the entire political universe of the Gilded Age.

6

FICTIONS OF THE REAL

I

"Realism," complained Hamilton Wright Mabie, erstwhile critic for the *Christian Union*, seemed bent on "crowding the world of fiction with commonplace people, whom one could positively avoid coming into contact with in real life; people without native sweetness or strength, without acquired culture or accomplishments, without the touch of the ideal which makes the commonplace significant and worthy of study." In such chiding remarks, the voices of gentility insisted on their view of art: on one side, "culture," "sweetness," "the ideal"; on the other, crowds of "commonplace people," with a broad hint of city streets and slums. Fiction, the critic implies, should display the good taste of gentlefolk; it should "avoid" vulgarity by the simple device of refusing to recognize it. Like the refined gentry, art should protect itself from common life, should concern itself with "ideal" characters, pure thoughts, and noble emotions.

Although gentility had strengthened its hold on institutions of education and art, publishing and philanthropy, nevertheless critics and editors frequently took a defensive tone, challenged as much by new currents of art and literature as by vulgar politics and business. "Realism" seemed such a threat, the term naming not so much a single consistent movement as a tendency among some painters and writers to depict contemporary life without moralistic condescension. Of course, the threats seem relatively timid now compared to the rise of modernist experiment and innovation in the arts which reached New York from Europe

182

early in the twentieth century. In painting, for example, convention still held strong. Artists took their typical subjects from the familiar academic modes of landscape, genre, and allegory, excluding signs of contemporary conflict and disturbance. Fashionable salon art favored scenes of leisure, of polite ease amid comfortable surroundings; a passive enjoyment of sunshine and beaches, of rich interiors, of rural scenes glazed with nostalgia, struck the most frequent note. To be sure, exceptions appeared: John Ferguson Weir's industrial interiors in the 1870's, Thomas Pollock Anshutz's remarkable picture of lounging workers in "Ironworkers: Noontime" (1882), and Robert Kohler's dramatic "The Strike" (1886). But not until the "Ash Can School" at the turn of the century would a concerted movement appear to depict city life in its daily unheroic scenes.

In the works of the two most prominent realists of the period, Winslow Homer and Thomas Eakins, a greater range of subject matter and a more strenuous original vision did appear as striking exceptions. Homer's variety of subject was perhaps the most extensive among established easel painters, embracing figures intent in work or sport: fishermen and women mending nets, seamen battling roiling high waters, huntsmen tracking their prey, country children at chores and games. Homer's canvases seem free of thematic concerns, certainly of moral judgments, idealizations, or simple interpretations, but they often hint at philosophical reflections on man's vulnerable condition in nature and the consequently enduring value of activity, of play as much as labor. Eakins's work was often even more overtly athletic, isolating single figures—boxers, wrestlers, rowers—as lonely performers of skill and endurance. Eakins's pictures disclose a world scrutinized in fine detail, with exacting analytical rigor. As a teacher as well as an artist, he insisted on studying anatomy directly from human models, and defied the prudery of art schools in his native Philadelphia in employing nude models. He participated as a nude subject in the photographer Eadweard Muybridge's experiments in recording the human figure in motion at the University of Pennsylvania in the 1890's.

Eakins's unflinching acceptance of the body, encouraged by his friendship with the older Walt Whitman, troubled his relations with the established art world. His famous "The Gross Clinic" (1875) was consigned to the medical section of the Centennial

183

Exposition in Philadelphia in 1876, excluded from the fine-arts exhibition because of the daring of its subject: the eminent surgeon Samuel Gross performing an operation while lecturing to a class. The canvas showed in detail an incision into a living body, and portrayed a range of responses in the audience, from fascination to horror. The picture also manifested Eakins's affinity with science, with its objectivity and rules of analysis: qualities he strived to achieve in his own art. Increasingly, Eakins turned to portraiture and the study of character; many of his canvases of performers, doctors, writers, businessmen, and their wives seem themselves surgical incisions, pictures of inward strain, disappointment, loneliness. Honesty of report, faithfulness to the act of seeing, refusal to idealize, disciplined accuracy: these features epitomized Eakins's realism, his break with the strictures of gentility, and his kinship with the rising rebellious spirit of the age.

II

The "realist feels in every nerve the equality of things and the unity of men," wrote William Dean Howells in the late 1880's. As for the complaints of genteel critics, he observed that "the aristocratic spirit," having lost its place of honor, now sheltered itself in aestheticism: "The pride of caste is becoming the pride of taste; but, as before, it is averse to the mass of men; it consents to know them only in some conventionalized and artificial guise." By contrast, "democracy in literature is the reverse of all this. It wishes to know and to tell the truth." Realists want to know the world as it really is, to create a world of fiction congruent with "real life." Thus, the literary battle lines were drawn, in Howells's mind, on a distinct political terrain. Realism represented nothing less than the extension of democracy into the precincts of fiction.

Howells launched monthly polemics against the aristocratic spirit from his seat in the "Editor's Study" of *Harper's Monthly* in the late 1880's and 1890's, a steady flow of reviews and screeds in defense of a fiction of the real. The target was not difficult to fix, but he well understood the superior resources of the enemy. Public taste, he complained, remained in vassalage to false values, preferring easy pleasures of shallow "romance" to the more exacting demands of the real. As he sensed defeat, his tone grew

184

bitter and resigned. "By far the greatest number of people in the world," he lamented in 1899, "even the civilized world, are people of weak and childish imagination, pleased with gross fables, fond of prodigies, heroes, heroines, portents and impracticalities, without self-knowledge, and without the wish for it." The public imagination seemed to resist the healthier doses of reality, the general reader remaining a "spoiled child" spurning instruction. "I suppose we shall have to wait," Howells conceded sadly in a *New York Times* interview with Stephen Crane in 1894.

Howells waged a battle on behalf of literary principles he had begun to practice in his novels of the 1880's, fictions in which he wished not only to open his pages to the real but also to persuade his readers that reading was a moral exercise, a serious exertion of civic faculties. "The novelist has a grave duty to his reader," he wrote, a duty of no small consequence to the republic. In this regard, Howells's campaign for realism resembled other campaigns for culture, for public enlightenment and elevation, for a restored middle ground. The "real" his touchstone of value, "false" became his deepest term of disdain, directed especially against those "innutritious" novels "that merely tickle our prejudices and lull our judgment, or that coddle our sensibilities, or pamper our gross appetites for the marvelous . . . clog the soul with unwholesome vapors of all kinds." As fearful of "barbarism" (from the unmentionable worlds of dime fiction and sordid adventure) as he was contemptuous of arrested aesthetic sensibilities (in genteel sentimental romance), Howells takes his place among the legions of nervous intellectuals seeking a role for themselves and a sense of control in what he named at the turn of the century "our deeply incorporated civilization." But if, under the banner of realism, he stands within those ranks, the banner itself marked a difference; while it may have clad him in a certain insulating virtue of its own, it also tempted him perilously close to the edge of his middle-class convictions and values. As a doctrine, realism gave Howells a stand on an imagined middle ground. In literary practice, however, it often caused that ground to shift under his feet.

Realism served Howells less as a doctrine and more as a conviction of rectitude. As he told Stephen Crane in 1894, realism was a corrective to faulty vision, a way of disclosing what is really *there.* The realist novel is "made for the benefit of people who have no true use of their eyes." Its aim is "to picture the daily life in the most exact terms possible, with an absolute and clear sense of proportion." True fiction "adjusts the proportions," "preserves the balances," and thus "lessons are to be taught and reforms won. When people are introduced to each other they will see the resemblances, and won't want to fight so badly." Seeing, picturing, recognizing: these represent realism's mode of reconciliation, the seriousness and gravity of its service to the republic.

Howells had arrived at his commitment to the healing powers of realism in the course of the troubled 1880's. In that decade, he moved from Boston and his post as chief editor of the prestigious *Atlantic Monthly*, to New York and eventually to the editorship of *Harper's Monthly*. The move corresponded to a shift in his own fiction, away from the courtship romances and polite travel narratives he had mastered in the 1870's, toward the novel of social realism in *A Modern Instance* (1882), *The Rise of Silas Lapham* (1885), *The Minister's Charge* (1887), *Annie Kilburn* (1889), and *A Hazard of New Fortunes* (1890). The change in residence and mode of fiction truly marked a major turn for Howells. As a young aspiring writer in rural Ohio before the Civil War, he had learned through self-education to adulate both the Republican Party and the high literary culture of New England, of Emerson, Lowell, and Longfellow. Rewarded with the position of consul in Venice for his campaign biography of Lincoln, he missed serving in the Civil War but gained enough of a reputation by his travel writings to return to a highly prized job on the staff of the *Atlantic*, tapped by the elder Brahmins as their adopted Western son. Even after his move to New York, Howells continued to cherish the Boston ideal. In its day, he wrote at the end of the century, Boston held together "a group of authors as we shall hardly see here again for hundreds of years." Moreover, "there was such regard for them and their calling, not only in good society, but among the extremely well-read people of the whole intelligent city, as hardly another community has shown."

Boston nourished a belief in the seriousness of literature, in the elevating influence of fine writing and reading, which remained a deep assumption of Howells's realism and a frequent theme of conversation within his novels. "I wonder what the average literature of non-cultivated people is," says the young Corey to his father, the old Boston Brahmin, in *The Rise of Silas Lapham*. The question concerns the young man's growing acquaintance with the Laphams, a country family newly rich on the weight of their father's success as a paint manufacturer. Living now in Boston, they seek acceptance in "society," and their unpolished ways, their lack of cultivation, and their conspicuous wealth pose a problem for the cultivated elite. "I don't suppose that we who have the habit of reading, and at least a nodding acquaintance with literature," replies the father, "can imagine the bestial darkness of the great mass of people—even people whose houses are rich and whose linen is purple and fine." The son agrees but ventures the opinion that the Laphams are nevertheless "intelligent people. They are very quick, and they are shrewd and sensible." "I have no doubt that some of the Sioux are so," Bromfield Corey retorts. "But that is not saying they are civilized. All civilization comes through literature now, especially in our country. A Greek got his civilization by talking and looking, and in some measure a Parisian may still do it. But we, who live remote from history and monuments, we must read or we must barbarise."

The elder Corey's words find echoes in Howells's own defense of literature: we must read or we must barbarize. But realism proposes a kind of reading, a way of seeing, which will mollify Corey's too stringent judgments; it will propose a more balanced view in which Silas Lapham's basic moral soundness will appear in true proportion to his country roughness and *arriviste* vulgarity (itself a result of a misplaced desire, on behalf of his daughters, to "rise" in Boston society). Throughout the novel, dialogue and action disclose how false readings misprepare people for real predicaments, the daily plights of normal existence, just as they prejudge inner character by social appearance.

In its narration, *Silas Lapham* asserts itself as the very model of the kind of reading and seeing the world needs badly: a pedagogy as well as a story. In this process of pointing to itself as an example of the realism missing from the human relations it portrays, the novel relies on the good Reverend Sewall, another Brahmin, intimate of the Coreys, yet also a sympathetic adviser to the Laphams. Sewall instructs the reader as well as his friends to beware of the false lessons of sentimental fiction. For the most part, he explains, novelists have had a "noxious" influence, fastening onto love and marriage "in a monstrous disproportion," praising self-sacrifice even when inappropriate. Considering their influence now that fiction forms "the whole intellectual experience of more people" than does religion, "novelists might be the greatest help to us if they painted life as it is, and human feelings in their true proportion and relation." For this they must overcome their abhorrence of the commonplace—"that light, impalpable, aerial essence which they've never got into their confounded books yet," exclaims yet another clear-eyed character. "The novelist who could interpret the commonplace feelings of commonplace people would have the answer to 'the riddle of the painful earth' on his tongue"—as Sewall attempts to interpret Lapham to the Coreys; as the novel itself attempts to interpret the entire Corey–Lapham world and all its misunderstandings, small and large.

The high value of reading, then, in the high culture of Boston, provided a key component in Howells's restorative realism. But the notion of reading as a corrective seeing, a true perspective, implied additional assumptions, not always in rapport with each other. When Howells insisted that "realism is nothing more and nothing less than the truthful treatment of material," it was partly to quiet alarms that realism held in store a revolution in letters, morals, and possibly society, hinted at by Flaubert in *Madame Bovary.* But "truthful treatment" does link Howells's realism with that of European writers in one significant regard. Appearing first in France in the 1830's, the term "realism" came to signify a general rejection in the arts of academic models, a defiance of the standards of symmetry and harmony on behalf of firsthand experience, direct observation of the visible world. In literature, its effects showed especially in the novel, in its "complete emancipation," in Eric Auerbach's words, from the neoclassical doctrine of "levels of style" according to which "everyday practical reality" and lower-class people "could find a place in literature only within the frame of a low or intermediate kind of style, that is to say, as either grotesquely comic or pleasant, light, colorful, and elegant entertainment." Thus, continues Auerbach, realism came to mean "the serious treatment of every reality, the rise of more extensive and socially inferior human groups to the position of subject matter for problematic-existential representation." In short, realism freed the "low" from the hold of the "high," permitting rough-edged slang-speaking characters like

Silas Lapham to be taken seriously as having genuine problems and true consciousness.

"But let fiction cease to lie about life," demanded Howells. "Let it portray men and women as they are, actuated by the motives and the passions in the measure we all know." Moreover, "let it speak the dialect, the language, that most Americans know —the language of unaffected people everywhere." Howells well understood that simply to allow characters low on the social scale to speak with the same freedom as what he dubbed "grammatical characters" constituted a kind of revolution, an overturning of those ingrained conventions which still guided popular novels. Moreover, because those conventions of linguistic representation worked hand in hand with the ever-present convention of the romantic-courtship plot, freedom of speech alone implied a radical change in the status of that plot, if not a complete elimination of it. Thus, Sewall's attack on the "monstrous disproportion" of the courtship-marriage plot served also to justify a novel about Silas Lapham's mundane "rise" in the first place.

A discourse of the "low," in dialect and vernacular speech, had already found a place in American writing, in the Southwestern humorous tales published in the East before the Civil War, in "local color" stories which had begun to appear in the 1850's and broadened into a major current in the postwar decades, and even in very popular sentimental romances such as Susan Warner's *The Wide, Wide World* (1850). But by and large, the low remained low, subordinated by plot and other devices of social designation to what can be called a discourse of respectability—a mode of writing which takes as its own the speech and social perspective of its "grammatical characters": a subordination found in varying degrees in Bret Harte's California mining-camp stories and poems, James Whitcomb Riley's Indian Hoosier poems, the Uncle Remus tales of Joel Chandler Harris, George Washington Cable's Creole stories, Mary Murfree's treatment of rural Southern whites, the New England regional fictions of Mary Wilkins and Sarah Orne Jewett. With few exceptions, dialect either appeared within a grammatical framework or otherwise made clear it was intended for a grammatically proper reader. This placement of speech in such a way that it is unmistakably recognized as "low," as culturally inferior to the *writing* of the narrator, owed as much to economics as to the social attitudes of writers (most of them middle or upper class in origins), an effect of prudential considerations in a literary marketplace controlled largely by major Eastern periodicals like *Atlantic, Century,* and *Harper's.* In the 1880's, the monthlies had evolved a remarkable authority over the production of fiction. Realism suited their purposes of reaching a national audience as long as it was tempered to accord with the predominant Protestant morality they assumed among their readers. For the privilege of publication and payment, regional writers were expected to present *themselves* at least, even if not their characters, as standing within that morality, that national discourse of propriety.

Not until Mark Twain's *Adventures of Huckleberry Finn* (1884), told entirely in the vernacular voice of an illiterate outcaste boy of the Mississippi valley, did the linguistic freedom implicit in realism come to fruition in America. From the outset, Mark Twain had circumvented the journals and the respectable publishing houses often (like *Atlantic* and *Harper's* and *Scribner's*) tied directly to the journals, by publishing his books on a subscription basis, sold door-to-door by traveling agents, reaching a nonliterary audience almost as large as that of dime novels and story papers sold at newsstands. Stamped thus with the onus of popularity, less an "author" than an entertainer, a personality, a "humorist," Mark Twain began his career outside the circle of respectability, and soon found a begrudging genteel acceptance. In the linguistic experiment of *Huckleberry Finn,* he found a freedom for the realistic telling of tales of insanity, murder, thievery, betrayal, feuding and lynching, and brutalities of racism without precedent in American fiction: without precedent, and unique until the appearance in 1900 of Theodore Dreiser, who in *Sister Carrie* and later novels would abandon respectability altogether, along with the very notion of "high" and "low," romantic plots, and the entire apparatus of reconciliation that lay at the heart of Howells's enterprise.

In 1895, Howells defended the growing use of dialect as indicating "the wider diffusion of the impulse to get the whole of American life into our fiction." *Huck Finn* and *Sister Carrie* suggest that getting "into" fiction entailed more than the deft inclusion of vernacular speech. Howells, who rarely employed dialect, confined the vernacular to dialogue: his narratives remained securely within the discourse of respectability, as in *Silas Lapham,* with the important modification that Silas is allowed a major, not merely a comic or incidental role, a role, moreover, which serves to correct the social, moral, and *literary* perspective of grammatical characters like Bromfield Corey and the reader. For it is clear from the narrator's own ease of discourse that he addresses the Coreys among his readers, not the Silas Laphams, who are not yet presumed to have developed a taste for serious fiction. Howells remains, then, within the circle, attempting to revise its vision from within.

And this posture, of standing within, of staking his risks on the middle ground, involved Howells in what has appeared to later critics as a fatal flaw in his realism: his permitting respectability to censor his observations and insights. This reservation, however, mislocates the contradiction. In fact, Howells revised the notion of realism to fit his own role, the role of fashioning serious fiction as an anodyne for the rifts he observed in the social fabric, the growing tensions between old and new ways of life. "Fidelity to experience and probability of motive" represented to Howells fidelity to the true underlying shape of American experience. Realism will always find "consolation and delight" in "real life" because, Howells believed, real life, in America at least, was at bottom truly governed by a moral universe. Neither callousness nor dishonesty led him in 1886, the year of the Haymarket crisis whose outcome would so agitate his convictions as to make of him a Christian socialist and in the 1890's a utopian novelist, to write: "In a land where journeymen carpenters and plumbers strike for four dollars a day the sum of hunger and cold is certainly very small, and the wrong from class to class is also inappreciable. We invite our novelists, therefore, to concern themselves with the more smiling aspects of life, which are the more American." What was "peculiarly American," he continued, was "the large, cheerful average of health and success and happy life."

The contradiction in his notion of realism may be found rather in his fictions: not in his beliefs but in his practices. The Reverend Sewall holds that fiction, however paradoxical, should be *true*, that novels should paint life "as it is." Howells himself stressed perspective, balanced and proportioned seeing; that is, *picture*. Picture implies the making of a form, and also the closure of an event: that is, it implies *plot*. By Howells's notion of "real life," balance, proportion, picture, and plot inhere in reality it-

191

self: all a matter of proper seeing. Yet, seeing is not, for him, description alone; realism is "false to itself" when it "maps life instead of picturing it." A true-to-life picture, then, will seem credible because life itself contains that picture, that form, that symmetry of plot.

So goes the theory. In practice, in his novels of the 1880's especially, Howells frequently felt he needed to force his picture into its proportions and balances even if by acts of arbitrary plotting, by transparent devices of romance such as the Corey-Lapham marriage, and Silas's quite unbusinesslike renunciation of the opportunity to revenge himself against a former crooked partner and make a handsome pile of money in the bargain: a renunciation which wins him the admiration of the Coreys as having in the end "behaved very well—like a gentleman." The denouement entails destruction of a scapegoat, the crooked partner Rogers, as indeed, in *A Modern Instance* and *A Hazard of New Fortunes*, acts of violence—the killing of Bartley and of Conrad Dreyfus—serve as punishments or sacrifices essential to the balance and proportion of the picture, of the plot. Moreover, the romantic-courtship element, which Howells never entirely abandoned, serves the same end by another course, the reverse of violence and murder: the regenerative powers of the good woman, of emotional and domestic love. For the sake of the moral order he assumed realism would disclose, it was essential that characters reap their just rewards, that good come to the good and bad to the bad—even at the cost of plausibility. Too often Howells contrived devices—chance encounters, changes of heart, sacrificial acts—to ensure a relatively benign outcome, if not exactly a happy ending, then at least a morally pleasing one. Thus, Howells resorted often to "romance" to preserve the moral assurances of his "realism."

Realism, then, brings Howells to the point where, in spite of himself, his fictions of the real disclose the unresolved gaps and rifts within the traditional world view he wishes to maintain, to correct and discipline. That outlook no longer possessed the resources of self-renewal, of creative accommodation to the new shape of its world. Resorting to romance, Howells conceded, without acknowledgment, the fundament of illusion on which his realism rested: the illusion and romance of "America" itself.

For Howells, realism and America were always interchangeable terms, the one informing and assuring the other of that ultimate coming-out-all-right which held together the middle-class Protestant view. In response to Matthew Arnold's remark that America lacked "distinction," Howells respectfully if illogically replied that "somehow, the idea that we call America has realized itself so far that we already have identification rather than distinction." This means: "Such beauty and such grandeur as we have is common beauty, common grandeur, or the beauty and grandeur in which the quality of solidarity so prevails that neither distinguishes itself to the disadvantage of anything else." Howells remarks improbably that America invites "the artist to the study and the appreciation of the common, and to the portrayal in every art of those finer and higher aspects which unite rather than sever mankind, if he would thrive in our new order of things." As solidarity, as order, as higher and finer aspects which unite, "America" is thus America's own romance—what Melville would call in another connection, in the same troubled days at the end of the 1880's, "the symmetry of form attainable in pure fiction."

III

"My mother called them all *lies*," Penelope Lapham says to Tom Corey about novels. " 'They're certainly fictions,' said Corey, smiling." But fictions, in the best of cases, Howells would add, are also true. His campaign for realism had on one important side the high motive of establishing precisely this, the authority and legitimacy of serious fiction as a serious enterprise. Realism held within itself a defense of literature: a defense as much against the idealists' claim that art belonged to a "higher" sphere, as against traditional moral scruples, like Mrs. Lapham's, against novels and novel reading.

Like James, Howells was especially vexed by the apparent anomaly of serious literature, fictions with truth-telling claims, in a culture ruled by business values, by images of success and failure. The role of reading in *Silas Lapham*, of journalism in *A Modern Instance*, of the founding of a new periodical of letters, arts, and opinion in *A Hazard of New Fortunes*, embodied that

193

concern; the novels can be taken as examinations of the predicament of serious writing as well as pedagogies of serious reading. A critical predicament, central in *A Hazard of New Fortunes*, was the changed economic situation of the writer as a social type, a vocational category. Until the Civil War, Howells explained in an essay at the end of the century, "The Man of Letters as a Man of Business," few writers could hope for economic independence from literary income alone. Now, because of "the prosperity of the magazines," it is possible for writers to "live prettily enough," chiefly by sale of serial publications to journals. Still, the man of letters retains a "low grade among business men." This is because "literature is still an infant industry," book publication making "nothing like the return to the author the magazine makes." Also, even among "the highest class" of magazine readers, the "love of pure literature," as opposed to opinion, science, travel, and so on, has been "growing less and less," hardly strong enough "to justify the best business talent in devoting itself" to letters. For those seeking financial success, writing remains a poor investment of time and effort, though indeed storytelling is now a recognized trade, occasionally lucrative for those willing to produce "the sort of fiction which corresponds in literature to the circus and the variety theatre." Even the best-known serious writers often earn less than "a rising young physician," a fact "humiliating to an author in the presence of a nation of business men like ours."

The humiliation points to the mixed feelings rampant in Howells's essay. At the outset he had established as a basic premise the bizarre anomaly of art in a world of business. The artist knows "there is something false and vulgar" in the practice of selling art, something obscenely wrong in the conception of artworks as commodities, in the poet's use of his emotions, for example, "to pay his provision bills." "The work which cannot be truly priced in money cannot be truly paid in money." Yet there is no doubt that "Literature is Business as well as Art, and almost as soon." As things stand, in fact, "business is the only human solidarity; we are all bound together with that chain, whatever interests and tastes and principles separate us." The reference to circus-like fiction, however, cuts across the image of a solidarity of writers, for it implies that the artist is also perforce an entrepreneur and entertainer, a competitor. Even though "literature has no objective value really, but only a subjective value," authors have become "largely matters of fashion, like this style of bonnet, or that shape of gown."

In the shape of competition, serious writers preserve the subjective value, while circus-like writers produce the commodities, like sentimental romances and what Henry James excluded from "legitimate fiction" altogether, the dime novel or "sensation novel." The competitive scene, as James described it in "The Question of Opportunities" (1898), was "subdivided as a chessboard, with each little square confessing only to its own *kind* of accessibility." With "divisions and boundaries," he wrote, increasing stratification of readerships by social class, by level and interest, "the very force of conditions" compelled American writers to react against the possibility of any single literary mode, "any taste or tone," establishing itself as the "general" fashion, by staking out individual claims. If the process continued, he foresaw, "we may get individual publics positively more sifted and evolved than anywhere else, shoals of fish rising for more delicate bait." It was this that Howells faced with misgiving: further fragmentation of the social world and further diminishment of both the earning power and the cultural influence of that "pure" and serious writing on which a restored middle ground, a revived America, depended. And so his double-fronted campaign, against the "gross fables," prodigies and marvels of the popular, and for novels of enlightenment and instruction, of reflective consciousness. Unless novels tend "to make the race better and kinder," he wrote, they cannot be "regarded as serious"; they are "lower than the rudest crafts that feed and house and clothe, for except they do this office they are idle; and they cannot do this except from and through the truth." The function is both practical and religious: "Let all the hidden things be brought into the sun, and let every day be the day of judgment. If the sermon cannot any longer serve this end, let the novel do it." His defense of the realist novel is a defense, then, of civilized mind itself: "I confess that I should suspect an unreality, an insincerity in a mature and educated person whom I found liking an unreal, an insincere novel."

Yet, "in the actual conditions," Howells concludes his essay on "The Man of Letters as a Man of Business," the artist is "anomalous," no better than an amusement for the "classes," unknown

195

and unregarded among the "masses": "the common people do not hear him gladly or hear him at all." Howells brings to a close this essay of complaint with a remarkable unexpected image—unexpected, yet once announced, a perfectly apt figure of speech.

In the end, the writer is "an artist merely, and is allied to the great mass of wage-earners who are paid for the labor they have put into the thing done ... who live by doing and making a thing, and not by marketing a thing after some other man has done it or made it." In the last analysis, the author "is merely a working-man, and is under the rule that governs the working-man's life," the rule that he must earn his bread by the sweat of his brow. "I wish that I could make all my fellow-artists realize," he writes, "that economically they are the same as mechanics, farmers, day-laborers." The solidarity of business, which had assumed each individual writer to be an entrepreneur competing with his goods in the market, now appears as a solidarity of labor, a solidarity, moreover, which figures forth a broad community of producers strikingly like that of the antebellum free-labor doctrine, the revived America of Populism, of Bellamy's "Nationalism," of Christian socialism. "It ought to be our glory that we produce something," Howells exults, and "we ought to feel the tie that binds us to all the toilers of the shop and field, not as a galling chain, but as a mystic bond also uniting us to Him who works hitherto and evermore." The bond is nothing less than sacral America itself, now a distant hope of incarnation rather than an immediate prospect: "Perhaps the artist of the future will see in the flesh the accomplishment of that human equality of which the instinct has been divinely planted in the human soul."

Thus, the artist of the real is the artist of "America", a figure which not surprisingly submerges the competitiveness out of which realism had defined its own zealous mission against the degradations of circus and variety-house fiction. If the marketplace has made wage workers out of artists, against the grain of their essentially subjective work, then the solidarity of producers ought to dissolve the competition, reattach the artist to the sacred body of the nation, at least as a future prospect. Certainly a compelling image, nevertheless it evades the very insight it embodies. For the burden of Howells's essay is that the artist *must* be a businessman in a business world, must sell his wares not as a wage slave but as an independent entrepreneur, directly into a competitive market. This is precisely the goal of Howells's realism: to take a competitive stance among competing modes, and yet insist on it as the only true mode, the only serious fiction. Thus, Howells's realism bears the mark of the very competition it condemns as alien to art and the instinct of equality.

And while Howells's own condemnation raged most angrily against the best sellers of the age, sentimental romances like *Ben-Hur, Little Lord Fauntleroy, Trilby,* his reference to circuses and "gross fables" also excluded the story-paper fiction which represented the reading of perhaps the majority of urban Americans. Published as pamphlets in mass quantities, without even the pretense of qualifying as "book," as belonging to culture, such fiction represented one of the most ephemeral commodities of the era. Dime fiction was indeed the product of proletarian labor—hundreds of authors working anonymously in factory-like quarters in New York, reported Edward Bok of the *Ladies' Home Journal* in 1892. Such a writer "turns into a veritable machine," paid at piece rates by the story or the word. As early as 1864, the *North American Review* took notice of their sales, "almost unprecedented in the annals of booksellers," obtaining "greater popularity than any other series of works of fiction published in America." Writing in Howells's *Atlantic Monthly* in 1879, novelist W. H. Bishop called "story-paper literature" the "greatest literary movement, in bulk, of the age, and worthy of every serious consideration for itself." It was a phenomenon, Bishop urged on his polite readers, which "cannot be overlooked."

Precisely because of its conditions of production, its popularity, its serving no other objective ends than the sale of quickly consumable commodities of entertainment and distraction, dime fiction was not susceptible to formal literary criticism; its producers did not enjoy "careers" subject to critical reception and the honor of reviews. They were Howells's lowest order of literary producers: the undisguised hacks. And their product thus raised the deepest, most unsettling fears among respectable critics: that for the young readers of such sensational and fantastic fiction, the line between fiction and real life might indeed be entirely obliterated. Ranging from the evangelical rhetoric of Anthony Comstock's *Traps for the Young* (1883), to newspaper and

197

journal editorials and commentary, the commonest fear was that young people would take the "pernicious stories of the 'dime novel' class" as models for themselves. According to Comstock, crusader for the Suppression of Vice, "these stories . . . disparage honest toil and make real life a drudge and a burden. What young man will serve an apprenticeship, working early and late, if his mind is filled with the idea that sudden wealth may be acquired by following the hero of the story?"

Editorial writers often described youngsters shooting themselves or others "during a period of mental aberration caused by reading dime novels." The fear was not only of random aberrant violence. In 1878, *Scribner's Monthly* worried about the "effects on society" of fiction so outrageously antisocial: "stories about hunting, Indian warfare, California desperado life, pirates, wild sea adventure, horrors (torture and snake stories), gamblers, practical jokes, the life of vagabond boys, and the wild behavior of dissipated boys in great cities." The magazine worried especially about the social effects of typical characterizations of authority: "all teachers, of course, are sneaks and blackguards"; "fathers and sons are natural enemies"; vagabond life is "interesting and enticing," while "respectable home life . . . is not depicted at all." Held up to admiration are "low people who live by their wits . . . heroes and heroines of bar-rooms, concert saloons, variety theatres, and negro minstrel troupes." The police are "all stupid louts," and the law not to be minded. It is impossible "that so much corruption should be afloat and not exert some influence."

Less moralistic, less fearful of personal disasters following an afternoon immersed in a tale of lurid adventure, Bishop viewed the story papers from a perspective similar to Howells's realism. The worst aspect of this fiction is its implausibility. "The admiration grows," he writes, "for the craving which can swallow, without misgiving, so grand a tissue of extravagances, inaneness, contradictions, and want of probability." Villains display "no redeeming traits," and the good are always good. Characters are "never exhibited attending to the ordinary duties of existence." To be sure, there are elements of genuine popularity: living persons and current events frequently appear, as well as "a great many poor people." Indeed, "the capitalist is occasionally abused." But, "though written almost exclusively for the use of the lower classes of society, the story papers are not accurate pictures of their life." Their fault lies, in short, in their not being realist novels.

More benign than other critics, Bishop also proposes a program of reform. All things considered, he writes, the story papers "are not an unmixed blessing." They "reward virtue and punish vice." "They encourage a chivalrous devotion to woman." And, most of all, they represent among the masses a "taste for reading" which, "however perverted, is connected with something noble, with an interest outside of the small domain of self." With their popularity, their profound hold on their vast audiences, perhaps story-paper fiction "offers a solution to the problem of how the literature of the masses is to be improved." Certainly, Bishop argues, "the enormous extent of this imaginative craving" will demand objects of satisfaction. "Lack of culture is a continuous childhood," he explains, and most of the present audience "is not reflective." But an improved popular literature may hold the key to an improved culture.

Dime novels consisted of a baffling melange of storytelling devices, overlapping plots, hidden identities, disguises, long-lost heirs. Violence was rife: fistfights, knifings, shootings, acts of treachery, cowardice, and bravery. Bishop is probably correct in supposing an absence of "misgiving" among their readers. They were read rapidly, probably with a rising pulse beat. What lay behind the appeal of such fictions of the unreal remained obscure, inaccessible at least to literary reformers and intellectuals like Howells. Embracing dime fiction along with sentimental romance under the same heading of "injurious" literature, Howells described it as "the emptiest dissipation," a kind of "opium-eating," drugging the brain and leaving the reader "weaker and crazier for the debauch," in "dumb and passive need." His own imagery of excoriation grew more extreme at the height of his campaign for realism in the late 1880's, depicting fictions "which imagine a world where the sins of sense are unvisited by the penalties which follow, swift or slow, but inexorably sure, in the real world," as "deadly poison: these do kill." Such pervasive appetite for poison, for opium, could only imply a state of barbarism. It is a "palpable error," he insisted, "to regard civilization as inclusive of all the members of a civilized community." Many still "live in a state of more or less evident savagery with respect to their habits, their morals, and the propensities . . . Many more yet are savage in their tastes, as they show by the decoration of their houses and persons, and by their choice of books and picture."

Obviously, it is not to these savage Americans Howells addressed his essays in *Harper's* or his novels. Howells's language of contempt indicates his abandonment of the popular. Whatever the reasons, the story papers expressed to him a mass consciousness at profound odds with realism, with culture itself. They stood as "low" to "high," and thus challenged Howells and others to their task of defining a level, a stratum of their own, a Central Park of the imagination, where civilized acts might be performed in the "light of common day" upon a greensward of measured vistas and balanced views: a communal spectacle of a revived Republic. It was for Howells as for Olmsted a matter of "civilization" or "savagery": we read, or we barbarize.

The virtually Manichaean antithesis of the alternatives arose from the depth of Howells's investment in the concept of America, of republican equality and solidarity. Fully capable of discerning how untenable the concept was fast becoming in the face of a rigidifying class structure and open class strife—how fragile the supporting moral universe seemed to be against social injustice and mechanization—he nevertheless persisted in his belief. "I'm not in a very good mood with 'America' myself," he wrote to Henry James in 1888.

It seems to be the most grotesquely illogical thing under the sun; and I suppose I love it less because it won't let me love it more. I should hardly like to trust pen and ink with all the audacity of my social ideas; but after fifty years of optimistic content with "civilization" and its ability to come out all right in the end, I now abhor it, and feel that it is coming out all wrong in the end, unless it bases itself anew on a real equality. Meantime I wear a fur-lined overcoat, and live in all the luxury my money can buy.

Blaming the word "America" as "illogical," Howells could only pass off his own illogicality with a self-deprecatory remark, burying his abhorrence in the persisting faith that the old America might yet "base itself anew on a real equality." Herein lay his desperate hope for a fiction of the real.

IV

"The symmetry of form attainable in pure fiction cannot so readily be achieved in a narration essentially having less to do with fable than with fact. Truth uncompromisingly told will always have its ragged edges." So wrote Herman Melville in *Billy Budd, Sailor*, the tale he called an "inside narrative," unfinished and unpublished at his death in 1891. Melville had endured the Gilded Age in virtual silence, unknown, unread, a ghost of the past performing a daily round of chores at the New York Custom House. It seems unlikely he attended to Howells's campaign for realism, but in these two sentences from his final tale the chief dilemma of a fiction of the real comes powerfully to the fore.

Howells proved unable or unwilling to accept the raggedness of "truth uncompromisingly told," retreating always into the symmetry of a fiction he held "pure," including the illogical fiction of "America." To be sure, the strains and tensions and the violence of his age make their way into his novels. Indeed, in the fictions of Howells, James, Mark Twain, in the regional stories of Kate Chopin, Mary Wilkins, E. W. Howe, Hamlin Garland, in the new "naturalism" of Crane and Frank Norris and Dreiser in the 1890's, a ragged picture does emerge, of lost hopes, hypocrisy, narrowed and constricted lives, grinding frustrations of poverty and isolation. The report is relieved, especially in the regional fiction, by acts of courage, a surviving residue of older ways, rural customs and habits and speech. But the major picture included a keen lament for the passing of an older, more secure and reliable way of life, one based on ingrained assumptions about the possibilities of freedom. The discovery of social constraints, of the incursions of history on the idyll of Huck and Jim on their raft, or of vile manipulation on Isabel Archer's belief (in James's *Portrait of a Lady*) in a perfect freedom of choice and self-determination, tainted much of the fiction of the age with sorrow, bitterness, cynicism. In worlds of greed and plotting, James's heroes and heroines learn what their author himself insisted in his writings on fiction: that experience is always social,

201

that freedom only manifests itself within human relations. On the whole, realism portrayed the old American credo of a community of autonomous natural beings as a sad illusion. Howells's problems in arriving at satisfactory conclusions to his novels, like Mark Twain's last-minute resort to romantic plot at the end of *Adventures of Huckleberry Finn,* reflect the intellectual difficulty of absorbing that lesson, of creating fictions of fact rather than fable.

Under Howells's tutelage, writers embraced more unsettling contemporary fact than the audiences of respectable literature had been accustomed to reading. Yet fact consistently battled with fable in his own works, and in the end Howells narrowed his range, addressing an imaginary audience, a "literary elect" who might serve as a saving remnant against the future when the solidarity of writer and reader might be realized. "I believe," he confessed in a lecture in 1899, "that it is far from these nervous centres that the author finds his closest, truest, liveliest appreciation. For my part I like to think of my stories, if they are so blest, as befriending the loneliness of outlying farms, dull villages, distant exile."

From his own internal exile within the nervous city, Herman Melville had his say in the privacy of his cryptic tale of Billy Budd, without a hope of reaching living readers, high or low or middle.

Written late in the 1880's, *Billy Budd* turns to an event more than a generation earlier, the Somers Mutiny of 1842, in which a member of Melville's family joined the tribunal in sentencing to death a young offender against the ship's military discipline. Set "in the time before steamships," before the harsh industrial conflicts in the years in which Melville wrote, the tale bristles with personal implication for the aging writer whose family had thirty years earlier worried for his sanity. But the story of the "fated" Billy, a common sailor consigned to death by a possibly deranged captain during the naval wars between revolutionary France and counterrevolutionary England, also reflects on the turbulence of Melville's own times. The tale is set amid a turbulence which Melville is at pains to describe as not so much an external threat of French victory over England, "a Power then all but the sole free conservative one of the Old World," but an internal one of "insurrection" in the British fleet. Just months

202

before the events, British sailors had rebelled at Spithead and Nore, signaling their mutiny by running up the royal flag "with the union and cross wiped out," thus "transmuting the flag of founded law and freedom defined, into the enemy's red meteor of unbridled and unbounded revolt." Growing out of "reasonable discontent" over "glaring abuses," the revolt flamed into an "irrational combustion," a "distempering irruption of contagious fever." It was a time, like the days and months following the summer of 1877, or Haymarket in 1886, when the red banner terrified established authority, portending even further unbounded revolt. Officers at sea felt compelled "to stand with drawn swords behind the men working the guns."

The similarities of historical moment—of mass unrest and challenges to authority, of issues brought to law and settled by authorized force—resound too insistently to be ignored. Certainly, this is not to say that Melville intended his tale to serve as an explicit commentary on the current events of his own declining years. Free of any direct allusion to contemporary affairs, the narrative does speak of the Great Mutiny at Nore as similar to "some other events in every age befalling states everywhere, including America," but it seems likely that Melville has in mind the Civil War, which elsewhere he had described as a mutiny against the Republic. Moreover, to what extent does the tale even concern itself with its own larger historical moment? True, Billy's story begins with an act—his impressment in the open sea—pointedly described as an example of abuse not redressed by the settlement at Nore. Snatched from the *Rights-of-Man*, a homeward-bound merchant ship named in honor of Thomas Paine, Billy is coerced into the King's service aboard the outward-bound HMS *Bellipotent*, a 74-gun warrior ship rushing to join the royal fleet awaiting battle with the French. The "inside narrative," writes Melville, will have "little concernment" with the actual maneuvers of the ship, but surely the revolutionary moment, and especially Britain's fear of the Red Flag, will contribute in no small way to Billy's end. The larger history will fade imperceptibly but nonetheless decisively into the drama of Billy, Claggart, and Starry Vere.

What concern us, then, are not so much the parallels between the represented history of the tale and that of Melville's America, but the reflection on history itself, on the impingement of an outside on an inside narrative. The tale recounts an act, a doubled act within an outside history: Billy's killing of Claggart, Vere's killing of Billy. It also recounts a continuing act of interpretation.

Billy Budd, the "Handsome Sailor," seems the incarnation of a "natural" goodness, the corporeal form of an otherworldly innocence. And Claggart, the "master-at-arms," seems a predestined opposite and foe, demonism incarnate as human malice, envy, and spite. In Claggart lurked some element of unmotivated evil the narrator cannot explain except by evoking, if only figuratively, the "mystery of iniquity" of the old Calvinist doctrine. Claggart seemed by nature "bad," while Billy "had none of that intuitive knowledge of the bad which in natures not good or incompletely so foreruns experience." Are Billy and Claggart, then, moral types, fables fallen into a world of fact? When Billy strikes out in speechless rage at Claggart's false accusation that the young sailor had plotted mutiny, and kills his superior officer at one blow, Captain Vere grasps instantly the fatal conjunction of fable and fact. "Struck dead by an angel of God! Yet the angel must hang!" He must hang, moreover, and hang at once, as Vere would argue before his own disbelieving officers, precisely because of those angelic features which arouse so powerful a current of sympathy. Vere had witnessed the false accusation and the deadly blow with rising fatherly feelings. But then, momentarily "eclipsed" by emotion, he emerged from his spell "with quite another aspect." "The father in him . . . was replaced by the military disciplinarian."

Did Vere act precipitously? After all, as members of the drumhead court themselves argued, Billy might have been held over in chains until a regular court might be convened. There is no doubt that Vere acts in a state of extreme distress. But what does his condition signify? Just as Vere performs an act of interpretation on Billy and Claggart, so the reader is constrained to interpret Vere, who indeed proves a more intractable case of ambiguity. "Who in the rainbow can draw the line where the violet tint ends and the orange tint begins?" asks the narrator. "Distinctly we see the difference of the colors, but where exactly does the one first blendingly enter into the other? So with sanity and insanity." The case is left to the reader: whether Vere must be considered insane or not "everyone must determine for himself by such

204

light as this narrative may afford." Was it insanity, or guilt, or some stoic sense of impersonal tragedy which drove Vere, at the moment of his own death after a successful battle with the French ship the *Athée*, to murmur "words inexplicable to his attendant: 'Billy Budd, Billy Budd' "? Does the narrative finally afford sufficient light to clarify Vere's condition, or to make his final words explicable?

The narrative cloaks all questions of motive, of meaning, in a cunning uncertainty. Only the outside narrative, the chronicle of mere events, remains incontrovertible. Everything inside seems equivocal, murky, elusive. And it is precisely the encroaching sense of the inside world's ultimate obscurity which would have brought discomfort and protest from those among Melville's readers still faithful to inherited notions of an America, a city on a hill, in which reason and nature might achieve a perfect harmony. Such believers would fiercely reject Vere's instant condemnation of Billy. To hang an angel for performing his Father's work: what more violent desecration of the harmony once implied by the "rights of man" and by popular Christian belief?

Vere meets these objections without flinching. What springs to our attention in the following passage is not only a grim justification but its basis in a distinction of realms uncommon in popular American political thought:

How can we adjudge to summary and shameful death a fellow creature innocent before God, and whom we feel to be so?—Does that state it aright? You sign sad assent. Well, I too feel that, the full force of that. It is Nature. But do these buttons that we wear attest that our allegiance is to Nature? No, to the King. Though the ocean, which is inviolate Nature primeval, though this be the element where we move and have our being as sailors, yet as the King's officers lies our duty in a sphere correspondingly natural? So little is that true, that in receiving our commissions we in the most important regards ceased to be natural free agents . . . Our vowed responsibility is in this: That however pitilessly that law may operate in many instances, we nevertheless adhere to it and administer it.

Not "nature" but "king" defines duty, not natural reason or natural law but the *state*, the arbitrary power whose authority, signified by the officers' buttons, runs like the King's yarn throughout the society. Finally, it is the irreconciliability of Nature and King which seals Billy's fate: the fate of "fable" in a world of "fact."

Billy would have had a home in the old imagined America of a natural law supporting a naturally reasonable society. But once impressed on the *Bellipotent,* he left behind all familiar meanings and unambiguous relations. The force which tore him from the haven of the *Rights-of-Man* represented the hard facts of warfare, class conflict, malice, intrigue, unrelenting law: in short, *history.* Meanings no longer secure, motives hidden at impenetrable depths, the very name Billy Budd "inexplicable": just so, his story in the end lies twisted and perverted in "official" accounts in the press. Moreover, neither the death of Billy nor that of Vere discloses any ultimate meaning, any symmetry of form. As Michael Rogin has argued cogently about this very political tale, the state no longer promises redemption. "Lying between two guns, as nipped in the vice of fate," Billy lies a victim of an order which, in the face of his utter innocence, cannot justify itself except by evoking "order" itself, form and symmetry for their own sake. And is not Vere himself also caught in that same nipping vice?

Of course, Melville writes about an earlier era, a distant event. But still, *Billy Budd* invites us to take it as Melville's final, undelivered message to his countrymen and fellow writers. In the light of the narrative, the historical world can no longer be mistaken as hospitable to the American fable of a *natural* innocence and solidarity. History discloses itself as the realm of power, the laws and iron weapons of the state set against the receding utopia of the "rights of man." Not in nature but in the King's yarn lay the hidden meaning of the law. So much is clear from the buttons on Vere's coat, and from the sight of Billy hanging from the yard-arm. But so much, in treating of narratives inside larger events, remains unclear. Melville's message thus includes a severe commentary on interpretation itself, on the ways of knowing and judging behavior. Melville's message, translated freely, argues not only that the state must be seen as distinct from "nature," grounded in power and social interest, but also that the process of seeing and knowing must be freed from "fable," from utopian wish. To perceive their new world, Melville implies, Americans must reckon with ragged edges, the cunning currents and deceits of history.

There is an even deeper message in Billy's fate. Just as the state no longer grounds itself in natural reason, neither does it even claim to represent a shared community of interest. That community known in the tale as "the ship's populace" finds itself utterly separate from the ruling state, subordinate to it, coerced by external law, the apparatus of the master-at-arms and his unholy crew of enforcers and spies. The populace is free only to obey or disobey, accept or rebel. Rewards and punishments remain wholly material: ultimately, life and death. There is no hint of redemption, of self-fulfillment in obedience. What survives in the tale, then, is not the power of the guns or of the coercive yardarm, but "Billy in the Darbies," the concluding ballad, a "rude utterance" from an "artless *poetic* temperament," testifying in "low" art to the separate and enduringly compassionate vision of "the ship's populace." Under the strict governance of the state, yet distinct from it in a very profound way, the sailors appear in Melville's narrative as a community of work and play in which a mutual predicament fostered a law of its own, a social law of sympathy and compassion. Billy Budd is their hero, the human image of their own precarious history. Only the poem at the end renders the name explicable.

7

WHITE CITY

I

"October 12. —*The Discovery*. —It was wonderful to find America, but it would have been more wonderful to miss it." Pudd'nhead Wilson's mordant calendar entry in Mark Twain's bleak comedy of race and class, *Pudd'nhead Wilson*, with its wicked pun on "wonderful," may well have seemed apt to at least some of the book's readers when it appeared in 1894. It was the year of the great railway strike which spread like a prairie fire from its origins in Pullman, Illinois. An epic insurgence of sympathy in the form of a national boycott in support of the Pullman strikers, the event pitted the United States Army against the American Railway Union, and the clash resulted in the most destructive civil violence since the Civil War. But the previous summer, when close to 30 million people had trekked by railroad to visit the Fair staged in Chicago on reclaimed swamplands on the shores of Lake Michigan, in commemoration of the four hundredth anniversary of that same discovery, Pudd'nhead's coy remark would not have made a hit. Surely Chauncy M. Depew's view of the occasion carried the day. In his oration at the dedication ceremonies in October 1892 (the Fair itself would not open its gates until May of the following year), the New York senator and industrialist summed up the common belief: "This day belongs not to America, but to the World. The results of the event it commemorates are the heritage of the people of every race and clime. We celebrate the emancipation of man." Of course, what he meant, and what the Fair would proclaim, is that America

208

represents the world, is itself the world's heritage, itself the "emancipation of man." Inviting the world to come and see (though not to stay: Depew included a timely warning against unrestricted immigration, against admitting "those who come to undermine our institutions and subvert our laws"), White City would display just how wonderful America had become.

How shall we take this event, which lasted but a summer—an oasis of fantasy and fable at a time of crisis and impending violence? Given its time and place, the Fair invites ironic scrutiny as few other events and objects in the age. Not the gesture alone of planting a new "city upon a hill" for the world to admire, but the accidental setting of that gesture between the financial panic of 1893 and the strike of 1894 makes White City seem a fitting conclusion of an age. The fruition of the alliance between "the word Culture" and corporate powers, it closes out an era. But it also inaugurates another. It lays bare a plan for a future. Like the Gilded Age, White City straddles a divide: a consummation and a new beginning.

We shall take it as a pedagogy, a model and a lesson not only of what the future might look like but, just as important, how it might be brought about. And in our analysis we shall look not only at what it says but at what it fails to say, what it keeps hidden. For example, as a model city it taught a lesson in the coordination of spaces and structures: some 400 buildings covering almost 700 acres of once swampy land dredged and filled and inlaid with canals, lagoons, plazas, and promenades, and a preserve of woods. Based on Olmsted's unifying ground plan, it taught the public utility of beauty, the coordination of art with the latest mechanical wonders: railroads, dynamos, electrical bulbs. It was, of course, a city without residences, though it offered advice in great detail about how families might live in cities of the near future: the model electrical kitchen, for example. How did its manifest harmony of parts (and in the central Court of Honor, of architectural style, height of buildings, color: a uniform whiteness) come about? The overt message stressed the structure of authority, a structure which gave to the Director of Works, Daniel H. Burnham, a free hand in selecting designers, architects, engineers, and approving their plans. Burnham's task seemed a model "commission," aloof from politics and practical economics, answerable only to the corporation which employed it: a private entity created by the laws of the state of Illinois as "World's Columbian Exposition" and authorized to raise capital by selling stock certificates. The Official Manual of the Fair consisted of the bylaws of this body, an account of its structure (board of directors elected by stockholders, standing committees), many lists of names of the prominent Chicago citizens among its ranks (businessmen, bankers, lawyers), and a complete text of the Act of Congress which authorized a "World's Columbian Commission" of appointed officials to deal with the corporation in matters of selection of site and specification of buildings and exhibits. The overt message about the origins of the Fair appeared, then, in the chain of authority devolving from legislative acts to private enterprise, a structure which gave the Department of Works its own authority and freedom to coordinate spaces and buildings according to its own lights.

The manual did not mention "labor." But one covert message about how a model future might be built lies in Walter Wyckoff's account of his experiences as a "road builder" on the fairgrounds in the spring of 1892. A Princeton graduate who had undertaken an "experiment" of tramping across the country to learn firsthand how the world looks and feels from the point of view of a working stiff, Wyckoff published his extraordinary narrative of hard knocks and wrenched perspectives in *Scribner's* and then in two volumes. In the second, *The Workers: An Experiment in Reality: The West* (1899), he described his experiences as a laborer on the fairgrounds. His employment there was a happy reprieve after a bleak winter of unemployment on the streets of Chicago. Now he finds himself with "wholesome labor in the open air," and has no complaints. He lives in a temporary "hotel" on the site "of the future 'court of honor' " with about four hundred other workers. They include "half a score of nationalities and of as many trades," including the unskilled, "who work in gangs." "Housed and fed in this one house," they seem altogether in an ideal situation. Yet the picture contains an ambiguous note: "Guarded by sentries and high barriers from unsought contact with all beyond, great gangs of us, healthy, robust men, live and labor in a marvelous artificial world. No sight of misery disturbs us, nor of despairing poverty out in vain search for employment." Regimentation on one hand, artificial security on the other: the picture suggests that White City's proposal for a future includes a distinct solution to the "labor problem." "Work is everywhere abundant and well paid and directed with the highest skill. And here, amid delicate, web-like frames of steel which are being clothed upon with forms of exquisite beauty, and among broad, dreary wastes of arid dunes and marshy pools which are being transformed by our labor into gardens of flowers and velvet lawns joined by graceful bridges over wide lagoons, we work our eight hours a day in peaceful security and in absolute confidence of our pay." A work force tranquilized by security, by beauty of environment, and by barriers and sentries which protect it from "unsought contact with all beyond": such is the utopia of labor implied.

Of such weavings of the overt and covert is White City made. By design, the Fair set itself against what lay beyond its gates. It enforced its lessons by contrast. The irony of opening its gates almost at the exact moment in May 1893 when banks and factories closed theirs in the worst financial panic of the nation's history only highlights the contrast, the dialogue of opposites between the Fair and the surrounding city, between White City and the great city of Chicago. As Julian Ralph pointed out in *Chicago and the World's Fair* (1893), a book written for Harper's and "approved by the Department of Publicity," Chicago displayed an energy and an exuberance in need of discipline: its politics, for example, showing the worst features of the spoils system, while its parks, governed by a commission above politics (responsible business leaders appointed by the county or state, not the city itself), represented a hopeful direction. With its own corporate structure, its chain of command, and its contented labor force (in fact, a number of strikes delayed construction), White City would show how a place like Chicago might be governed as well as how it might look. Just as the ground plan of the Fair implicitly rebuked the monotonous grid of Chicago's streets, so the Department of Works and its master plan rebuked the rule of mere competition, of commercial domination over beauty and order. By model and example, White City might thus inaugurate a new Chicago, a new urban world.

Much has been written about that master plan and its execution: Burnham's single-mindedness, for example, in choosing a uniform neoclassicism in uniform whiteness for the Court of Honor, and his preference for New York architects over local

211

Chicago firms who in the previous several years had pioneered in original skyscraper designs. In architectural histories, the story of the White City is riddled with "ifs": if John Wellborn Root, Burnham's partner, had not died before he had a chance to influence the shape of the Fair; if Root and Louis Sullivan had been able to take charge, how different the results might have been. As it is, Burnham's name has been tainted with charges of betrayal, of turning against the regional Chicago School in favor of the Paris-trained New York group and their elegant academicism. Sullivan charged many years later that the Fair set back American architecture an entire generation. Whether it did or not, more important is the implicit notion in White City of an architecture, an art and a culture, appropriate to the immediate future. More important than the battle of styles between the New York and Chicago schools is the conception embodied in the total design of White City of how space might be ordered and life organized.

Like the structure of the organizational command behind it, the Fair took its stand on symmetry of form, most strikingly in the Court of Honor, a harmonious arrangement of the major buildings on orthogonal axes alongside bodies of water and open plazas. Here, symmetry proclaimed the immediate message, the underlying spatial form speaking directly to the senses through the prestige of neoclassical monumentality. The message joined form to monument, each building and each vista serving as an image of the whole. Here, symmetry asserted itself as an unmistakable conquering presence. But the Court of Honor represented only one portion of the master plan. Less immediately apparent was the symmetrical order of the entire fairgrounds, the design embracing a diversity of buildings, styles, exhibitions, and events. As a style, neoclassicism was reserved for the Court of Honor. But radiating from that center, a principle of balance and order governed the entire fairgrounds.

In the Rand McNally *Handbook* (Andrew McNally was one of the chief backers of the Fair and member of the board of directors), Daniel Burnham explained to the public how the Fair's unfamiliar organization of space should be understood. After describing the work of transforming the "desolate wilderness" and "dreary landscape" of the original site, he wrote:

Three distinct motives are apparent in the grouping of the buildings. Those about the Grand Basin—the Administration, Manufactures, Agriculture, Machinery, Electricity, Mines, and also the Art Building—are essentially dignified in style; those lying farther to the north—the Horticultural, Transportation [Sullivan's contribution], and Fisheries—being less formal, blend readily with the more or less homelike headquarters buildings of the States and foreign governments, which are grouped among the trees of the extreme northern portion of the grounds. Upon the Midway Plaisance no distinct order is followed, it being instead a most unusual collection of almost every type of architecture known to man—oriental villages, Chinese bazaars, tropical settlements, ice railways, the ponderous Ferris wheel, and reproductions of ancient cities. All these are combined to form the lighter and more fantastic side of the Fair.

It might seem peculiar that Burnham should describe the Midway, with its mixture of modern machinery and vernacular buildings, as fantastic "reproductions," implying that the real and the original were to be found in the academic classicism of the Court of Honor. But the spatial divisions proclaimed just what Burnham implied, that reality must be sought in the ideality of high art. The Court of Honor provided the center around which the rest of White City was organized in hierarchical degree; indeed, the carnival atmosphere of the Midway Plaisance confirmed by contrast the dignity of the center. And, of course, the center represented America through its exhibitions, the outlying exotic Midway stood for the rest of the world in subordinate relation.

The design, then, encompassed a schematic set of contrasts, and by this it further promulgated its message of unity through subordination. But the heart of the message did not lie in the geometric form alone; it lay in the fact that the formal center of the Fair was derived from "art," from "culture." The Fair insinuated this primacy at every turn. Its organized spaces and classified exhibitions were an intellectual edifice indispensable to the message, as were the religious, educational, and scholarly events of the World's Congress Auxiliary. The motto of these events and meetings scheduled throughout Chicago during the months of the Fair articulated the message of White City: "Not Matter, But Mind; Not Things, But Men." If the Fair displayed matter and things, the Congress reflected on their meaning. Or-

213

ganized into twenty departments and 225 divisions, the Congress represented the incorporation of mind and spirit with matter and things, of culture with material progress. Under classifications such as Temperance, Moral and Social Reform, Social and Economic Science, Labor, Religion, and Woman's Progress, the Congress named those intellectual and social categories through which progress might be discerned and further problems identified: problems which remain to be solved in the spirit of unity, of "congress." The many discussions and scholarly exchanges—the session of the American Historical Association at which Frederick Jackson Turner read his epochal paper on the frontier, for example—represented culture in its intellectual practice, as fully integrated into the vision of White City as were the plastic arts in the master plan. The Congress served, in the overall design, as the intellectual equivalent of the visible art which made matter and things palpable on the fairgrounds.

"Not Matter, But Mind; Not Things, But Men": the art of White City took the same motto. The distinctions in the motto were critical, reinforced everywhere in White City as part of the exposition's basic message. By itself, matter stood at a distance from art; the products of labor and science occupied a realm of their own. But art provided the mode of presentation, the vehicle, the medium through which material progress manifests itself, and manifests itself precisely as serving the same goals as art: the progress of the human spirit. Here, too, a subtle contrast functioned as method. Just as the departments of the Congress represented a conceptual map of the realm of mind and spirit, so the division of the Fair's exhibitions into twelve departments mapped out the activities that constitute civilized society: agriculture, mining, machinery, transportation, invention, and so on. Quite apart from the location and style of the buildings housing each exhibition, the classification system served as a guide to one meaning: the material. Exhibitions provided further breakdowns of categories into the names of corporate business: General Electric, Westinghouse, Krupp of Germany. Progress thus appeared in the form of goods produced by capitalist enterprise, adding the name of private ownership to the products of labor. The substance of the exhibitions offered, then, not simple matter and things but matter and things as commercial products.

Between the abstract name of the department and the specific name of a company may have seemed to lie a contradiction: one proclaiming an activity of society as a whole, the other a certain system of production, distribution, and ownership. Virtually alone in recognizing this split, Edward Bellamy wrote: "The underlying motive of the whole exhibition, under a sham pretence of patriotism is business, advertising with a view to individual money-making." Certainly, the mode of presentation hardly disguised the commercial trade-fair aspect of White City, as a marketplace of display and sales. And neither was the "art," also a superimposed name (the name of antique styles recovered by academic research as "neoclassicism"), designed to deny and disguise its own act of concealing on the outside the steel frameworks which were the true support of buildings. "The engineering has been of a magnitude never reached before," wrote Burnham. Machinery Hall, built by a Boston firm, covered a floor space of more than seventeen acres, its roof supported by "vast arched trusses which," states the Rand McNally *Handbook*, "are built separately of iron and steel in such a manner that they may be taken down and sold for use as railroad train-houses or State exposition buildings." It housed "a monster elevated traveling crane" and a 2,000 horsepower engine running two dynamos, "each lighting 10,000 incandescent lights." The use of alternating-current electrical power to illuminate the entire fairgrounds was one of the event's unique achievements. What did the building look like? The design, "thoroughly classical in all of its details," was "copied from the best types of the Spanish Renaissance." Like all the principal buildings of the Court, it was covered with a composite plaster-like material called "staff." Painted white, staff was applied throughout the Court, as Burnham writes, on "sculpture, ornamentation of almost every kind, the construction of balustrades, vases, facing for docks." It was staff which permitted what one observer called the "architectual spree" of the Fair: the facing of steel-frame buildings with an allusive façade, an illusion of marble and classic monumentality. Staff provided the means of covering steel with architecture, the mechanical with the artistic, and, especially in the incrustation throughout the Court of allegorical statuary attached to buildings, the material with the spiritual.

Over the eastern entrance of the Machinery Hall appeared a pediment with "Columbia" seated on a throne, bearing a sword in one hand and a palm of peace in the other (a motif similar to the commanding female figure of the Republic, Columbia, dressed in gold, at one end of the central lagoon, carrying a globe surmounted by an American eagle in one hand, and a liberty pole and cap in the other). "Honor" stands on her left, "Wealth" at her feet, "throwing fruits and flowers out of a horn of plenty." In addition to a group of inventors, the pediment includes "two groups of lions, representing brute force subdued by human genius, which is represented by two children." Buildings were composed, then, as pictures of art, thus establishing the place of culture in relation to the activities of society embodied by the exhibits within.

A model of the true, ideal shape of reality, and in the methods of attaining that shape, the World's Columbian Exposition made itself relevant almost exactly to the extent that the world outside its gates did not conform to its symmetry. What may strike us as ironies are instead contradictions held in momentary balance—not a confusion of values, as historians have suggested, but an effort to incorporate contrary and diverse values under the unity of a system of culture in support of a system of society. The architect Henry Van Brunt, writing in *Century* before the Fair opened, made the matter explicit:

In order, therefore, to present a complete and symmetrical picture of modern civilization, it is necessary that the Columbian Exposition should not only bring together evidences of the amazing material productiveness which, within the century, has effected a complete transformation in the external aspects of life, but should force into equal prominence, if possible, corresponding evidences that the finer instincts of humanity have not suffered complete eclipse in this grosser prosperity, and that, in this headlong race, art has not been left entirely behind. The management of the Exposition is justified in placing machinery, agricultural appliances and products, manufactures and the liberal arts, the wonderful industrial results of scientific investigation, and other evidences of practical progress, in the midst of a parallel display shaped entirely by sentiment and appealing to a fundamentally different set of emotions. It is the high function of architecture not only to adorn this triumph of materialism, but to condone, explain and supplement it, so that some elements of "sweetness and light" may be brought forward to counterbalance the boastful Philistinism of our times.

216

The Fair seemed thus an Arnoldian program of social unity through culture. "Was it real, or only apparent?" Henry Adams was not certain that the "look of unity" worn by White City represented a genuine and lasting "rupture in historical sequence." But, he wrote, "one's personal universe hung on the answer, for, if the rupture was real and the new American world could take this sharp and conscious twist toward ideals, one's personal friends would come in, at last, as winners in the great American chariot-race for fame."

"Look here, old fellow," one of Adams's close friends, the sculptor Augustus Saint-Gaudens, was reported to have said to Burnham during a planning session, "do you realize that this is the greatest meeting of artists since the Fifteenth Century?" In its completed form, White City seemed indeed the triumph of a distinct community of artists, architects, scholars, and patrons: a community whose social commitment to the reforming power of beauty had grown and deepened during the crisis of the Gilded Age. In March, before the opening of the Fair, they gathered in Madison Square Garden in New York to pay tribute to Burnham, and among the more than two hundred guests were names high on the list of Arnold's apostolate: Charles Eliot Norton, the editor and poet Richard Watson Gilder, the inevitable E. L. Godkin, Olmsted, President of Johns Hopkins Daniel Coit Gilman, the architects Richard Hunt and Charles McKim, men of practical affairs like the businessmen Henry Villard, Marshall Field, Lyman Gage, and Abram Hewitt—and the admiring William Dean Howells. Norton spoke of the general design of the Fair as "noble, original, and satisfactory," and of the Court of Honor as "a splendid display of monumental architecture," showing how well "our ablest architects have studied the work of the past." On such occasions, the voices of culture rang loud in self-praise, for the Fair proclaimed, at last, their role.

That role appeared as the making of a landscape of fantasy in which goods might be displayed as progress, as emblems of a beneficent future. The final message of the Fair concerned the method of making such a future: through a corporate alliance of business, culture, and the state. But another part of the message was precisely to keep that alliance aloof, not so much hidden and disguised but above reproach, beyond criticism. And, for this function, art and culture served simply to dazzle the senses in

217

visible "beauty," to bathe the mind in delight. "I went to the fair at once," wrote Owen Wister in his diary, "and before I had walked for two minutes, a bewilderment at the gloriousness of everything seized me . . . until my mind was dazzled to a standstill." Delight to the point of bewilderment: such seemed the work of high art. "I studied nothing, looked at no detail, but merely got at the total consummate beauty and grandeur of the thing: —which is like a great White Spirit evoked by Chicago out of the blue water upon whose shore it reposes." So wrote Wister, enthralled by the White Spirit. Just such responses to the ordering and tranquilizing effects of the highest art William James must have had in mind in explaining in a letter to his brother Henry that, though he would not go to Chicago, "*everyone* says one ought to sell all one has and mortgage one's soul to go there; it is esteemed such a revelation of beauty. People cast away all sin and baseness, burst into tears and grow religious etc., under the influence!!"

The influence of beauty arrayed as public monuments had a somewhat similar effect even on critics of the social order which lay beyond the gates of the Fair. White City, wrote Henry Demarest Lloyd, "revealed to the people possibilities of social beauty, utility, and harmony of which they had not even been able to dream." Its image of coordination and cooperation for the end simply of beauty was a vision to lighten "the prosaic drudgery of their lives." Even Eugene V. Debs spoke of "the lofty ideal" of the Fair, its "healthful influences . . . upon the national character." He made these observations in an editorial in the *Locomotive Firemen's Magazine* against a plan to keep the fairgrounds closed on the Sabbath, thereby depriving many working people of the chance to look "upon the beautiful in art as well as nature, a form of worship," Debs remarked, "entirely devoid of cant and hypocrisy, superior to any worship narrowed by creeds and dogmas." In another article during the summer, Debs would describe the Fair as primarily a tribute to labor. But for one moment at least White City seemed to him a secular church, exactly the place for Sunday worship.

It was left to William Dean Howells to draw the appropriate conclusion. Writing as the "Altrurian Traveler" in his utopian novel of angry social criticism then running serially in *Cosmopolitan*, Howells exempted the Fair from his assaults on selfish-

218

ness and greed, holding it up as the very model for a better future: "glorious capitals which will whiten the hills and shores of the east and the borderless plains of the west." He is reminded of home, the Altruria Howells portrays as the true, the original, the real America:

> *Of the effect, of the visible, tangible result, what*
> *better can I say than that in its presence I felt myself*
> *again in Altruria? The tears came, and the pillared porches*
> *swam against my vision; through the hard nasal American tones,*
> *the liquid notes of our own speech stole to my inner ear; I*
> *saw under the careworn masks of the competitive crowds, the*
> *peace, the rest of the dear Altrurian face; the gay tints of*
> *our own simple costumes eclipsed the different versions of*
> *the Paris fashions about me. I was at home once more, and*
> *my heart overflowed with patriotic rapture in this strange*
> *land so remote from ours in everything, that at times Altruria*
> *really seems to me the dream which the Americans think it.*

The future latent in White City seemed to Howells to be an America that once was.

Henry Adams, on the other hand, persisted in viewing the Fair in his usual hard light of politics and power, drawing quite different conclusions for the future. In spite of the "Babel of loose and ill-joined . . . thoughts and half-thoughts and experimental outcries" he detected on the fairgrounds, "Chicago was the first expression of American thought as a unity." The meaning of that apparent unity and its effect on him became clear when he returned to Washington in time to learn that Congress had resolved the long-standing money controversy by repealing the Silver Act and confirming a single gold standard, at the behest of bankers and capitalists. Realizing that his own "antiquated dislike of bankers and capitalistic society" had made him "little better than a crank," Adams recorded that now, especially after the Fair, he seemed better able to accept the new realities. "All one's friends, all one's best citizens, had joined the banks to force submission to capitalism," he wrote, finally resolving the hesitation and vacillation of the American people between "two forces, one simply industrial, the other capitalistic, centralizing, mechanical." Chicago had represented to him, subliminally at least, the defeat of the "simply industrial," the final victory of the centralizing, mechanical, and incorporated society of capitalism. Indeed, if capitalism "were to be run at all, it must be run by capital and by capitalistic methods; for nothing could surpass the nonsensity of trying to run so complex and so concentrated a machine by Southern and Western farmers in grotesque alliance with city day-laborers." And that exactly proved the lasting lesson of Chicago, of White City: that the new society required the corporate version of "capitalistic methods," including the array of culture before the senses. In the glow of White City, Populism looked as grotesque as the notion of direct rule by "the people" seemed now a "nonsensity."

II

The message of the Columbian Fair may have been clear, but actual lessons varied with perspective. If it stood for culture, its symmetry indicated relative positions of value, even of inclusion and exclusion. American blacks stood beyond the gates, petitions for an exhibition, a building, or a separate department all rejected. They were denied participation in the Fair, in its administration, on the National Commission, even on the construction force and ground crews (except as menials). Indians found themselves included among the exhibitions of the ethnology department, part of a display (in Julian Ralph's words) "to exemplify the primitive modes of life, customs, and arts of the native peoples of the world." Quoting the chief of that department, Ralph writes that native Americans will appear as "a living picture . . . each family to be living in its native habitation; the people to be dressed in native costume, surrounded by characteristic household utensils, implements, and weapons, and engaged in their native occupations and manufactures": not exactly a Wild West show, but nevertheless a spectacle of the "savage" in a lower state of progress. Prominent blacks organized an independent "Jubilee" or "Colored People's Day," at which the distinguished Frederick Douglass renamed White City "a whited sepulcher." Former slave, author, and statesman, Douglass attended the Fair as commissioner from Haiti—not as citizen of his own country. In his speech at the "Jubilee" he clarified one of the lessons of the distinctions incorporated into the Fair's spatial scheme, the contrasts between the Court of Honor and the Old World customs

and folkways, the African, Asian, and Islamic people sprawling
in their costumes along the Midway Plaisance: "As if to shame
the Negro, the Dahomians are here to exhibit the Negro as a
repulsive savage." Yet a significant portion of the civilization
celebrated in White City, Douglass pointed out, represented the
labor of black Americans.

Images implied and stated of blacks and Indians served the
total pedagogy. No social image served more significantly, however, than that of women. This was the moment, as the Fair
proclaimed, when women (like artists) came into their own. By
the initiating Act of Congress, a Board of Lady Managers served
alongside the World's Columbian Commission. A separate department both of exhibition and of the World's Congress, the
world of women furthermore possessed a building of its own: a
building, moreover, designed by a female architect (the only
American building whose design was open to competition), decorated, arranged, and furnished entirely by women. At the Congress, more than three hundred women read papers on a variety
of topics concerning the history and social position of their gender: Elizabeth Cady Stanton on suffrage, Susan B. Anthony on
politics, Jane Addams on housework and factory work. Cham-
pions of women's political rights and of radical reform were
accorded places at the Congress, as indeed were advocates of
single-tax and public ownership at other sessions. But they did
not appear among the more socially proper figures of the Lady
Managers, nor did militant notes ring prominently in the exhibitions. Instead, the prevailing note was domesticity, the unique,
and uniquely virtuous, powers of women as mothers, homemak-
ers, teachers, and cooks.

The very prominence of women at the Fair heightened the
ambiguities in their conceived role. The Women's Building, designed by Sophia Hayden in a harmonious neoclassical style,
struck the artist Candace Wheeler favorably as "the most peacefully human of all the buildings . . . like a man's ideal of woman
—delicate, dignified, pure, and fair to look upon." Adorned with
murals representing "The Primitive Woman" (by Mary Mac-
Monnies) and "Modern Woman" (by Mary Cassatt)—the one
welcoming her man home from the hunt, the other engaged in
happy pursuits of art, of music and dance—the building occupied
the significant site of the exact junction between the Court of

Honor and the Midway Plaisance, just at the point of transition from the official view of reality to the world of exotic amusement, of pleasure. Housing exhibits of domestic labor, virtue, and order —exhibits of the ordering hand of women—the building represented the conceptual opposite, the most pointed moral contrast, to the excitements of the Midway. Similarly, the dominating sixty-foot statue by Daniel Chester French of a female figure representing the Republic presiding over the Court of Honor taught the populace what to make of the Midway's own "World's Congress of Beauties," a parade of belly dancers and "Forty Ladies from Forty Countries."

Labor, too, was represented, but in a manner finally not entirely pleasing to Eugene Debs. Praising the Fair for its educational value, Debs echoed Frederick Douglass in his reversal of the hierarchical placement of labor and culture: "The Fair, after all, was the sublimest testimony the world has ever heard or seen, in all the centuries of the civilizing, elevating, liberalizing force of labor. Everywhere, from the turnstiles through which the millions passed to review the wonders of the Fair—over all, above all, surrounding all, the imagination, without an effort, could see written, as vivid as electric light, the announcement that the Columbian Fair is monumental of the achievements of labor." How clearly this lesson was in fact written in the fantastic sky of the Fair is hard to tell, but certainly the architects of the Court did their best to conceal the message. Debs's meaning, however, lay at a deeper level than the merely tangible signs of human labor in physical constructions; it lay in a theory of political economy denied implicitly throughout the structures of the Fair, its organizing and controlling corporation, and its design: "We are quite willing to admit the alliance between money and labor in the accomplishments of great undertakings, but this must be said, because it is true that the greater credit is due to labor, because it is the creator of the capital with which, where justice holds the scales, it is in ceaseless harmony."

But where in fact did justice hold the scales? Within the year, Debs was indicted and jailed for refusing to obey a federal injunction against the boycott by the American Railway Union of the major railroad lines. Called in support of a bitter strike by members of ARU against the Pullman Palace Car Company, the sympathy boycott led to the firing of participating workers, and the halting of rail traffic across the land. President Cleveland had issued an injunction on the pretext of protecting the flow of mail, and over the protests of Governor Altgeld of Illinois, ordered troops to restore order. Anger and bitterness—at the successive wage cuts at Pullman, the intervention of the government on the side of the railroad companies—brought Chicago to near hysteria in June and July of 1894, just one year after the wonders of the Fair. Incited by fear of wider class conflict and conflagration, community support of the strikers began to wane, the boycott lost its strength, the Pullman workers their strike, and the American Railway Union sank to defeat. After serving his six months' sentence in 1895, Debs left jail a socialist, arguing now for government ownership of capital as the only solution to the social crisis, the only way to restore justice to labor, its rights in the wealth it produces.

The Pullman strike, its burning railroad cars, and the path of ugly violence it traced through Chicago, seems the most dramatic external instance of history playing tricks on the White City. What starker contradiction than the strike and the themes of the Fair? But the relation of events lay even deeper. The model industrial town of Pullman and White City articulated quite similar intentions. Pullman, too, arose from a design, a planned community conceived by a single architect, S. S. Beman (responsible for the Mines and Mining building at the Fair), who designed the factories and homes and supervised construction. The aim was to create an environment conducive to steady work, good morals, and industrial peace. The community had attracted world attention as an experiment in industrial relations, and in 1885 the economist Richard T. Ely visited the town to see for himself whether Pullman succeeded "from a social standpoint." A liberal reformer sympathetic to socialism, Ely reported his findings in an article in *Harper's New Monthly Magazine*. Did Pullman fulfill the ideal of helping each individual "to participate as fully as his nature will allow, in the advantages of the existing civilization?" The report was mixed.

The first impression of the town gave Ely a striking contrast with the typical "Coketown" image of industrial centers: "Not a dilapidated doorstep nor a broken window." The streets were in perfect condition, with young, promising shade trees. The

223

prospect pleased the eye. "Unity of design and an unexpected variety charm us as we saunter through the town." Green lawns and a pleasant diversity of style lent the dwellings of workers an unexpected look. "French roofs, square roofs, dormer-windows, turrets, sharp points, blunt points, triangles, irregular quadrangles, are devices resorted to in the upper stories to avoid the appearance of unbroken uniformity." Everything about the architecture is praiseworthy and desirable. Moreover, the town provides a public square, an "Arcade and Market-house"—and an elegantly furnished library "with Wilton carpets and plush-covered chairs." "It is avowedly part of the design of Pullman to surround laborers as far as possible with all the privileges of large wealth," writes Ely, wondering what the "ordinary artisan, unaccustomed in his own home to such extravagance," must think of this. But Mr. Pullman believes in "the commercial value of beauty," as his world-renowned sleeping cars indicate. He intends his town to be at once a "philanthropic undertaking" and "a profitable investment," and this conjunction of ends gives Ely his theme. Does it really pay, in all senses, to "provide beautiful homes for laborers, accompanied with all the conditions requisite for wholesome living both for the body and the mind?"

The Pullman venture preceded White City. It applied culture to "the social problem," as a calculated "investment" for the sake of obedience and acquiescence. But aestheticism of the sort represented by the design of the town, Ely implies, is alien to the daily lives, and especially to the work experience of Pullman's employees. The very aim to "elevate" laborers carries troublesome paternalistic overtones. In fact, looking more closely at the social order of the town, Ely discovers that "the citizen is surrounded by constant restraint and restriction and everything is done for him, nothing by him." "It is benevolent, well-wishing feudalism, which desires the happiness of the people, but in such way as shall please the authorities." He finds "an all-pervading feeling of insecurity. Nobody regards Pullman as a real home." Has culture forged "new bonds of dependence?" "There is repression here as elsewhere of any marked individuality," Ely concludes, and adds a chilling prophetic image: "Everything tends to stamp upon residents, as upon the town, the character expressed in 'machine-made.' "

In a pamphlet prepared by the Pullman Company for visitors

224

to the White City, the unnamed writer explains that Pullman is "a town . . . where all that is ugly, and discordant and demoralizing, is eliminated, and all that inspires to self-respect, to thrift and to cleanliness of thought is generously provided." George Pullman was a member of the executive committee of the Chicago Company, subscribed $100,000 to the corporation, and mounted an impressive display in the Transportation Building designed by Louis Sullivan: not only two tracks of Pullman cars, but, just inside Sullivan's "golden door," a plaster replica of the town. The town and the Fair replicate each other in illuminating ways, and the events of the year after the dismantling of the Fair also dismantled the notion that in culture alone resides a power to enforce obedience, to teach acquiescence and consent. In the end, it took armed federal troops to rescue Pullman from the failure of its ideal.

III

And what of Sullivan's doorway, often praised as the only original creation of the architecture of the Fair? In his *Autobiography of an Idea* (1924) the aged pioneer of modern building and prophet of democracy vented his ire against White City: "an appalling calamity," causing at least fifty years of damage to American architecture. It was "an imposition of the spurious . . . a naked exhibition of charlantry in the higher feudal and domineering culture." Its idea of culture was a "virus," "snobbish and alien to the land." Under different circumstances, "there might have arisen a gorgeous Garden City, reflex of one mind, truly interpreting the aspirations and the heart's desire of the many, every detail carefully considered, every function given its due form, with the sense of humanity at its best, a suffusing atmosphere: and within the Garden City might be built another city to remain and endure as a memorial within the parkland by the blue waters, oriented toward the rising sun, a token of a covenant of things to be, a symbol of the city's basic significance as offspring of the prairie, the lake and the portage." Sullivan's reproach to the Fair rests on an alternative vision, owing much to Whitman's call for a culture of democracy.

What sort of alternative did Sullivan's "golden doorway" represent, the portal which opened upon Pullman's exhibit, and hundreds of others, including several impressive cannon and guns and rifles from the Gun and Armor Works of the Bethlehem Iron Company? It was clearly out of keeping with the classicism of the Court, though still a recognizable classical form, a Roman arch cut into a wall. The rounded arch recedes in smaller concentric arches, much decorated with Sullivan's unique floral ornamentation, and covered with bright gold leaf. Was it an expression of a wheel, of a basic element of transportation? Or of unity? Or simply of a doorway into a hall of mechanical wonders? Some jaundiced observers took the "golden doorway" as "a symbol of the Gilded Age itself"; H. C. Bunner remarked in *Scribner's* that it "does the completest justice to the Pullman car end of our civilization." The comment touches the heart of Sullivan's dilemma: is a serious architecture of celebration possible in a society whose functions have become corporate business, "capitalistic," as Adams wrote, rather than "simply industrial?"

In the retrospect of *An Autobiography of an Idea*, White City precipitated Sullivan's dilemma of vocation. It was, in his eyes, a dilemma of culture itself, a shift in the direction of American architecture away from the path he and Root, following the lead of H. H. Richardson (who had died in 1886), had wished to take. Sullivan understood that original direction as toward a native organic architecture, a kind of building which, being both native and organic, would represent the highest responsibility of the architect: as he put it in *Kindergarten Chats* (published in 1918, though written in 1901), "to initiate such buildings as shall correspond to the real needs of the people." Democracy, the people, democratic culture: these terms fall throughout Sullivan's copious writings (all the more copious as his active career declined). In an early lecture of 1885, Sullivan had called for a native expression in architecture, a "national style" answering to "the wishes of the public, and ministering to its conceptions of the beautiful and the useful." Such a style would be organic in the sense of representing both the social function of the building (as the golden door *represents* a portal) and the structural purposes of the parts of the building, especially those parts normally consigned by architects to their engineers. In the concept "form follows function," Sullivan vested his ambitions for an architecture true to its place, its purpose, and the needs of its public. Such buildings would not be mere scaffoldings for pictures of ancient buildings, clusters of stylistic allusions to traditions irrelevant to America. Their ornamentation, for example, would not be "stuck on" but would flow organically (and, in the case of his own original language of ornaments, would draw upon floral forms) from the artist's feeling for his work. "A building which is truly a work of art," he wrote in *Engineering Magazine* (August 1892), "is in its nature, essence and physical being an emotional expression . . . it must have, almost literally, life." Both "mass-composition" and ornamentation must "spring from the same source of feeling." Such buildings, replacing the "feudal and hence now artificial system of thinking and feeling" being foisted on Americans, would contribute to the making of "Democratic-Culture." Indeed, "America is the only land in the whole earth," he wrote in 1901, "wherein a dream like this may be realized; for here alone tradition is without shackles, and the soul of man free to grow, to mature, to seek its own."

In an essay on the Fair, the noted architectural critic Montgomery Schuyler quoted Burnham as saying: "The intellectual reflex of the Exposition will be shown in a demand for better architecture, and designers will be obliged to abandon their incoherent originalities and study the ancient masters of buildings." The remark has been interpreted as a rebuke to the followers of Richardson, and to Sullivan especially for the exuberance of his tall buildings, the Wainwright and Guaranty buildings, and the massive Chicago Auditorium with its richly ornamented interior and its high, elegant tower (all of these, together with the Transportation Building, executed by Sullivan in partnership with Dankmar Adler). But the issue between Sullivan and Burnham (fought out in Sullivan's monologue of 1924) was more than a difference over style, between Richardson's mode of Romanesque in brick and masonry and the academic neoclassicism Burnham came to champion during and after the Fair. The deeper issues concerned both the character and the social function of public buildings, their role as pedagogies of culture. Burnham's views would capture the day, and in the City Beautiful movement of the next twenty years (after 1893) would leave their mark in public structures and spaces, in park systems and boulevards, throughout the nation. Though finding a fulfillment in the career of Frank Lloyd Wright, Sullivan's views in 1893 would suffer a defeat, not unlike and in some ways strikingly similar to

227

that of Populism. For architect and embattled farmer alike evoked as their final authority the name of "the people."

In Sullivan's voice, however, like Whitman's, the name rang more with an abstract hope than with any specific experience of closeness with a public his buildings served. Writing most rapturously about the form in which he achieved his greatest triumphs, the skyscraper, Sullivan betrays a failure to reckon with new social realities, the very realities which Burnham seemed much better to understand and to serve. In "The Tall Office Building Artistically Considered" (1896), Sullivan speaks of "social conditions" which have resulted "in a demand for the erection of tall buildings." What these conditions are he claims it is not his purpose to discuss: "I accept them as the fact." Instead, he turns to the technical conditions, the physical problems posed by the tall building. His account of the problems and of the organic (or functional) principles for their solution is as eloquent as were his actual solutions of the 1890's. But it is clear that while he refuses to discuss the social meaning of the tall office building, he does conceive of the form as an expression of individual power: materialistic, to be sure, but capable of transformation through art into a spiritual expression—an expression, moreover (in his words), "of the people, by the people, and for the people." A physical problem of technics, the tall building is also an opportunity to express an emotion. The emotional power of the skyscraper lies in its sheer height, its loftiness. "This loftiness is to the artist-nature its thrilling aspect. It is the very open organtone of its appeal. It must be in turn the dominant chord of his expression of it, the true excitant of his imagination." Obeying that impulse to celebrate height and aspiration, the artist will create "a living form of speech, a natural form of utterance . . . an architecture that will soon become a fine art in the true, the best sense of the word, an art that will live because it will be of the people, for the people, and by the people."

It is hard to imagine words, in 1896, more deeply out of touch with the new corporate world of merging trusts and monopolies, of concentrated political power, than these elegant but sad cries of belief. Sullivan wished to celebrate business enterprise as heroic activity: a notion inherited from an earlier age of laissez-faire, of epic individual efforts. Richardson had seemed to show the way in his sole commercial building, the great Marshall Field

Wholesale Store in Chicago (now demolished) of 1885, about which Sullivan wrote: "Four-square and brown, it stands, in physical fact a monument to trade, to the organized commercial spirit, to the power and progress of the age, to the strength and resource of individuality and force of character." Richardson's use of Romanesque forms not as ornamentation but as forms expressing the inner structure of the building, and especially the properties of his materials, his granites and brown stones, seemed to suggest a direction: not toward a specific style but toward expressive design. By the 1890's, Richardson's exclusive use of masonry walls had become outmoded by the use of steel frameworks. Sullivan persisted in the spirit of Richardson, designing his buildings from the inside out, as celebrations of what he believed remained the organic relation of business enterprise to the life of "the people." All deviations from such a high sacral calling aroused his raging condemnation. "Such structures are *profoundly anti-social,*" he howled about an academically designed New York skyscraper in 1901. With their "growl of a glutton for the Dollar," they "are undermining American life." Thus did the imitative architecture desired by corporate clients eventually clarify for Sullivan the character of those "social conditions" crying for the erection of towers.

His golden door may well have seemed an ironic touch on the imperial façades of White City, but the hint remained ambiguous; a clearer set of implications about the meaning of the Court, as events of the following summer would disclose, lay just through Sullivan's portal, in the model of Pullman. Montgomery Schuyler, admirer and articulate expounder of the Chicago School, cast his own ironical and judicious eye on the same glittering scene, and reached closer to the heart of White City, to the secret of its spectacle. Schuyler attributed the "success" of "the cloud-capped towers and the gorgeous palaces" to three specific elements of design: unity, magnitude, and illusion. The three terms name the very devices of imperial spectacle. Unity comes from the classical forms which, having "lost touch with their origin, become *simply forms* [my emphasis], which can be used without a suggestion of any real structure or any particular material." Insubstantiality, then, is the very essence of White City unity: forms without substance. And, in place of substance, magnitude, "inordinate dimensions" distracting from the empty gestures of façades: "the magnitude of the buildings was everywhere forced upon the sense." As for illusion, even "a casual glance" reveals that these are "examples not of work-a-day building, but of holiday building, that the purpose of their erection is festal and temporary." This is precisely the point. The illusion reveals itself as illusion, "a triumph of occasional architecture." That very fact, the ephemerality of the show, made White City all the more *ideal:* the momentary realization of a dream. "They have realized in plaster that gives us the illusion of monumental masonry," Schuyler concludes, "a painter's dream of Roman architecture."

IV

The imperial implications of that Roman dream would soon materialize in more brutal forms, in the Cuban and Philippine invasions of 1898, in McKinley's "Open Door" to incorporation beyond these shores. The "whole present tendency of American life is centrifugal," noted Howells at the end of the century, but "I do not attempt to say how it will be when, in order to spread ourselves over the earth, and convincingly to preach the blessings of our deeply incorporated civilization by the mouths of our eight-inch guns, the mind of the nation shall be politically centred at some capital." Preoccupied with Altruria at the time, Howells did not seem to notice that White City had already anticipated such a central capital for the "mind of the nation." For a summer's moment, White City had seemed the fruition of a nation, a culture, a whole society: the celestial city of man set upon a hill for all the world to behold. It seemed the triumph of America itself, the old republican ideal. But dressed now in empty Roman orders, that ideal had taken on another look and signified another meaning: the alliance and incorporation of business, politics, industry, and culture. The spectacle proclaimed order, unity, coherence—and mutuality now in the form of hierarchy. White City manifested the conversion of the old ideal, its transvaluation into not a communal but a corporate enterprise. Business and politics provided the structure, the legitimacy of power, the chain of command. Industrial technology provided the physical power, forces of nature mastered and chained to human will, typified by tens of thousands of electric bulbs controlled by a single switch. And culture served as the presiding genius, orchestrating design and style, coordinating effort. Illumination, clarity of design, a perfectly comprehensible ground plan dividing the Fair into distinct regions—all such signs of lucidity seemed to proclaim mystery overcome by an artfully composed reality: a reality composed, that is, in the mode of theatrical display, of *spectacle.* White City seemed to make everything clear, everything available. This indeed had been the prime function of industrial expositions in the nineteenth century, to display the fruits of production as universal culture, to construct of the performances of economy a modern spectacle. Moreover, in choosing neoclassicism as its dominant style, White City made obvious allusion to European Baroque, to the monumental neoclassicism of capital cities in which radial avenues, open plazas, and façades of columns signified royal power, the authority of the state on display.

White City implied not only a new form of urban experience but a new way of experiencing the urban world: spectacle. Visitors to the Fair found themselves as *spectators,* witnesses to an unanswerable performance which they had no hand in producing or maintaining. The Fair was delivered to them, made available to them. And delivered, moreover, not as an actual place, a real city, but as a frank illusion, a picture of what a city, a real society, might look like. White City represented itself *as* a representation, an admitted sham. Yet that sham, it insisted, held a truer vision of the real than did the troubled world sprawling beyond its gates.

In sum, White City seemed to have settled the question of the true and real meaning of America. It seemed the victory of elites in business, politics, and culture over dissident but divided voices of labor, farmers, immigrants, blacks and women. Elite culture installed itself as official doctrine of the Court, claiming dominion over the "low" confined to the outskirts of the Midway. In retrospect, the Fair has seemed not only a culmination of the efforts of ruling groups since the Civil War to win hegemony over the emerging national culture but a prophetic symbol of the coming defeat of Populism and its alternative culture, the alternative "America" it proposed. White City expressed the very outlook later manifested by McKinley and the Republican banner of "peace, prosperity, progress and patriotism," as well as the overseas crusades to spread the blessings of "our deeply incorporated civilization." The power to say what was real, what was America, seemed now safely in the hands of property, wealth, and "the word Culture."

But the ragged edges of 1894 implied that even in defeat advocates of "union" over "corporation" retained their vision, their voice, and enough power to unsettle the image of a peaceful corporate order. At stake in the sympathy boycott of the American Railway Union was more than a legal right, but a way of life and a world view. Arguing before the Supreme Court in October 1894, in defense of Eugene Debs, who had been speedily convicted of violating a federal injunction against the boycott, Clarence Darrow presented the legal issue in the light of a broader defense of the right of workingmen to associate in the first place. It makes no difference whether the members of the American Railway Union were themselves personally at odds with the Pullman Company, he argued. "They doubtless believed that their fellow laborers were unjustly treated, and did not desire to handle the cars of a corporation that was unjustly treating their brothers who were engaged in a struggle with this company." It was the very right to consider each other "brothers" that Darrow insisted upon. "The right to cease labor for the benefit of their fellows" lay at the heart of labor unions. "If no man could strike except he were personally aggrieved, there could be no strike of a combination of workingmen," he explained. For "the theory on which all labor organizations are based is that workingmen have a common interest, and that 'an injury to one is the concern of all.' " "Mutual aid" is "the very object of combination and association." To deny this principle, which indeed the court would do in denying Darrow's plea, "would leave each individual worker completely isolated and unaided to fight his battle alone against the combined capital everywhere vigilant and aggressive, to add to its own profit by reducing the wages and conditions of those who work."

The crux of Darrow's losing argument lay in his joining this familiar notion of mutuality with a developing concept of collective rights which lay "beyond equality." He put the issue pointedly. "Politically and theoretically the laborer is now a freeman, the equal of the employer, the equal of the lawyer or the judge.

But freedom does not consist alone in political rights, or in theories of government, or in theories as to man's relations with the state." Effective freedom lay in the right of workers to combine and act in union, in solidarity. "The present system of industry" makes this larger freedom essential, for "so long as steam and electricity are applied to machines in any such manner as at present," and "hundreds and thousands of men must work for single employers," "great masses of men working together to a common end, and subject to regulations from a common head" must enjoy the right of collective action for mutual aid. Political economy itself raised the old mutuality to a new, more radical condition: the need for solidarity among an entire class of people. It was this need which welled up out of Pullman and spread along the railroad network across the land, as it had more spontaneously in 1877. The need arose from conditions, Darrow argued, which lay at the base of industrial life. It also arose from motives, principles, beliefs—from an entire culture—at sharp odds with the implied obedience and deference, the ethos of incorporation celebrated at Pullman and at White City. "No doubt it is difficult for some people to understand a motive sufficiently high," he concluded, "to cause men to lay down their employment not to serve themselves but to help some one else. But until this is understood, the teachings of religionists and moralists will have been in vain."

Darrow spoke out of the accumulated experience of labor, of workers and farmers in the age of incorporation, evoking the spirit of the Knights of Labor as well as the Farmers' Alliance. He spoke in a losing cause before the highest court in 1894, describing a vision of a new political concept arising from a culture of common need. In more figurative language, Eugene Debs invoked that same vision in images sharply at odds with the culture of Pullman and White City. Pausing for a moment to reflect on the events of 1894 while still in their midst, Debs wrote, in "Labor Strikes and Their Lessons" (published by John Swinton in his 1894 volume on the Pullman strike): "on one hand, a great corporation, rich to plethora, rioting in luxuries, plutocratic, proud, and powerful." And on the other, "not a picture of houses and lands, lawns and landscape, 'sacred grass,' violets and rose-trees, sparkling fountains and singing birds. and an

233

atmosphere burdened with the aroma of flowers, but of human beings living amidst such surroundings and toiling for a pittance doled out to them by their employers—as a Heber might say: 'Where every prospect pleases,' and only man is wretched." "Every honest patriotic American" should understand the need to resist such "brazen heartlessness." Indeed, the "great lesson" of the strike at Pullman is "that it arouses wide-spread sympathy." Debs continued:

This fellowship for the woes of others—this desire to help the unfortunate; this exhibition of a divine principle, which makes the declaration plausible that "man was made a little lower than God," and without which man would rank lower than the devil by several degrees—should be accepted as at once the hope of civilization and the supreme glory of manhood. And yet this exhibition of sympathy aroused by the Pullman strike is harped upon by press and pulpit as the one atrocious feature of the strike. Epithets, calumny, denunciation in every form that malice or mendacity could invent have been poured forth in a vitriol tide to scathe those who advocated and practised the Christ-like virtue of sympathy The crime of the American Railway Union was the practical exhibition of sympathy for the Pullman employees.

Thus did the events of 1894 reveal to Debs and Darrow not only corporations (and the state) pitted against striking workers, but a clash of cultures: the pleasing prospect against the bonds of sympathy, of solidarity.

That tension would persist in America, submerged in periods of prosperity and wartime nationalism, only to reappear at moments of stress and crisis: the Depression of the 1930's, the agitations of the 1960's and 1970's. To be sure, since World War II a larger number of workers have shared in the abundance of an incorporated America and have seemed to accept its cultural premises. A wider diffusion of comfort and the goods of culture (as well as education) seems to have overshadowed the vista of a solidarity grounded not in consumption but in equality, the dignity of labor, and the sympathy of common need. Yet it seems evident, almost a hundred years since White City and its aftermath at Pullman, that the question remains unresolved. In the conflict of perspectives disclosed in Chicago in 1893–94 lay one of the deepest and most abiding issues accompanying the incorporation of America.

REVISED AND EXPANDED
BIBLIOGRAPHICAL ESSAY

This revised and expanded bibliographical essay keeps intact the original bibliography while adding to each section brief and selective accounts of important scholarship since 1982. Additional bibliographical references are available in the cited readings.

GENERAL WORKS

Scholars have produced a spate of works on Gilded Age economic growth, politics, immigration and labor, cities, towns and farms, but relatively few efforts at interpretive synthesis. Robert H. Wiebe, *The Search for Order, 1877–1920* (New York, 1967) remains the most prominent work of synthesis: a challenging argument that Americans experienced a loss of bearings as their society of "island communities" began to break up after the Civil War. More concerned with emerging patterns of popular life, Daniel Boorstin focuses on the "democratizing" influences of new technologies and institutions in *The Americans: The Democratic Experience* (New York, 1973), which also contains bibliographical notes indispensable for a cultural history of the period. H. Wayne Morgan's volume in the Pelican History of the United States (Vol. 4), *Unity and Culture: The United States 1877–1900* (Middlesex, England, 1971), is a useful brief survey of developments in industry, politics, culture, and diplomacy. Lewis Mumford's *Brown Decades: A Study of the Arts of America 1865–1895* (New York, 1931) remains unsurpassed as an interpretation of styles and currents in architecture, city design, painting, literature, and philosophy. Howard Mumford Jones provides an invaluable panorama of the era in *The Age of Energy: Varieties of American Experience 1865–1915* (New York, 1971). Two valuable collections of contemporary documents, with interpretative introductions, are Alan Trachtenberg, ed., *Democratic Vistas 1865–1880* (New York, 1970) and Neil Harris, ed., *The Land of Contrasts 1880–1901* (New York, 1970). For a basic history of the period, W. R. Brock's essay on the United States in Vol. XI of *The New Cambridge Modern History: Material Progress and World-Wide Problems 1870–1898* (Cambridge, England, 1962) is an excellent introduction. Still the most useful general treatment of industrialization and its social effects is Thomas C. Cochran and William Miller, *The Age of Enterprise* (rev. ed., New York, 1961). For a lucid survey of the economic history of the era, see Stuart Bruchey, *Growth of the Modern American Economy* (New York, 1975). The relevant chapters of William Appleman Williams, *The Contours of American History* (Cleveland, 1961) and Gabriel Kolko, *Main Currents in Modern American History* (New York, 1976) should be consulted for important discussions of the relations among economic interest, politics, and ideology. Valuable essays by major scholars on business, politics, labor, and culture are included in H. Wayne Morgan, ed., *The Gilded Age: A Reappraisal* (Syracuse, 1970). Robert Higgs, *The Transformation of the American Economy, 1865–1914* (New York, 1971) is also useful and illuminating for the nonspecialist. Large economic patterns and their social, political, and cultural ramifications are treated in Carl Degler's excellent brief introduction, *The Age of the Economic Revolution 1876–1900* (Glenview, Illinois, 1967).

For a world perspective on the developments in the United States in the early part of this period, see E. J. Hobsbawm, *The Age of Capital 1848–1875* (New York, 1975). Karl Polanyi, *The Great Transformation: The Political and Economic Origins of Our Time* (New York, 1944) is an essential work on the emergence of a marketplace economy and its effects upon nineteenth-century European thought.

While the Gilded Age remains an important field for scholarly research, there have been few efforts at new interpretative syntheses of the period as a whole. Not focused exclusively on the Gilded Age, James Livingston's *Pragmatism and the Political Economy of Cultural Revolution, 1850–1940* (Chapel Hill, 1997) proposes the strongest recent reinterpretation of the shift from proprietary to corporate capitalism. An original and subtle work that draws as much on literature (Whitman and Dreiser) and philosophy (William James and John Dewey) as on political economy, it proposes that this radical shift in the late nineteenth century opened fresh possibilities for personal liberation and social change. See also Livingston's "The Social Analysis of Economic History and Theory: Conjectures on Late Nineteenth-Century American Development," *The American Historical Review* (February 1987), 69–95. Scott R. Bowman, *The Modern Corporation and American Political Thought: Law,*

Power, and Ideology (University Park, Pennsylvania, 1996), which focuses on economic and political power as the key elements in the regime of the large corporation, is especially valuable for its discussion of the legal fiction of the corporation as a single person and of "corporate liberalism." This term was first used by Martin Sklar, to whom Livingston and Bowman and all students of the corporate order are indebted. See Sklar, *The Corporate Reconstruction of American Capitalism, 1890–1916* (New York, 1988) and *The United States as a Developing Country: Studies in U.S. History in the Progressive Era and the 1920s* (New York, 1992). One of Sklar's cardinal insights is that incorporation has resulted in a "mix" of capitalism and socialism; it thus foretells a democratic alternative to unmitigated capitalism.

For more general works in Gilded Age studies, see Joshua Brown's valuable visual history, *Beyond the Lines: Pictorial Reporting, Everyday Life, and the Crisis of Gilded-Age America* (Berkeley, 2002). See also Lewis O. Saum, *The Popular Mood of America, 1860–1890* (Lincoln, Nebraska, 1990); George Cotkin, *Reluctant Modernism: American Thought and Culture, 1880–1900* (New York, 1992); Louis L. Stevenson, *The Victorian Homefront: American Thought and Culture, 1860–1880* (Ithaca, New York, 2001); Rebecca Edwards, *New Spirits: Americans in the Gilded Age, 1865–1905* (New York, 2006); and Thomas Schlereth, *Victorian America: Transformations in Everyday Life, 1875–1915* (New York, 1991).

On the occasion of its twentieth anniversary in 2002, *The Incorporation of America* was the subject of a panel at the annual meeting of the Modern Language Association. Papers from that panel, published together in 2003, in many ways comprise a succinct summary of twenty-five years of discussion, particularly in American literary and cultural studies. See *American Literary History* 15, no. 4, "Forum on Alan Trachtenberg's *The Incorporation of America*," Brook Thomas, "Culture, Society, and *The Incorporation of America*," David Leverenz, "Trachtenberg, Haskell, & Livingston, Inc.," James Livingston, "Incorporation and the Disciplines," David R. Shumway, "Incorporation and the Myths of American Culture," Alan Trachtenberg, "*The Incorporation of America* Today."

1. THE WESTWARD ROUTE

A continuing subject of controversy, Frederick Jackson Turner's "Frontier Thesis" has provided the single most important view of the West in American historiography. In *Turner and Beard: American Historical Writing Reconsidered* (New York, 1960), especially Part II, "The Historical Background of Turner's Frontier Essay," Lee Benson views the thesis in the intellectual and social setting of the late nineteenth century, stressing the importance of changes in transportation and communication on Turner's conception of the frontier. Richard Hofstadter, *The Progressive Historians: Turner, Beard, Parrington* (New York, 1968) also places Turner in relation to the intellectual climate of his times and examines his influence on historiography. The most influential discussion of Turner as mythmaker and of the West as a whole as a cultural symbol has been Henry Nash Smith, *Virgin Land: The American West as Symbol and Myth* (Cambridge, 1950). For general narrative accounts of the Western movement, see R. A. Billington, *Westward Expansion* (4th ed., New York, 1974) and Richard A. Bartlett, *The New Country: A Social History of the American Frontier 1776–1890* (New York, 1974). The authoritative account of the influence of terrain and climate upon settlement is W. P. Webb, *The Great Plains* (New York, 1931). For a comprehensive discussion of government and railroad surveys and expeditions, and the role of the military in these undertakings, see William H. Goetzmann, *Exploration and Empire: The Explorer and the Scientist in the Winning of the American West* (New York, 1966). The politics and cultural multiplicity of the Southwestern Territories receive definitive treatment in Howard R. Lamar, *The Far Southwest, 1846–1912: A Territorial History* (New Haven, 1966). For more particular aspects of regional settlement and enterprise, see F. A. Shannon, *The Farmer's Last Frontier 1860–1897* (New York, 1945); E. S. Osgood, *The Days of the Cattleman* (Minneapolis, 1929); Lewis Atherton, *The Cattle Kings* (Bloomington, 1961); Eugene Gressley, *Bankers and Cattlemen* (New York, 1966); and W. S. Greever, *The Bonanza West: The Story of the Western Mining Rushes 1848–1900* (Norman, Oklahoma, 1963).

An important study of the role of the West in the experience of Eastern intellectuals is G. Edward White, *The Eastern Establishment and the Western Experience: The West of Frederick Remington, Theodore Roosevelt, and Owen Wister* (New Haven, 1968). Christopher Lasch's well-known essay, "The Moral and Intellectual Rehabilitation of the Ruling Class," in *The World of Nations* (New York, 1973), is relevant. For the imperial motives within the Western settlement, see Frederick Merk, *Manifest Destiny and Mission in American History: A Reinterpretation* (New York, 1963). Lively and cogent discussion of the evangelical aspects of the rhetoric of the West can be found in E. L. Tuveson, *The Redeemer Nation: The Idea of America's Millennial Role* (Chicago, 1968). Sacvan Bercovitch's original interpretation of the Protestant elements in the idea of America as a whole is developed with clarity and force in *The American Jeremiad* (Madison, 1978).

For a provocative discussion of the cultural meanings of the "Western," see John G. Cawelti, *The Six-Gun Mystique* (Bowling Green, 1975); see also Cawelti's more theoretical discussion of the genres of popular writing, *Adventure, Mystery, and Romance* (Chicago, 1976). On dime-novel Westerns in particular, see Merle Curti, "Dime Novels and the American Tradition," in *Probing Our Past* (New York, 1955); and Dixon Wecter, "The Dime Novel and Buffalo Bill," in *The Hero in America* (New York, 1941). A more general treatment of the figure of the cowboy is William W. Savage Jr., *The Cowboy Hero: His Image in American History and Culture* (Norman, Oklahoma, 1979).

For general histories of the North American Indian, see Paul Radin, *The Story of the American Indian* (rev. ed., New York, 1944); John Collier, *The Indians of America* (New York, 1947); and Jennings C. Wise (ed. and rev. by Vine Deloria Jr.), *The Red Man in the New World Drama: A Politico-Legal Study with a Pageantry of American Indian History* (New York, 1971). Important recent anthropological studies can be found in Eleanor Burke Leacock and Nancy Oestreich Lurie, eds., *North American Indians in Historical Perspective* (New York, 1971). Eleanor Burke Leacock's edition of Lewis Henry Morgan's *Ancient Society* (New York, 1963) provides an invaluable introduction and headnotes. A standard work on the image of the Indian in American cultural history is Roy Harvey Pearce, *Savagism and Civilization: A Study of the Indian and the American Mind* (Baltimore, 1953); an excellent recent treatment of the same theme in a broader historical perspective is Robert F. Berkhofer, *The White Man's Indian: Images of the American Indian from Columbus to the Present* (New York, 1978). The authoritative study of Indian policy in these years is Francis P. Prucha, *American Indian Policy in Crisis: Christian Reformers and the Indian 1865–1900* (Norman, Oklahoma, 1976), and, also by Prucha, the indispensable collections, *Documents of Indian Policy* (Lincoln, Nebraska, 1975) and *Americanizing the American Indian: Writings of the "Friends of the Indian" 1880–1900* (Cambridge, 1973).

The "new" Western history that emerged in the 1980's is marked by a break with the Turner thesis and the "myth" of the frontier as the testing ground of democracy. In its place has emerged an emphasis on the diversity of frontier experience and on frontier settlement as a form of imperial conquest. William Cronon's masterful *Nature's Metropolis: Chicago and the Great West* (New York, 1991) introduces "environmental" or "ecological" history; it stresses the role of natural resources—grain, lumber, meat—in altering the relations between country and city and thus overcoming that strict dichotomy of the older historiography. Patricia Nelson Limerick's *Legacy of Conquest: The Unbroken Past of the American West* (New York, 1987) heralded a new realism about the West. "Conquest" tells a different story from "settlement" and the popular myths of Hollywood Westerns. The new approach to Western history is also strongly represented by Richard White, *A New History of the American West* (Norman, Oklahoma, 1991), and Robert V. Hine and John Mack Faragher,

The American West: A New Interpretive History (New Haven, 2000). Recent re-evaluations of Frederick Jackson Turner and his once-commanding "frontier thesis" can be found in Richard Slotkin, *Fatal Environment: The Myth of the Frontier in the Age of Industrialization, 1800–1890* (New York, 1985); John Mack Faragher, *Rereading Frederick Jackson Turner: "The Significance of the Frontier in American History" and Other Essays*, with commentary by John Mack Faragher (New York, 1994); and James R. Grossman, ed., *The Frontier in American Culture*, an exhibition at the Newberry Library, August 26, 1994–January 7, 1995, with essays by Richard White and Patricia Nelson Limerick (Berkeley, 1994). Convenient collections of essays in the new mode of Western history include William Cronon et al., eds., *Under an Open Sky: Rethinking America's Western Past* (New York, 1992); Patricia Nelson Limerick et al., eds., *Trails: Toward a New Western History* (Lawrence, Kansas, 1991); and Richard White and John M. Findley, eds., *Power and Place in the North American West* (Seattle, 1999). David M. Wrobel, *End of American Exceptionalism: Frontier Anxiety from the Old West to the New Deal* (Lawrence, Kansas, 1993), and Martha A. Sandweiss, *Print the Legend: Photography and the American West* (New Haven, 2002), take up additional facets of ideology and visual culture.

No writer has been more important and effective in presenting a North American Indian perspective on the age of incorporation than Vine Deloria Jr. *American Indians, American Justice* (Austin, 1983) and *The Nations Within: The Past and Future of American Indian Sovereignty* (New York, 1984), both by Deloria and Clifford Lytle, are particularly useful for their detailed historical discussion of legal and moral issues. Brian W. Dippie's *The Vanishing American: White Attitudes and U.S. Indian Policy* (Lawrence, Kansas, 1982) is a major study of popular myths and official policies. Chapters dealing with the link between conquest of native tribes and overseas imperialism make Richard Drinnon's eloquent *Facing West: The Metaphysics of Indian-Hating and Empire-Building* (Norman, Oklahoma, 1990) extremely relevant to the study of Gilded Age incorporation. So too is the superb chapter "Reading the Savage Mind" in Helen Carr's *Inventing the American Primitive: Politics, Gender and the Representation of Native American Literary Tradition, 1789–1936* (New York, 1996). Richard White's incisive studies of the decline of traditional Indian cultures in *Roots of Dependency: Subsistence, Environment, and Social Change among the Choctaws, Pawnees, and Navajos* (Lincoln, Nebraska, 1983) makes a signal contribution.

Two important works on institutional ethnology and American Indians are Curtis M. Hinsley, *The Smithsonian and the American Indian: Making a Moral Anthropology in Victorian America* (Washington, D.C., 1981), and Robert E. Beider, *Science Encounters the Indian, 1820–1880*

(Norman, Oklahoma, 1986). See also Steven Conn's institutional histories, *Museums and American Intellectual Life, 1876–1926* (Chicago, 1999) and *History's Shadow: Native Americans and Historical Consciousness in the Nineteenth Century* (Chicago, 2004). Frederick E. Hoxie's *Final Promise: The Campaign to Assimilate the Indians, 1880–1920* (Lincoln, Nebraska, 1984) is the definitive work on the Dawes Act and the reservation system. See also Hoxie's *Parading Through History: The Making of the Crow Nation in America, 1805–1935* (Lincoln, Nebraska, 1995). Robert M. Utley's epochal *The Lance and the Shield: The Life and Times of Sitting Bull* (New York, 1993) re-creates warrior cultures of the Plains. On the role of government boarding schools in imposing assimilation, see Dona F. Lindsey, *Indians at Hampton Institute, 1877–1923* (Urbana, Illinois, 1995), and David Wallace Adams, *Education for Extinction: American Indians and the Boarding School Experience, 1875–1928* (Lawrence, Kansas, 1995). In *Individuality Incorporated: Indians and the Multicultural Modern* (Durham, North Carolina, 2004), Joel Pfister reconsiders the role of schooling in the assault against traditional communal cultures on behalf of "individuality."

2. MECHANIZATION TAKES COMMAND

On the whole, scholars have concerned themselves more with specific technological innovations than with the cultural effects of technological change. The work from which this chapter takes its title, Siegfried Giedion's *Mechanization Takes Command* (New York, 1948), remains the foremost examination of the impact of mechanical process on human activities and perceptions; although the book is global in its coverage, it draws many of its primary examples from the American experience, especially in regard to the assembly line, the industrialization of agriculture and meat production, the interiors of railroads and households, the mechanization of bathrooms and bathing. Concerned less with actual mechanization than with the place of technology in the cultural imagination (both popular and literary), Leo Marx's *The Machine in the Garden: Technology and the Pastoral Ideal in America* (New York, 1964) maintains that Americans in general have tended to view machines in the light of inherited landscape values: as instruments either of fulfillment or of destruction of the pastoral ideal. Although the book deals chiefly with antebellum writers, its discussions of Mark Twain and Henry Adams are pertinent to these years. For a suggestive study of the role of machinery in European popular culture in the same years, see Dolf Sternberger, *Panorama of the 19th Century* (New York, 1977). For an excellent study of generally favorable responses to the machine, see John Kasson, *Civilizing the Machine: Technology and Republican Values in*

America 1776–1900 (New York, 1976), especially the chapters on machine design and on utopian writings. The changing place of advanced technology in the world's fairs of the period is charted usefully by John Cawelti in "America on Display: The World's Fairs of 1876, 1893, 1933," in Frederic C. Jaher, ed., *The Age of Industrialism in America* (New York, 1968). And for more general responses to industrialization in the later years of the period, see the helpful summary in Samuel P. Hays, *The Response to Industrialism 1885–1914* (Chicago, 1957).

A good place to begin further reading on the processes of mechanization itself, in industrial production and in transportation, is David S. Landes, *The Unbound Prometheus: Technological Change and Industrial Development in Western Europe from 1750 to the Present* (Cambridge, England, 1969), which draws often on American materials. A useful overview can be found in Edward C. Kirkland, *Men, Cities, and Transportation: A Study in New England History 1820–1900* (Cambridge, 1948). Indispensable for its treatment of the role of railroads in fostering industrialization in the earlier period is George R. Taylor, *The Transportation Revolution 1815–1860* (New York, 1951). For a concise account of railroads, the major mechanized industry of the era, see Taylor and Irene D. Neu, *The American Railroad Network* (Cambridge, 1956). In *Railroads and American Economic Growth* (Baltimore, 1964), Robert Fogel challenges the conventional wisdom regarding the exact role of railroads in American economic growth in these years. For a factual account of the introduction of standard time zones, see W. F. Allen, *Short History of Standard Time and Its Adoption in North America in 1883* (New York, 1904). An original discussion of the culture of the railroad in the nineteenth century, with a brilliant chapter on the American experience, is Wolfgang Schivelbusch, *The Railway Journey: Trains and Travel in the 19th Century* (New York, 1979).

An important comparative discussion of the incentives toward technological change is H. J. Habakkuk, *American and British Technology in the Nineteenth Century* (Cambridge, England, 1962). The writings of Nathan Rosenberg on the role of technology in American economic history are original and indispensable. See especially his *Technology and American Economic Growth* (New York, 1972), *Perspectives on Technology* (New York, 1976), especially "Technological Change in the Machine Tool Industry 1840–1910," and his "Technological Interdependence in the American Economy," *Technology and Culture* (1979), 25–49. Useful discussions of the application of electrical power can be found in Richard B. Du Boff, "The Introduction of Electric Power in American Manufacturing," *Economic History Review* (December 1967), 509–18; and Thomas P. Hughes, "The Electrification of America: The System Builders," *Technology and Culture* (1979), 124–61. On Thomas A. Edison, see Matthew Josephson's biography, *Edison* (New York, 1959) and Wyn Wachhorst, *Thomas Alva Edison: An American Myth* (Cambridge, 1981). For a critical study of the role of the engineering profession in shaping corporate capitalism, see David F. Noble, *America by Design: Science, Technology, and the Rise of Corporate Capitalism* (New York, 1977). In his review of Noble's book, Richard Du Boff continues the argument against the notion of a "neutral" technology; see "The 'Bias' of Technology: Corporate Capital and the Engineers, 1880–1930," *Monthly Review* (October 1978), 19–28. For additional essays on the changing role of formal science in industry in these years, see George H. Daniels, ed., *Nineteenth-Century American Science: A Reappraisal* (Evanston, 1972), especially Edwin Layton, "Mirror-Image Twins: The Communities of Science and Technology," and Carroll Pursell, "Science and Industry." Also, Alexandra Oleson and John Vos, eds., *The Organization of Knowledge in Modern America 1860–1920* (Baltimore, 1979), especially John Rae, "The Application of Science to Industry," and Louis Galambos, "The American Economy and the Reorganization of the Sources of Knowledge." On the effects of mechanization under corporate conditions, Harry Braverman's *Labor and Monopoly Capital: The Degradation of Work in the 20th Century* (New York, 1974) is of vital importance.

For discussions of the place of technology within utopian thought and science fiction, see Neil Harris, "Utopian Fiction and Its Discontents," in Richard Bushman et al., eds., *Uprooted Americans: Essays to Honor Oscar Handlin* (Boston, 1979); John L. Thomas, "Utopia for an Urban Age: Henry George, Henry Demarest Lloyd, Edward Bellamy," *Perspectives in American History* (1972); H. Bruce Franklin, *Future Perfect: American Science Fiction of the Nineteenth Century* (New York, 1966); Darko Suvin, *Metamorphoses of Science Fiction: On the Poetics and History of a Literary Genre* (New Haven, 1979).

Walter Licht's *Industrializing America: The Nineteenth Century* (Baltimore, 1995) cannot be surpassed for its description of the main developments of industrialization and its synthesis of the main currents into a brief, readable survey. On the application of industrial technology to the organization of "mass production," see David Hounshell, *From the American System to Mass Production, 1800–1932: The Development of Manufacturing Technology in the United States* (Baltimore, 1984). For an expert collection of cogent essays on the subject, see Steven Tolliday, ed., *The Rise and Fall of Mass Production*, 2 vols. (Northampton, Massachusetts, 1998). Reconsiderations of technological determinism are presented in Merritt Roe Smith and Leo Marx, eds., *Does Technology Drive History? The Dilemma of Technological Determinism* (Cambridge, Massachusetts, 1994). Thomas P. Hughes, *American Genesis: A Century of*

Invention and Technological Enthusiasm (New York, 1989), offers a pertinent history of mechanical invention in the century starting in 1870. One of the most productive scholars in the field of technology studies has been David Nye, whose *America as Second Creation: Technology and Narratives of New Beginnings* (Cambridge, Massachusetts, 2003) is particularly relevant to the themes of this book. In addition, see his *American Technological Sublime* (Cambridge, Massachusetts, 1994), *Electrifying America: Social Meanings of a New Technology, 1880–1940* (Cambridge, Massachusetts, 1990), and *Invented Self: An Anti-Biography from Documents of Thomas A. Edison* (Odense, Denmark, 1983). Another recent study of Thomas Edison, *The Languages of Edison's Light* (Cambridge, Massachusetts, 1999) by Charles Bazerman, is particularly valuable for its rhetorical analyses. Howard P. Segal's *Technological Utopianism in American Culture* (Chicago, 1985) takes another tack in exploring implications of technology for thinking about the future.

For a lively narrative of effects of the railroad on city and country landscapes in the United States, see John Stilgoe, *Metropolitan Corridor: Railroads and the American Scene* (New Haven, 1985). Walter Licht's *Working for the Railroad: The Organization of Work in the Nineteenth Century* (Princeton, 1983), a rich study in social history, explores the effects of the railroad on the organization of work. Steven W. Usselman's *Regulating Railroad Innovation: Business, Technology, and Politics in America, 1849–1920* (New York, 2002) examines in close detail how the complex railroad system emerged through competition, innovation, and political manipulation. Taking another approach to the effect of railroads is Leo Marx and Susan Daly, eds., *The Railroad in American Art: Representations of Technological Change* (Cambridge, Massachusetts, 1988). Elspeth Brown's brilliant *The Corporate Eye: Photography and the Rationalization of American Commercial Culture, 1884–1929* (Baltimore, 2005) offers a path-breaking study of new technologies of photography applied to time-study agendas of incorporation.

3. CAPITAL AND LABOR

The authoritative discussion of the free-labor ideology that guided the Republican Party is Eric Foner, *Free Soil, Free Labor, Free Men: The Ideology of the Republican Party Before the Civil War* (New York, 1970). The changing relations among labor, business, and the Republican Party after the Civil War are subjected to close and searching scrutiny in David Montgomery, *Beyond Equality: Labor and the Radical Republicans 1862–1872* (New York, 1967). C. Vann Woodward, *Reunion and Reaction: The Compromise of 1877 and the End of Reconstruction* (Boston, 1951) is indispensable for its analysis of the link between economic policy and national party politics, especially the role of corporate business-men in resolving the presidential deadlock in 1877. For a broad summary of economic policy and practices, see Edward C. Kirkland, *Industry Comes of Age: Business, Labor and Public Policy 1860–1897* (New York, 1961).

Changes in the popular free-labor doctrine are examined in Daniel T. Rodgers, *The Work Ethic in Industrial America 1850–1920* (Chicago, 1978). See also Irvin G. Wylie, *The Self-Made Man in America* (New York, 1954) and John Cawelti, *Apostles of the Self-Made Man: Changing Concepts of Success in America* (Chicago, 1965); Moses Rischin, ed., *The American Gospel of Success, Individual and Beyond* (Chicago, 1965); Sigmund Diamond, *The Reputation of the American Businessman* (Cambridge, 1955).

For a lively, critical account of the most prominent men of business, see Matthew Josephson, *The Robber Barons: The Great American Capitalists 1861–1901* (New York, 1934). Entrepreneurial historians have questioned Josephson's influential portrait. See Thomas C. Cochran, "The Legend of the Robber Barons," *Explorations in Entrepreneurial History* (May 1949), 1–7; William Miller, ed., *Men in Business* (Cambridge, 1952); John Chamberlain, *The Enterprising Americans: A Business History of the United States* (New York, 1963); L. M. Hacker, *The World of Andrew Carnegie 1865–1901* (Philadelphia, 1967). The relations between old and new wealth are examined in a particular case by Gabriel Kolko in "Brahmins and Business, 1870–1914: A Hypothesis on the Social Basis of Success in American History," in Kurt H. Wolff and Barrington Moore Jr., eds., *The Critical Spirit: Essays in Honor of Herbert Marcuse* (Boston, 1967). For the life and business activities of John D. Rockefeller, see Allan Nevins, *John D. Rockefeller*, 2 vols. (New York, 1940), and Ida M. Tarbell, *The History of the Standard Oil Company* (New York, 1904). Leading ideas held by businessmen are succinctly explored in Edward C. Kirkland, *Dream and Thought in the Business Community 1860–1900* (Ithaca, 1956). The standard study of the "survival of the fittest" theme is Richard Hofstadter, *Social Darwinism in American Thought* (rev. ed., Boston, 1955). See also Sidney Fine, *Laissez Faire and the General Welfare State: A Study of Conflict in American Thought 1865–1901* (Ann Arbor, 1956). For economic thought in general, the definitive study is Joseph Dorfman, *The Economic Mind in American Civilization*, Vol. III (New York, 1949).

On the emergence of corporate forms of business organization, Alfred D. Chandler, *The Visible Hand: The Managerial Revolution in American Business* (Cambridge, 1977) is thorough, incisive, and lucid. Thomas C. Cochran discusses significant changes prior to the Civil War in "Business Organization and the Development of an Industrial Discipline," in

Harold F. Williamson, ed., *The Growth of the American Economy* (New York, 1944). A clear and useful account of the financial situation after the Civil War, pertinent to incorporation, can be found in Sidney Ratner, James H. Sollow, and Richard Sylla, *The Evolution of the American Economy: Growth, Welfare, and Decision-Making* (New York, 1979), especially chap. 15, "The Financial System under Stress." For a very helpful general essay on incorporation, see Edward S. Mason, "Corporation," in *International Encyclopedia of the Social Sciences* (New York, 1968). For background essential to this period, see Oscar Handlin and Mary F. Handlin, "Origins of the American Business Corporation," *Journal of Economic History* (1945), 1–23. George Heberton Evans Jr., *Business Incorporations in the United States 1800–1943* (National Bureau of Economic Research, 1948) provides basic statistical information. An excellent, rather theoretical review of the legal and political status of corporations is James Willard Hurst, *The Legitimacy of the Business Corporation in the Law of the United States 1780–1970* (Charlottesville, 1970).

For a succinct and pithy narrative of labor in these years, see David Montgomery, "Labor in the Industrial Era," in Richard B. Morris, ed., *U.S. Department of Labor History of the American Worker* (Washington, D.C., 1976). A suggestive overview of the character of class conflict in these years is provided by Leon Fink in "Class Conflict in the Gilded Age: The Figure and the Phantom," *Radical History Review* (Fall/Winter 1975), 56–73. Although dated, Norman Ware's *The Labor Movement in the United States 1860–1895* (New York, 1929) remains a good general study of the period, as does the more recent brief study, Melvyn Dubofsky's *Industrialism and the American Worker 1865–1920* (New York, 1975). Gerald N. Grob, *Workers and Utopia: A Study of Ideological Conflict in the American Labor Movement 1865–1900* (Evanston, 1961) interprets the labor movement in these years in light of the conflict between reformism and trade unionism, while David Montgomery, in *Workers' Control in America: Studies in the History of Work, Technology, and Labor Struggles* (Cambridge, England, 1979), calls into question the validity of such polarization by focusing on specific struggles for control of the workplace in the late nineteenth century, suggesting that a principled rejection of the wage system remained a strong current even in trade-union actions, an argument he continues in "Strikes in Nineteenth-Century America," *Social Science History* (February 1980), 81–104, and "Labor and the Republic in Industrial America 1860–1920," *Le Mouvement Social* (April–May 1980). For an excellent account of changing workplace conditions and forms during the nineteenth century, see Daniel Nelson, *Managers and Workers: Origins of the New Factory System in the United States 1820–1920* (Madison, 1975). And for descriptions and discussions of major labor conflicts of the period, see Robert V. Bruce, *1877: Year of Violence* (Indianapolis, 1959); Philip S. Foner, *The Great Labor Uprising of 1877* (New York, 1977); Henry David, *The History of the Haymarket Affair: A Study in the American Social-Revolutionary and Labor Movements* (New York, 1936); and Leo Wolff, *Lockout: The Story of the Homestead Strike of 1892* (New York, 1965).

A major impetus toward study of working-class cultures under the strain of industrialization and urbanization is found in the work of Herbert Gutman, especially his essays collected in *Work, Culture and Society in Industrializing America* (New York, 1977). A first-rate example of recent community studies that attend to issues of ethnicity as well as class is Alan Dawley, *Class and Community: The Industrial Revolution in Lynn* (Cambridge, 1976). See also Eric Foner, "Class, Ethnicity, and Radicalism in the Gilded Age: The Land League and Irish-America," *Marxist Perspectives* (Summer 1978), 6–55; Harmut Keil and Heinz Ickstadt, "Elemente einer deutschen Arbeiterkultur in Chicago zwischen 1880 und 1890," *Geschicte und Gesellschaft* (1979), 103–24, and "A Forgotten Piece of Working-class Literature: Gustav Lyser's Satire of the Hewitt Hearing of 1878," *Labor History* (Winter 1979), 127–40. On immigration in general in these years, the standard works are M. L. Hansen, *The Immigrant in American History* (Cambridge, 1948); Oscar Handlin, *The Uprooted* (Boston, 1951); and for reactions on the part of older Americans, John Higham, *Strangers in the Land: Patterns of American Nativism 1860–1925* (New Brunswick, 1953).

On black Americans as members of the industrial working class, see S. D. Spero and A. L. Harris, *The Black Worker: The Negro and the Labor Movement* (1931), and the early selections in Julius Jacobson, ed., *The Negro and the American Labor Movement* (New York, 1968). Philip S. Foner's *Women and the American Labor Movement* (New York, 1979) is a comprehensive study of women and unions. See also Carol Hymowitz and Michaele Weissman, *A History of Women in America* (New York, 1978) and W. Elliot Brownlee and Mary M. Brownlee, *Women in the American Economy: A Documentary History 1675–1929* (New Haven, 1976).

The struggles of workers to maintain and extend control over their working conditions, their successes, and their more prominent defeats continue as major themes in labor history. In *The Fall of the House of Labor: The Workplace, the State, and American Labor Activism, 1865–1925* (New York, 1987) and *Citizen Worker: The Experience of Workers in the United States with Democracy and the Free Market during the Nineteenth Century* (New York, 1993), David Montgomery continues his cutting-edge studies of the workplace and working-class politics. See also Bruce Laurie, *Artisans into Workers: Labor in Nineteenth-Century America* (New

York, 1989) and Nell Irvin Painter, *Standing at Armageddon: The United States, 1877–1919* (New York, 1987). *Eight Hours for What We Will: Workers and Leisure in an Industrial City, 1870–1920* (New York, 1983) by Roy Rosenzweig stresses the cultural dimensions of the working-class experience, especially the emergence of commercial institutions of leisure. The campaign for an eight-hour day and Chicago's Haymarket Square bombing in 1886 are treated freshly by James Green in *Death in the Haymarket: A Story of Chicago, the First Labor Movement, and the Bombing That Divided Gilded Age America* (New York, 2006).

Immigration in the making of the U.S. industrial working class and urban population is treated in a number of important works. See John Bodnar, *The Transplanted: A History of Immigrants in Urban America* (Bloomington, Indiana, 1985); Elizabeth Ewen, *Immigrant Women in the Land of Dollars: Life and Culture on the Lower East Side, 1890–1925* (New York, 1985); Roger Daniels, *Coming to America: A History of Immigration and Ethnicity in American Life* (New York, 1990); James Barret, "Americanization from the Bottom Up: Immigrants and the Remaking of the Working Class in the United States, 1880–1930," *Journal of American History* (December 1992); and Matthew Frye Jacobson, *Whiteness of a Different Color: European Immigrants and the Alchemy of Race* (Cambridge, Massachusetts, 1998).

For the social documentation of labor in these years, see *Who Built America? From the Centennial Celebration of 1876 to the Great War of 1914* (New York, 1994), by Roy Rozenzweig and Steve Brier, with Josh Brown as visual editor. Alice Kessler-Harris's *Out to Work: A History of Wage-Earning Women in the United States* (New York, 1982) is an indispensable synthesis of women's and labor history. On the Knights of Labor in working-class culture in the Gilded Age, see Leon Fink, *Workingmen's Democracy: The Knights of Labor and American Politics* (Urbana, Illinois, 1983); Kim Voss, *The Making of American Exceptionalism: The Knights of Labor and Class Formation in the Nineteenth Century* (Ithaca, 1993); and Robert E. Weir, *Beyond Labor's Veil: The Culture of the Knights of Labor* (University Park, Pennsylvania, 1996). Other cogent studies of Gilded Age labor and politics are Victoria Charlotte Hattam, *Labor Visions and State Power: The Origins of Business Unionism in the United States* (Princeton, 1993), and Elizabeth Sanders, *Roots of Reform: Farmers, Workers, and the American State, 1877–1917* (Chicago, 1999).

Oliver Zunz's *Making America Corporate, 1870–1920* (Chicago, 1990) exemplifies organizational history, focusing on middle managers who invented themselves as a class of white-collar workers. The book follows the lead of Chandler's widely influential *The Visible Hand*, a formative (and formidable) work that put the "organizational synthesis" of the bureaucratic corporation at the heart of modern U.S. history, a direction from which other scholars have recently begun to veer away. While the "organizational" school tends to see the structure and the shaping social effects of the modern corporation as foregone conclusions following from rationalized technologies such as the railroad, Gerald Berk, in *Alternative Tracks: The Constitution of American Industrial Order, 1865–1917* (Baltimore, 1994), argues that the way corporations developed into national systems was not predetermined, that alternatives such as decentralized "regional republicanism" were briefly in play. In *The Political Economy of American Industrialization, 1877–1900* (New York, 2000), Richard Franklin Bensel examines the political-economic conditions that fostered incorporation and concludes that corporations and democracy can indeed coexist as compatible forms in modern society.

4. MYSTERIES OF THE GREAT CITY

A. M. Schlesinger, *The Rise of the City 1878–1898* (New York, 1933) remains a basic study of urban life in these years. Among the more recent general histories of American cities, Blake McKelvey, *The Urbanization of America 1860–1915* (New Brunswick, 1963) is particularly useful. It is still essential to consult the pioneering work in urban statistics, Adna F. Weber, *The Growth of Cities in the 19th Century* (New York, 1899). Sam Bass Warner Jr., *The Urban Wilderness* (New York, 1972) is particularly good on the impact of industrialization on urban form. See also his *Streetcar Suburbs: The Process of Growth in Boston 1870–1900* (Cambridge, 1962). For a readable text with valuable photographic documents, see Harold M. Mayer and Richard C. Wade, *Chicago: Growth of a Metropolis* (Chicago, 1969). For more particular social histories, stressing relations of class and immigrant groups, see Stephan Thernstrom, *Poverty and Progress: Social Mobility in a Nineteenth Century City* (Cambridge, 1964); Richard Sennett, *Families against the City: Middle Class Homes of Industrial Chicago 1872–1890* (Cambridge, 1970); Virginia Yans McLaughlin, *Family and Community: Italian Immigrants in Buffalo 1880–1930* (Ithaca, 1977); and Stephan Thernstrom and Richard Sennett, eds., *Nineteenth-Century Cities* (New Haven, 1969). A very useful discussion of responses to urban poverty is contained in Part One of Robert H. Bremner's *From the Depths: The Discovery of Poverty in the United States* (New York, 1956). On the accommodation of the churches to the city, consult the excellent study by Henry F. May, *Protestant Churches and Industrial America* (New York, 1949). For an important study of efforts by reformers toward social control, see Paul Boyer, *Urban Masses and Moral Order in America 1820–1920* (Cambridge, 1978).

Among the early investigations by sociologists, Robert E. Park and Ernest W. Burgess, *The City* (Chicago, 1925) still offers pertinent insights.

A concise and illuminating overview of evolving city forms in the nineteenth-century industrial world can be found in Françoise Choay, *The Modern City: Planning in the 19th Century* (New York, 1969). For a brief summary of major American trends and patterns, see Christopher Tunnard and Henry Hope Reed, *American Skyline: The Growth and Form of Our Cities and Towns* (New York, 1953). Predominantly a topographical discussion, John W. Reps, *The Making of Urban America: A History of City Planning in the United States* (Princeton, 1965) is indispensable. For an astute historical discussion of the city-parks movement, see Francesco Dal Co, "From Parks to the Region: Progressive Ideology and the Reforms of the American City," in Giorgio Ciucci et al., *The American City: From the Civil War to the New Deal* (Cambridge, 1979). Ross Miller offers an interesting argument about the anti-urban strain in Olmsted's work in "The Landscaper's Utopia Versus the City: A Mismatch," *New England Quarterly* (June 1976), 179–93. Useful selections (with introductions) of Olmsted's own writings are available in Albert Fein, ed., *Landscape into Cityscape* (Ithaca, 1968) and S. B. Sutton, ed., *Civilizing American Cities: A Selection of Frederick Law Olmsted's Writings on City Landscapes* (Cambridge, 1971). On Central Park in particular, see F. L. Olmsted Jr., and Theodora Kimball, eds., *Frederick Law Olmsted: Landscape Architect 1822–1903: Central Park* (New York, 1928).

For descriptive accounts and discussions of main currents in urban architecture in these years, see James Marston Fitch, *American Building: The Historical Forces That Shaped It* (Boston, 1966); Edgar Kaufman Jr., ed., *The Rise of an American Architecture* (New York, 1970); and Carl Condit, *The Chicago School of Architecture* (Chicago, 1963). On specific urban forms, see Carroll Meeks, *The Railroad Station: An Architectural History* (New Haven, 1956) and Alan Trachtenberg, *Brooklyn Bridge: Fact and Symbol* (New York, 1965). David P. Handlin, *The American Home: Architecture and Society 1815–1915* (Boston, 1979) is a comprehensive study of changing patterns of domestic architecture and interiors. More specialized in range but an excellent discussion of the cultural implications of domestic building is Gwendolyn Wright, *Moralism and the Model Home: Domestic Architecture and the Cultural Conflict in Chicago 1873–1913* (Chicago, 1980). On the application of modern technology to the home, see Reyner Banham's superb *The Architecture of the Well-Tempered Environment* (London, 1969) and May N. Stone, "The Plumbing Paradox: American Attitudes toward Late Nineteenth-Century Sanitary Arrangements," *Winterthur Portfolio* (Autumn 1979), 283–310.

For a provocative and compelling conception of "spectacle" in relation to consumerism, see Guy Debord, *Society of the Spectacle* (Detroit, 1970). Neil Harris's discussion of the changing form of circuses in these years appears in his *Humbug: The Art of P. T. Barnum* (Boston, 1973). John Kasson's *Amusing the Million: Coney Island at the Turn of the Century* (New York, 1978) is an excellent account of the emergence of the urban amusement park as a response to new social realities. On the new city journalism, see Frank Luther Mott, *American Journalism: A History 1860–1960* (New York, 1962) and Peter C. Marzio, *The Men and Machines of American Journalism* (Washington, D.C., 1973). On Stephen Crane's newspaper stories, see Alan Trachtenberg, "Experiments in Another Country: Stephen Crane's City Sketches," *Southern Review* (April 1974), 265–85. For historical accounts of advertising, see Frank Presbrey, *The History and Development of Advertising* (Garden City, 1929) and Frank Luther Mott, *A History of American Magazines*, Vol. 3 (Cambridge, 1938). Critical discussions of the place and effect of advertising in American culture can be found in David Potter, *People of Plenty: Economic Abundance and the American Character* (Chicago, 1954); Daniel Boorstin, *The Image: A Guide to Pseudo-Events in America* (Chicago, 1961); Marshall McLuhan, *The Mechanical Bride* (New York, 1951); and Leo Spitzer, "American Advertising Explained as Popular Art," in *Essays on English and American Literature* (Princeton, 1962). For a history of the department store, see H. Pasadermadjian's useful *The Department Store: Its Origins, Evolution and Economics* (London, 1954); Ralph M. Hower, *History of Macy's of New York 1858–1919* (Cambridge, 1943); and Harry E. Resseguie, "Alexander Turney Stewart and the Development of the Department Store 1823–1876," *Business History Review* (Autumn 1965). An excellent recent discussion is Susan Porter Benson, "Palace of Consumption and Machine for Selling: The American Department Store 1880–1940," *Radical History Review* (Fall 1979), 199–221.

Richard Sennett's meditations on changing forms of urban life remain pertinent to the study of Gilded Age cities. See his *Conscience of the Eye: The Design and Social Life of Cities* (New York, 1990) and *Flesh and Stone: The Body and the City in Western Civilization* (New York, 1994). Invaluable, too, are Neil Harris's studies of the place of cultural institutions and new architectural forms in the growth of U.S. cities; see his "Cultural Institutions and American Modernization," in *Cultural Excursions: Marketing Appetites and Cultural Tastes in Modern America* (Chicago, 1990), 96–110 and passim. See also the commentary on the establishment of cultural hierarchies by Lawrence W. Levine in *Highbrow Lowbrow: The Emergence of Cultural Hierarchy in America* (Cambridge, Massachusetts, 1988). On literary elites, see Thomas Bender, *New York: A History of Intellectual Life in New York City from 1750 to the Beginnings of Our Own*

Time (New York, 1987), Part Two, "Literary Culture." On urban elites in general see Frederick Cople Jaher, *Urban Establishment: Upper Strata in Boston, New York, Charleston, Chicago, and Los Angeles* (Urbana, Illinois, 1982). The formation of a distinct urban corporate elite is the important subject of Sven Beckert's *The Monied Metropolis: New York City and the Consolidation of the American Bourgeoisie, 1850–1896* (New York, 2001).

In *Empire City: The Making and Meaning of the New York City Landscape* (Philadelphia, 2002), David M. Scobey incisively examines how developments in real estate such as segregated commercial, recreational (Central Park), and residential spaces allowed for the emergence of New York as the center of corporate America's "bourgeois urbanism." See also Kenneth T. Jackson, "The Capital of Capitalism: the New York Metropolitan Region," in *Metropolis, 1890–1940*, ed. Anthony Sutcliffe (London, 1983). For a multidimensional historical study of Central Park, see Roy Rosenzweig and Elizabeth Blackmar, *The Park and the People: A History of Central Park* (Ithaca, 1992). For the cultural effect of another major urban construction of the period, see Richard Haw's excellent *The Brooklyn Bridge: A Cultural History* (New Brunswick, New Jersey, 2005). Ross Miller, *American Apocalypse: The Great Fire and the Myth of Chicago* (Chicago, 1990) studies the emergence of Chicago as a distinctive image in the discourse of the city. See also Carl S. Smith, *Chicago and the American Literary Imagination, 1880–1920* (Chicago, 1984). For a perspective from the point of view of class, see Richard Schneirov, *Labor and Urban Politics: Class Conflict and the Origins of Modern Liberalism in Chicago, 1864–1897* (Urbana, Illinois, 1998).

The place of the department store in cultural and intellectual history is the subject of William Leach's major study *Land of Desire: Merchants, Power, and the Rise of a New American Culture* (New York, 1993). For a social history with emphasis on women's history, see Susan Porter Benson, *Counter Cultures: Saleswomen, Managers, and Customers in American Department Stores, 1890–1940* (Urbana, Illinois, 1986). Jackson Lears's many-faceted study *Fables of Abundance: A Cultural History of Advertising in America* (New York, 1994) is essential reading on the origins and effects of advertising on urban life. Also see Lears's essay in *The Culture of Consumption: Critical Essays in American History, 1880–1980* (New York, 1983), and essays in the same volume by Christopher Wilson and Jean-Christophe Agnew. Also relevant to the emergence of mass consumption at the turn of the century is Susan Strasser, *Satisfaction Guaranteed: The Making of the American Mass Market* (New York, 1989). For a good introduction to the rising commercial culture of recreation in New York, see Lewis A. Erenberg, *Steppin' Out: New York Nightlife and the Transformation of American Culture* (Westport, Connecticut, 1981).

5. THE POLITICS OF CULTURE

Notoriously difficult to define to everyone's satisfaction, the word "culture" as used by social scientists tends to mean the whole way of life of a society, its everyday values and manners as well as its arts and religion, while humanists tend to use the word in the more restricted sense of the received tradition in the fine arts, literature, philosophy, and religion. Yet this distinction is not hard-and-fast. In his path-breaking book on literary and intellectual history, *Culture and Society 1780–1950* (New York, 1958), Raymond Williams traces the evolution of the term among writers and intellectuals in England, charting its changes in meaning as responses to industrialization. Williams's *Keywords: A Vocabulary of Culture and Society* (New York, 1976) offers compact biographies of words such as "culture" that have undergone similar changes in the modern era. See also his *Marxism and Literature* (New York, 1977), especially "Cultural Theory," for an important discussion of dominant, residual, and emergent cultures. For an extremely useful compendium of meanings chiefly in the social sciences, see *Culture: A Critical Review of Concepts and Definitions* (New York, 1952), by A. L. Kroeber and Clyde Kluckhohn. Robert Berkhofer provides a useful survey and analytical discussion of the uses of the culture concept in historiography in "Clio and the Culture Concept: Some Impressions of a Changing Relationship in American Historiography," in Louis Schneider and Charles Bonjean, eds., *The Idea of Culture in the Social Sciences* (Cambridge, England, 1973).

The changing perceptions and roles of intellectuals between the Civil War and World War I has received considerable attention, notably in T. J. Jackson Lears's magisterial *No Place of Grace: The Quest for Alternatives to Modern American Culture 1880–1920* (New York, 1981). George Fredrickson, in *The Inner Civil War: Northern Intellectuals and the Crisis of the Union* (New York, 1965), examines responses to the Civil War, particularly the emergence of elitist and anti-democratic currents. While his view of the period is based on an older notion of status anxiety, Stow Persons, in *The Decline of American Gentility* (New York, 1973), casts light on an implicit theory of mass society in the writings of genteel critics. The standard study of leading genteel editors and intellectuals is John Tomsich, *A Genteel Endeavor: American Culture and Politics in the Gilded Age* (Stanford, 1971). For the influence of English figures, see John Henry Raleigh, *Matthew Arnold and American Culture* (Berkeley, 1961) and Roger B. Stein, *John Ruskin and Aesthetic Thought in America, 1840–1900* (Cambridge, 1967). For an excellent biography of one of the leading spokesmen for genteel values, see Kermit Vanderbilt, *Charles Eliot Norton: Apostle of Culture in a Democracy* (Cambridge, 1959). Although largely concerned with antebellum figures, Ann Douglas's *The Feminization of American Culture* (New York, 1977) is a valuable investigation of the alliance of middle-class women and ministers in the formation of popular cultural values. John Higham's deservedly well-known essay, "The Reorientation of American Culture in the 1890s," in John Weiss, ed., *The Origins of Modern Consciousness* (Detroit, 1965), remains a useful treatment of major patterns in that decade.

For relevant discussions of education, see L. A. Cremin, *The Transformation of the School: Progressivism in American Education 1876–1957* (New York, 1961), and the more critical recent study by Samuel Bowles and Herbert Gintes, *Schooling in Capitalist America* (New York, 1976). For a useful account of higher education, see Frederick Rudolph, *The American College and University: A History* (New York, 1962). Richard Hofstadter and W. P. Metzger, *The Development of Academic Freedom in the United States* (New York, 1955) is an essential study, as is Richard Hofstadter, *Anti-Intellectualism in American Life* (New York, 1950). For a lively general study of professionalism and the adjustment it required in traditional individualist values, see Burton J. Bledstein, *The Culture of Professionalism: The Middle Class and the Development of Higher Education in America* (New York, 1976). More narrowly focused, Thomas L. Haskell links the rise of social science to deep changes within the economic structure in *The Emergence of Professional Social Science: The American Social Science Association and the Nineteenth Century Crisis of Authority* (Urbana, 1977). See also Dorothy Ross, "Socialism and American Liberalism: Academic Social Thought in the 1880s," *Perspectives on American History* (1977–78).

On the establishment of new cultural institutions, see the important study by Helen L. Horowitz, *Culture and the City: Cultural Philanthropy in Chicago from the 1880s to 1917* (Lexington, Kentucky, 1976). Neil Harris has been concerned with cultural change and its context in a number of valuable essays, including "The Gilded Age Revisited: Boston and the Museum Movement," *American Quarterly* (Winter 1962), 545–66; "Iconography and Intellectual History: The Half-Tone Effect," in John Higham and Paul K. Conkin, eds., *New Directions in American Intellectual History* (Baltimore, 1979); "The Lamp of Learning: Popular Lights and Shadows," in Olsen and Voss, eds., *The Organization of Knowledge in Modern America 1860–1920* (Baltimore, 1979). Also useful in the latter volume is John Y. Cole's "Storehouses and Workshops: American Libraries and the Uses of Knowledge."

For a clear and comprehensive survey of politics and policy making, see Morton Keller, *Affairs of State: Public Life in Late Nineteenth Century America* (Cambridge, 1977). Matthew Josephson's *The Politicos* (New York, 1938) is a colorful and detailed account of the ties between party politics and big business. For conventional party politics, see the excellent treatment by Robert D. Marcus, *Grand Old Party: Political Structure in the Gilded Age 1880–1896* (New York, 1971) and H. Wayne Morgan's more comprehensive *From Hayes to McKinley: National Party Politics 1877–1896* (Syracuse, 1969). And on the 1896 campaign, see Paul W. Glad, *McKinley, Bryan, and the People* (New York, 1964).

There has been a recent flood of studies of the major parties and electoral politics in these years, with a strong emphasis on cultural (chiefly ethnic and religious) factors. See the general interpretative essay by Samuel P. Hays, "Political Parties and the Community-Society Continuum," in William Nisbet Chamber and Walter Dean Burnham, eds., *The American Party System* (New York, 1975), as well as Geoffrey Blodgett, "A New Look at the Gilded Age: Politics in a Cultural Context," in Daniel W. Howe, ed., *Victorian America* (Philadelphia, 1976); Richard L. McCormick, "Ethno-Cultural Interpretations of Nineteenth Century American Voting Behavior," *Political Science Quarterly* (June 1974), 351–77; Robert Kelley, "Ideology and Political Culture from Jefferson to Nixon," *American Historical Review* (June 1977), 531–62. Important books on cultural aspects of electoral politics include Walter Dean Burnham, *Critical Elections and the Mainspring of American Politics* (New York, 1970); Paul Kleppner, *The Cross of Culture: A Social Analysis of Midwestern Politics 1850–1900* (New York, 1970) and *The Third Electoral System 1853–1892: Parties, Voters, and Political Culture* (Chapel Hill, 1979); Robert Kelley, *The Cultural Pattern in American Politics* (New York, 1979).

General studies of reform in these years can be found in Eric Goldman, *Rendezvous with Destiny* (New York, 1952) and Richard Hofstadter, *The Age of Reform* (New York, 1955). On the role of blacks in party politics, see R. W. Logan, *The Negro in American Life and Thought: The Nadir, 1877–1901* (New York, 1954). The place of "men of culture" in reform movements is treated intelligently by John G. Sproat, *"The Best Men": Liberal Reformers in the Gilded Age* (New York, 1968). See also Alexander B. Callow Jr., *The Tweed Ring* (New York, 1966); Seymour Mandelbaum, *Boss Tweed's New York* (New York, 1965); and Morton Keller's abundantly illustrated study of Tweed's nemesis, *The Art and Politics of Thomas Nast* (New York, 1968). The definitive study of civil-service reform is Ari Hoogenboom, *Outlawing the Spoils: A History of the Civil Service Reform Movement 1865–1883* (Urbana, 1968). On battles over monetary policy, see Irwin Unger, *The Greenback Era: A Social and Political History of American Finance 1865–1979* (Princeton, 1964). On third parties, Fred E. Haynes, *Third Party Movements since the Civil War* (Iowa City, 1916) is still a useful survey. An illuminating discussion of fusion politics can be found in Peter H. Argersinger, " 'A Place on the

Ballot': Fusion Politics and Antifusion Laws," *American Historical Review* (April 1980), 287–306. For the Henry George mayoral campaign of 1886, see the contemporary account by Louis F. Post and Fred C. Leubuscher, *Henry George's 1886 Campaign* (reprint, New York, 1961) and Allan Nevins, *Abram S. Hewitt* (New York, 1935).

The standard narrative work on Populism is J. D. Hicks, *The Populist Revolt* (Minneapolis, 1931). For essential background to Populism and the Farmer's Alliance, see Chester McArthur Destler, *American Radicalism 1865–1901: Essays and Documents* (New London, 1946). Lawrence Goodwyn's reappraisal, *Democratic Promise: The Populist Movement in America* (New York, 1976), is likely to establish itself as the definitive account. Goodwyn's sympathetic treatment of rural radicalism owes a good deal to C. Vann Woodward's earlier treatment in *Origins of the New South 1877–1913* (Baton Rouge, 1951). See also Woodward's important essay, "The Populist Heritage and the Intellectual," in *The Burden of Southern History* (Baton Rouge, 1960).

A major work on the enlarged role of the national state is Stephen Skowronek, *Building a New American State: The Expansion of National Administrative Capacities, 1877–1920* (New York, 1982). Rogers Smith, *Civic Ideals: Conflicting Visions of Citizenship in U.S. History* (New Haven, 1997) gives a thorough account of changing meanings and powers of citizenship. For enlightening discussion of ideas of democracy in the politics of the age, see Alan Dawley, *Struggles for Justice: Social Responsibility and the Liberal State* (Cambridge, Massachusetts, 1991), Chapter 1, "Gilded Age Liberty." James T. Kloppenberg's comparative study *Uncertain Victory: Social Democracy and Progressivism in European and American Thought, 1870–1920* (New York, 1986) provides an acute discussion of relevant political thought as well as a fresh perspective on the era. In *The Reconstruction of American Liberalism, 1865–1914* (Chapel Hill, 2002), Nancy Cohen considers the response of liberal reformers to the new challenge to democracy of the corporate form of property and power. In *The Decline of Popular Politics: The American North, 1865–1928* (New York, 1986), Michael McGerr examines voter registration to identify changing patterns of political participation. See also his rigorous study of the roots of Progressivism in these years, *Fierce Discontent: The Rise and Fall of the Progressive Movement in America, 1870–1920* (New York, 2003). Also relevant is Gretchen Ritter, *Goldbugs and Greenbacks: The Antimonopoly Tradition and the Politics of Finance, 1865–1896* (New York, 1997). For the social and political history of the rural South, see Steven Hahn's seminal works: *Roots of Southern Populism: Yeoman Farmers and the Transformation of the Georgia Upcountry, 1850–1890* (New York, 1983) and *Nation Under Our Feet: Black Political Struggles in the Rural South from Slavery to the Great Migration* (Cambridge, Massachusetts, 2003). On the continuing presence of the Civil War in public discourse and persistent racism, see David W. Blight, *Race and Reunion: The Civil War in American Memory* (Cambridge, Massachusetts, 2001). See also Tera W. Hunter, *To 'Joy my Freedom': Southern Black Women's Lives and Labors after the Civil War* (Cambridge, Massachusetts, 1997).

Rich in cultural change, the Gilded Age has inspired a rich array of cultural studies. For an investigation of the influence of the new corporate world on relations between the sexes, see Angel Kwolek-Folland, *Engendering Business: Men and Women in the Corporate Office, 1870–1930* (Baltimore, 1994). David Leverenz perceptively explores literary responses to the corporation as a problematic model of patriarchy in *Paternalism Incorporated: Fables of American Fatherhood, 1865–1940* (Ithaca, New York, 2003). Gail Bederman's *Manliness & Civilization: A Cultural History of Gender and Race in the United States, 1880–1917* (Chicago, 1995) considers the beleaguered masculinity of white supremacy movements. On intellectual and social sources of feminism in these years, see Rosalind Rosenberg, *Beyond Separate Spheres: Intellectual Roots of Modern Feminism* (New Haven, 1982), and Nancy Cott, *The Grounding of Modern Feminism* (New Haven, 1987). See also Beryl Satter's important study of intellectual and cultural change, *Each Mind a Kingdom: American Women, Sexual Purity, and the New Thought Movement, 1875–1920* (Berkeley, 1999). James Livingston's *Pragmatism, Feminism, and Democracy: Rethinking the Politics of American History* (New York, 2001) presents a challenging argument about the synchronicity of feminism and pragmatism as responses to openings for change in gender, selfhood, and politics accompanying incorporation. See too the lucid accounts of the thinking of late nineteenth-century New England Brahmins in Louis Menand, *The Metaphysical Club* (New York, 2001). On changing ideas of selfhood, see relevant chapters in Wilfred M. McClay, *Masterless: Self and Society in Modern America* (Chapel Hill, 1994), and Jeffrey P. Sklansky, *The Soul's Economy: Market Society and Selfhood in American Thought, 1820–1920* (Chapel Hill, 2002). Scott A. Sandage's *Born Losers: A History of Failure in America* (Cambridge, 2005) tells the other side of the story of "success" and "self-made" selfhood.

6. FICTIONS OF THE REAL

There are several good introductions to realism as a movement in European and American fiction, including F.W.J. Hemmings, ed., *The Age of Realism* (Baltimore, 1974) and Damian Grant, *Realism* (London, 1970). For a useful collection of documents, see George J. Becker, ed., *Documents of Modern Literary Realism* (Princeton, 1963). The classic study of the concept of "reality" in relation to literary convention is Eric Auerbach, *Mimesis: The Representation of Reality in Western Literature* (Princeton, 1953). And the major Marxist discussion, which sees realism as the essential mode of the novel, is Georg Lukács, *Studies in European Realism* (London, 1950), a discussion continued as a polemic against literary modernism in *The Meaning of Contemporary Realism* (London, 1962). Other useful general discussions include Harry Levin, "What Is Realism?" in *Comparative Literature* (1951), and René Wellek, "The Concept of Realism in Literary Scholarship," in *Concepts of Criticism* (New Haven, 1963).

For a superb study of realism in European (chiefly French) painting, and of its cultural setting, see Linda Nochlin, *Realism* (Middlesex, England, 1971). See also Axel von Saldern, *Triumph of Realism* (New York, 1967). For an excellent and incisive general survey, see the relevant chapters in Joshua C. Taylor, *The Fine Arts in America* (Chicago, 1979); also Oliver Larkin, *Art and Life in America* (New York, 1949). Patricia Hills, *The Painters' America: Rural and Urban Life, 1810–1910* (New York, 1974) contains valuable discussions of industrial and urban themes. A standard brief work on Winslow Homer is Lloyd Goodrich, *Winslow Homer* (New York, 1944). See also John Wilmerding's excellent monograph, *Winslow Homer* (New York, 1972). For a study of Thomas Eakins, see Lloyd Goodrich, *Thomas Eakins, His Life and Work* (New York, 1933).

Although left incomplete at his death in 1929, Vol. Three of Vernon L. Parrington's *Main Currents of American Thought* (New York, 1927, 1930), "The Beginnings of Critical Realism in America," remains the most comprehensive treatment of the social and political ideas informing literary realism in America. For a briefer general introduction, see Jay Martin, *Harvests of Change: American Literature, 1865–1914* (New York, 1967). Bernard Bowron's essay, "American Realism," in *Comparative Literature* (1951), remains the best brief discussion of features distinctive to American writing. Warner Berthoff, in *The Ferment of Realism: American Literature 1884–1919* (New York, 1965), offers a comprehensive and intelligent survey of writers and ideas, as does Larzer Ziff in *The American 1890s* (New York, 1966). The opening chapter of Alfred Kazin, *On Native Grounds* (New York, 1942), is also relevant.

On the literary culture of the post–Civil War years, see Henry Nash Smith, "The Scribbling Women and the Cosmic Success Story," *Critical Inquiry* (September 1974), 47–70, and *Democracy and the Novel* (New York, 1978). The chapter on Howells in the latter work is especially instructive. Smith's concern is largely with the demands of the literary marketplace on the serious efforts of Howells, Mark Twain, and Henry James. For discussions of the marketplace itself, see William Charvat

(Matthew J. Bruccoli, ed.), *The Profession of Authorship in America 1800–1870* (Columbus, Ohio, 1968), especially chaps. 14 and 15. On best sellers, the standard works are James D. Hart, *The Popular Book* (Berkeley, 1961); Frank Luther Mott, *Golden Multitudes* (New York, 1947); and Donald Sheehan, *This Was Publishing: A Chronicle of the Book Trade in the Gilded Age* (Bloomington, 1952). For Howells's own critical writings, consult the useful selection in Edwin H. Cady, ed., *W. D. Howells as Critic* (London, 1973). See also Everett Carter's valuable discussion in *Howells and the Age of Realism* (1954). For biographical studies of Howells, see Edwin Cady's two volumes, *The Road to Realism* (Syracuse, 1956) and *The Realist at War* (Syracuse, 1958), and Kenneth S. Lynn's *William Dean Howells: An American Life* (New York, 1971). On the political meanings of *Billy Budd*, see Michael Paul Rogin, *Subversive Genealogy: The Politics and Art of Herman Melville* (New York, 1983).

Several superb works on realism as a cultural discourse have appeared in recent years. Miles Orvell's original work of research and criticism, *The Real Thing: Imitation and Authenticity in American Culture, 1880–1940* (Chapel Hill, 1989), usefully covers a range of fields, including photography and material culture. A major interpretation of a painter and a writer, Michael Fried's *Realism, Writing, Disfiguration: On Thomas Eakins and Stephen Crane* (Chicago, 1987) offers a rigorously formalist discussion of realism. Other important cultural studies of realist painters of the period are Elizabeth B. Johns, *Thomas Eakins: The Heroism of Modern Life* (Princeton, 1983) and *Winslow Homer: The Nature of Observation* (Berkeley, 2002); David M. Lubin, *Act of Portrayal: Eakins, Sargent, James* (New Haven, 1985); and Martin A. Berger, *Man Made: Thomas Eakins and the Construction of Gilded Age Manhood* (Berkeley, 2000).

Michael Davitt Bell provides an invaluable overview of definitions in *The Problem of American Realism: Studies in the Cultural History of a Literary Idea* (Chicago, 1993). Amy Kaplan's *The Social Construction of American Realism* (Chicago, 1988) signaled a turn toward historicism and social criticism in the study of post–Civil War literary realism. Part II, "The Color Line," in Eric J. Sundquist's magisterial *To Wake the Nations: Race in the Making of American Literature* (Cambridge, Massachusetts, 1993) covers works by Mark Twain and Charles Chesnutt in the context of race relations. See also Kenneth W. Warren, *Black and White Strangers: Race and American Literary Realism* (Chicago, 1993). Walter Benn Michaels's *Gold Standard and the Logic of Naturalism: American Literature at the Turn of the Century* (Berkeley, 1987) sees realist and naturalist writers as more complicit in the turn toward incorporation than had been recognized. Also relevant to the definition and study of realism is Wai Chee Dimock's elegant treatment of "the juridical subject" in *Residues of Justice: Literature, Law, Philosophy* (Berkeley, 1996). In another important work concerned with literature and law, Brook Thomas sees realism as a studied critique of the promises of corporate capitalism; see *American Literary Realism and the Failed Promise of Contract* (Berkeley, 1997). Nancy Glazener, *Reading for Realism: The History of a U.S. Literary Institution, 1850–1910* (Durham, North Carolina, 1997), offers an ideological critique of realism by considering it as an ideal way of reading propagated by leading literary magazines. Also see Ellery Sedgwick, *The Atlantic Monthly, 1857–1909: Yankee Humanism at High Tide and Ebb* (Amherst, 1994).

7. WHITE CITY

On international exhibitions in Europe and America in the nineteenth century, see Frederick P. Pittera, *The Art and Science of International Fairs and Exhibitions* (1961) and *Fairs of the World* (1970). Useful historical discussions can also be found in Pittera's article on "Exhibitions and Fairs" in the *Encyclopedia Britannica* (1973), and in Guy Stanton Ford's "International Exhibitions" in the *Encyclopedia of the Social Sciences* (New York, 1933). On the American entries at various fairs, see Merle Curti's summary in "America at the World Fairs, 1851–1893," *Probing Our Past* (New York, 1955). The World's Columbian Exposition in Chicago in 1893 has as yet inspired only a modest body of scholarship. Two books with valuable materials are David F. Burg, *Chicago's White City* (Lexington, Kentucky, 1976) and R. Reid Badger, *The Great American Fair: The World's Columbian Exposition and American Culture* (Chicago, 1979), the latter an interesting effort to place the fair in the context of cultural values in crisis. Burnham's role, and the implicit political vision of his plan, is discussed perceptively by Mario Manieri-Elia in "Toward an 'Imperial City': Daniel Burnham and the City Beautiful Movement," in Giorgi Ciucci et al., *The American City: From the Civil War to the New Deal* (Cambridge, 1979). For a fuller discussion of Burnham in his career, see Thomas S. Hines, *Burnham of Chicago: Architect and Planner* (New York, 1974). A handy selection of views of the architecture of the fair is available in William A. Coles and Henry Hope Reed Jr., eds., *Architecture in America: A Battle of Styles* (New York, 1961). For the prevalence of academic classicism in the architecture, sculpture, painting, and interior design of the period as a whole, see The Brooklyn Museum, *The American Renaissance 1876–1917* (New York, 1979).

In "The White City: The Beginnings of a Planned Civilization in America," *Journal of the Illinois State Historical Society* (April 1934), 71–93, Maurice F. Neufeld discusses several of the social and political implications of the fair. The exclusion of blacks is discussed by August

Meier and Elliot Rudwick in "Black Man and the 'White City': Negroes and the Columbian Exposition, 1893," *Phylon* (1965), 354–61, and by Robert W. Rydell in "The World's Columbian Exposition of 1893: Racist Underpinnings of a Utopian Artifact," *Journal of American Culture* (Summer 1978), 253–75. See also Justus D. Doenecke, "Myths, Machines and Markets: The Columbian Exposition of 1893," *Journal of Popular Culture* (Winter 1972), 535–49.

For a fulsome and provocative treatment of the Chicago school of architecture, the effect of the fair, and the ideas of Sullivan and Frank Lloyd Wright, see Hugh Dalziel Duncan, *Culture and Democracy: The Struggle for Form in Society and Architecture in Chicago and the Middle West during the Life and Times of Louis H. Sullivan* (Totowa, New Jersey, 1965). A standard work on Sullivan's career is Hugh Morrison, *Louis Sullivan* (New York, 1935). See also the brief introduction to Sullivan, with excellent photographic illustrations, by Albert Bush-Brown, *Louis Sullivan* (New York, 1960), and the intellectual biography by Sherman Paul, *Louis Sullivan: An Architect in American Thought* (New York, 1962). For H. H. Richardson's work and career, consult Henry-Russell Hitchcock, *The Architecture of H. H. Richardson and His Times* (rev. ed., New York, 1961). On the Pullman community, its design and its social structure, see Stanley Buder, *Pullman: An Experiment in Industrial Order and Community Planning, 1880–1930* (New York, 1967); and on the strike, Almont Lindsey, *The Pullman Strike* (Chicago, 1942).

In *A Season of Renewal: The Columbian Exposition and Victorian America* (Westport, Connecticut, 2002), Dennis B. Downey interprets the Chicago fair as the answer to a cultural need expressed in the 1890's for renewal and renovation of the nation. James Gilbert's *Perfect Cities: Chicago's Utopias of 1893* (Chicago, 1991) thoughtfully views the Exposition and its tensions between White City and Midway in the context of other utopian efforts to impose order on an unruly social world: the guidebooks to the Exposition, George Pullman's nearby model industrial town named after himself, and the urban revival led by Dwight L. Moody. Commemorating the centenary of the exposition, Norman Bolotin and Christine Laing, *The Chicago World's Fair of 1893: The World's Columbian Exposition* (Washington, D.C., 1992), offers a richly illustrated panoramic view of the event and its constructed spaces. Julie K. Brown's *Contesting Images: Photography and the World's Columbian Exposition* (Tucson, 1994) provides a valuable compendium and critical study of the unprecedented role of photography in defining the experience of a specific event and place such as the fair. Neil Harris traces the influence of the Chicago fair in the design of subsequent fairs and on urban planning in the United States in "Great American Fairs and American Cities: The Role of Chicago's Columbian Exposition," in Harris,

Cultural Excursions: Marketing Appetites and Cultural Tastes in Modern America (Chicago, 1990), 111–31. For a discussion of social and ideological aspects of the Chicago fair in the context of other American world's fairs, see Robert W. Rydell's comprehensive *All the World's a Fair: Visions of Empire at American International Expositions, 1876–1916* (Chicago, 1984). Also relevant is the abundant and growing literature on U.S. imperialism and racism in the 1890's: see Reginald Horsman, *Race and Manifest Destiny: The Origins of American Racial Anglo-Saxonism* (Cambridge, Massachusetts, 1982), and Anders Stephanson, *Manifest Destiny: American Expansion and the Empire of Right* (New York, 1995).

INDEX

263

36 Morgan, Indians, property

45 Holmes Sr on "unconscious action of the mind"

59-60 railroad time, zones, etc

117 Holley, design of big plants to fit transportat"
"bldgs & inhabitants subordinate to the forms
of corporate industry."

123 spectator sports
125 "isolating information from experience"
130 electricity in home as "greatest environmental
revolution in .. history"
138 ad unique in art - its premise is falsehood...